Contents

We have developed and assembled the *Solutions Fieldbook* to help education stakeholders meet the increasing demands now placed on public schools. Both state and federal governments recognize that America's schools, controlled by locally elected boards of education, are falling behind in the race to meet the demands of a rapidly changing world. Too many students leave school woefully ill prepared to meet the challenges of the society and the workplace of the 21st-century Information Age.

We have published three school improvement writings:

1. *Game Time: The Educator's Playbook for the New Global Economy*, which emphasizes the economic importance of urging the public schools to practice continuous improvement, to produce a globally competitive workforce.
2. *Healing Public Schools: The Winning Prescription to Cure Their Chronic Illness*, which concentrates on using the well-established principles embodied in quality processes to achieve a high-reliability school organization.
3. *Solutions: Tools and Strategies for Schools*, which concentrates on student-centered information tools and data utilization to effectively implement school strategic plans.

The *Solutions Fieldbook* brings together that research and effort and addresses the *what* and *how* of:

- new challenges to education
- continuous improvement

- high-reliability organizations
- customer-centered schools
- quality processes and goals
- measuring progress
- performance management
- the balanced scorecard
- data warehousing
- benchmarking standards

First and foremost, the *Solutions Fieldbook* is designed for everyday use by both line and staff educators. It can also serve as a useful guide to motivating education stakeholders. More specifically, it is directed to:

- School administrators, department leaders, and school information officers seeking to introduce up-to-date school improvement methods and tools to a wide array of stakeholders;
- Colleges of education seeking to bring more disciplined-thinking principles into the art of teaching;
- Developers of university-level course materials for new teachers; and
- Developers of continuing education course materials for administrators and teachers.

The *Solutions Fieldbook* is structured so the reader can make ready use of its contents. It is just that—a fieldbook—in which readers can make margin notes and personalize its ideas for their own use and the use of their school colleagues. We hope the readers will find this a useful tool to help transform the management and teaching practices of their schools into tangible student achievement.

The Backdrop to Change

1. LOOKING BACK

Schools have changed in some ways. A century ago, student desks and chairs were bolted to the floor, facing front and center. Discipline was just as tight, with students needing individual permission even for a bathroom trip. Students and teachers addressed each other according to rule and teachers dressed formally. In the 20th century, classrooms gradually grew less rigidly organized, a trend that really picked up steam in the 1960s and 1970s.

Today, teachers are probably more considerate of student feelings than they were ten decades ago, and discipline is greatly relaxed. The tone of the classroom is less formal, the furniture can be moved around, and many lower-grade students sit in cooperative learning circles, facing each other. Teachers dress much more casually, and students are granted considerably more self-rule, now moving around more freely to do their work. And most seem able to hit the "john" whenever they wish.

Students also enter and leave the classroom at their own initiative to attend special classes or participate in other activities. Even teachers who still describe themselves as disciplinarians tolerate noise, side conversations, and levels of mischief that would have been quickly stamped out only a generation or two ago.

Classroom talk has also changed a great deal. Only a few decades ago, students and teachers worked within a fairly rigid format. Teachers put questions to the individual student, who was expected to answer on the spot. A premium was placed on both speed and precision. The teaching-learning exercise took place at a brisk clip. There was little or no room for students to develop an informed personal point of view, let alone to ask questions or discuss the matter. Students usually stood when called on to speak. They were also graded on posture and behavior. Today, student presentation as a discipline has disappeared from the school landscape—an extinct animal in education. When students are called upon to address the class, if ever, they do so quite informally.

Today, students manage more of their own instruction. The materials used have also changed. Now there are more texts, supplementary works, and trade books for students than in previous years. The materials are also diverse in style, format, content, and intended audience. They are designed better and presented more attractively than anything available even a few decades ago, let alone in 1900. Topping it off there is new instructional media—television, radio, audiotape, videotape, and computers—making their way into wider classroom use, many showing astounding instructional possibilities.

If these changes show promise for school reformers, other traditional instructional features refuse to give way. The egg-crate, age-graded organization of school life, inherited from the 19th-century school, is very much alive. So too is the snapshot approach to topic definition and content coverage. Concepts of knowledge seem to have changed little.

While education reformers have successfully changed the behavior, culture, and social organization of the classroom and improved learning materials, they have not yet come to grips with the core process features of classroom instruction. Cultural informality within the school and organizational breakdown within the classroom have left a trail of unreliable teaching practices for such basics as reading and math. And these unreliable practices remain dominant today.

After the USSR launched Sputnik in 1957, an unprecedented barrage of events, reports, and forums convinced stakeholders in American education of the urgent need to improve elementary and secondary schools. By the end of the 20th century, grave social, economic, and political problems were still begging for improvement in public schools. State legislatures rushed to pass hundreds of school-related statutes; existing school systems were criticized from every direction. Schools, like business and government, were being challenged to transform themselves to meet the needs of a different time,

At the very moments when the nation most needed a highly skilled workforce to prevent further losses in international trade, commerce, science, and technology, the public school systems were falling further and further behind in preparing students to join and become a productive member of a modern workforce. Millions of Americans, some already high school graduates, were discovered to be functionally illiterate, by minimal literacy measures. Business and the military were forced to spend tens of millions of dollars each year as a kind of "remedial school" for their newest employees and enlistees. American schools had seriously dropped the ball. The schools' failures were becoming an economic burden on employers and on the nation as a whole.

From its earliest days, a central aim of U.S. education has been to help the *individual* fulfill his or her capacities to become a thinking person, one who has learned how to learn. This process was understood to run from immaturity to maturity, from dependence to independence. Developing the self-instructing learner, who knows how to organize and guide his or her own learning experiences, is not a new goal.

In 1873 Herbert Spencer wrote, "In education, the process of self-development should be encouraged to the fullest extent. Children should be led to make their own investigations, and to draw their own inferences. They should be *told* as little as possible, and induced to *discover* as much as possible. Humanity has progressed solely by self-instruction; and . . . to achieve best results, each mind must progress somewhat after the same fashion."

—*Education: Intellectual, Moral, and Physical*

Along the way, reformers were making serious attempts to improve the public schools, long before computer-assisted and managed learning. In the 1920s, for example, Mary Ward, a supervisor of arithmetic in the San Francisco State Normal School (now San Francisco State University), suggested to her students that they prepare learning materials so that their pupils could proceed *at their own rate*. She found, for example, that the number of days needed by each child to master the "high-second-grade arithmetic" ranged from less than five to as many as 65 days.

Her university president, Frederic Burke, was enthusiastic about her instructional exercises for existing textbooks. Later, many of these exercises were used instead of texts. Individual instruction was widely used in the elementary school attached to the Normal School. A few prominent school systems took up the practice. But the practice could not be sustained. It was dissolved by the culture of schooling, defined as "the way we do things around here" that still continues to this day.

President Burke presented a serious indictment of the traditional classroom system used in schools. He felt that the class system was "modeled on the military system . . . constructed upon the assumption that a group of minds can be marshaled and controlled in growth in exactly the same manner that a military officer marshals and directs the bodily movements of a company of soldiers." The picture he paints is of a "solid unbreakable phalanx" marching in lockstep from grade to grade at a pace "set by the 'average' pupil—an algebraic myth born of inanimate figures and an addled pedagogy."

The history of education since World War II is full of examples of attempts at innovation. They meet with great enthusiasm at the outset but not for long. They fail to take root or become part of the mainstream of educational practice.

Typically, such "innovations" involve a small number of interested parties. Many are heavily—but temporarily—subsidized by outside funding. Quietly, they fade away after affecting only a few stakeholders. Educators with even limited on-the-job experience are heard to mutter, "This too shall pass," or "Here we go again," suggesting that educational change is viewed as something to be endured.

This experience of seeing new ideas repeatedly fail to take root may explain why many educators react to demands for educational change with the spirit of lukewarm milk. They usually reply that the major problem in education is the frequency of change. In many cases, change is confused with educational faddism.

If "change" is understood as something *distinctly different*, it is clear that public schools in America have not changed much in any meaningful way since their widespread inception in the 1800s. Significant changes in education, when they have occurred, have been driven by the needs of their time such as social pressures or legal forces that forced desegregation and collective bargaining.

Every few years, observers wryly note, some familiar pattern will reemerge and then, again, disappear. What, then, does it take to change a school system?

This Time It's Really Different

The present crisis in American education involves the erosion of public support as much as it does the glacial meltdown of monetary resources for schools. And the loss of public support can only lead to the further loss of financial support. In a way, school taxes and accountability for cost per proficient student (as opposed to cost per student) holds the potential explosiveness of a 21st-century Boston Tea Party.

Every day, and in so many ways, K–12 schools are driving concerned parents into looking for learning alternatives for their kids. Parents fear school violence, the inability of teachers to maintain classroom civility, more failures of improvement programs, and the possibility that their children will leave school without having mastered so much as the very basic skills.

This erosion of public support is a slippery slope. Whose money will sustain local schools, given that their chronic problems remain intractable or unattended? Why would parents and grandparents willingly support a new bond issue to build school facilities for professionals that seemingly are unable to deliver quality schooling? Which of us would be willing to allow ourselves to be taxed more to support an eroding public institution?

The 1980s

During the early 1980s, educators experienced a wave of demands for reform.

- Teachers and administrators needed to do *more* of what they had been doing, only do it *better*.
- The existing educational system was to be fine-tuned. It required *more* testing of teachers and students.
- Demands grew for *higher* standards for graduation and teacher certification.

- There was need for a *more* closely defined curriculum. School boards and staff began making *more* careful selection of textbooks.
- The call for *more* school accountability was finally beginning to be heard.

Coalitions of concerned citizens organized themselves. Parents, educators, elected officials, business and industry leaders, and private citizens all offered up quick solutions to *fix* broken schools. The quick fix for education was viewed primarily as a *people,* not a system, problem. The existing educational system would improve if people were just smarter and worked a lot harder.

By the mid-1980s, it became clearer that these approaches were aimed at fixing a badly fragmented system. Improvements prescribed from the top down were not changing the situation and ultimately did not. Demanding that educators do more of the same or do the same things better did not—and could not—produce the desired results.

To fix a broken and badly fragmented school meant changing the system. It literally meant putting "Humpty Dumpty" back together again. But the American educational system, originally designed to meet the agricultural age and later retrofitted to meet the needs of the industrial age, was now hopelessly out of date. It was ill prepared and could not meet the needs of an Information Age society.

2. NO CHILD LEFT BEHIND

The "No Child Left Behind" Act signed into law in January 2002 is the most important piece of federal education legislation since the Elementary and Secondary Education Act of 1965 (ESEA). The central aim is to tie federal dollars more closely to school and student performance.

The legislation requires schools to give students annual tests from the third through the eighth grades. The results are to be reported to parents and analyzed by race, gender, and other criteria. The act directs money at economically disadvantaged students and struggling schools. The 50 school districts with the highest percentage of such disadvantaged students will immediately get more federal cash.

The money comes with some strings attached, one of them being that parents of children at schools that continue to fail for several years win the right to transfer their children to better-performing public schools, as well as the money to buy after-school education for their children.

The measure includes a grab bag of other sensible ideas. It gives states a little more flexibility to move money among different federal programs. It sets a timetable for states to make sure that all teachers are qualified to teach their subjects (in terms of traditional school classroom practice, an earth-shattering and long-overdue idea!). And, it increases spending on reading instruction in the early grades for children with substandard English.

All of this comes as the culmination of an "accountability movement" that has gripped governors' mansions and state legislatures for the past two decades. But will this bill really improve education?

In some states (Texas and North Carolina) and cities (Chicago) the accountability movement has produced some big performance improvements. But by now we know that educational change is a slow-moving affair and the federal government accounts for only 7 percent of the monies spent on schools. The twin worries of educational reform continue to be (1) overblown expectations and (2) inevitable and often early disappointment.

The biggest weakness in this legislation is less about what it does than about what it does not deal with. It's as though a failing sports team were told to improve itself, raise its record of games won, and expect to be rewarded. The players want to win, but something stands in the way.

What this legislation totally ignores is the chronic problem of achieving system-wide improvement. In other words, current and traditional school systems have built-in features that literally bar their ability, not their willingness, to achieve "no child left behind."

Defining the Right Problem

The major barriers to system-wide improvement are described in what follows. We intend to show how the central aims of the new American education vision of *Every Kid a Winner*—the optimistic side of "no child left behind"—can be achieved.

There is little doubt that the new legislation radiates compassion. It is the biggest boost in federal spending on poor children in decades. Its pragmatism, expressed through a willingness to boost the size of federal government when it might help, and the bipartisanship expressed in its passage are cause for celebration. But it is doomed to disappoint and ultimately fail in achieving its epic educational vision unless education leaders confront the recurring causes of substandard performance that are built into *system* defects.

Why? Over the past several decades Americans have been asked to invest time, talent, and resources to improve our public schools. But the results have fallen well short of expectations and the reasons are now crystal clear. All of this effort and resources has tinkered around the edges instead of putting into action performance management *systems* for the schools.

No doubt, severe social problems have given education professionals some rough times. But such challenges can't be effectively dealt with except by tackling the systemic problems *in the schools themselves*.

Jack Bowsher,[1] former IBM education director, in his excellent book *Fix Schools First*, presents a first-rate account of major *system failings* of our public schools. He cites the major system failings in a compelling recital of *lacks*, specifically: (1) a coordinated curriculum; (2) grade-level standards and measurements for each grade level; (3) reliable teaching methods used as standard classroom practice; (4) reliable lesson plans as standard professional practice; (5) reliable classroom management skills; (6) adequate teaching materials; (7) adequate appraisal systems; (8) tutoring and catch-up systems; (9) time provisions for all students to learn; (10) fixed staff responsibility for student achievement; and, finally, (11) superintendents and principals regularly receiving reports on student progress and instituting corrective action in real time to overcome measured gaps in achievement.

Unless and until such basic system stumbling blocks to student achievement are dealt with, the efforts of 14,000 boards of education, their superintendents, their principals, and their teachers to meet the vision "no child left behind" are destined to fail.

Bowsher's Focus on System Failings

Lack of a Coordinated Curriculum

Few schools can answer the question, "What do you want students to know and be able to do after completing each grade level, and 13 years (K–12) of schooling?" A coordinated curriculum has learning and student achievement standards set up for *each* of the 13 grades and for graduation from the middle and high schools. This is absolutely essential if no child is to be left behind. Why? Because only then can each grade's tests and lessons become the foundation for the next grade. Only in such a system can students who come from different schools or places with varying levels of preparation and achievement be helped to master known requirements in knowledge and skills.

Schoolteachers themselves now have only a vague idea of what has been covered or must be covered in previous grades in their own schools. Wasted time, boring lessons, and left-behind kids are the inevitable results. Further, only a coordinated curriculum makes it possible for lessons learned in one subject (such as reading) to be reinforced in other classes, such as history and science. Without a coordinated curriculum, the school is at best merely a collection of independent one-room schoolhouses.

Lack of Grade-Level Standards and Measurements for Each Grade Level

If there is no coordinated curriculum, there will be no consistent grade-level standards. Students can't be measured by appropriate achievement tests. There can then be no grade-level assessment system. No surprise then that social promotion is so universally common.

Lack of Reliable Teaching Methods

Teaching that works reliably and not by chance to meet the standards of each grade level's subject matter always has six phases:

1. The learning and performance objectives required for students to achieve the standards are identified and widely communicated.
2. The nuts and bolts for learning subject content are acknowledged.

3. The classroom teaching lessons required for mastery are agreed upon.
4. The teaching strategies and motivational methods of teaching and learning are established and used.
5. The instructional materials and the classroom delivery system for those materials are developed or selected.
6. How the teacher decides whether students have learned the lessons (assessment documents) and what to do if there are gaps has been determined.

Teachers need to address all these points to achieve optimal student success. They establish a far different standard from the typical practice of creating lesson plans without regard to what others are doing.

Lack of Reliable Lesson Plans as Standard Professional Practice

Lesson planning that violates all of the essential principles described above is today's norm, and it is ineffective. Teachers usually develop their lesson plans during evening hours, on weekends, or between other tasks. This slap-dash situation leads to a tyranny of chance in which the student becomes the victim of "bad luck."

Lack of Reliable Classroom Management Skills

Too many teachers learn their classroom management skills "on the job." This subject is inadequately covered in colleges of education. In spite of this, many experienced teachers do an outstanding job of keeping students on track with few interruptions or distractions. Unfortunately, too many others do not. Students quickly pick up on this weakness, and the amount of learning for a grade can decrease by 25 to 50 percent as a result.

Lack of Targeted Teaching Materials

Targeted teaching materials need to be either the first or second most important line item in a school budget. Instead, all too often, they have the lowest priority. It takes classroom libraries with carefully selected books to assist reading development. Classrooms in many schools have very few books and the books they have are either donated or were selected because they were inexpensive. Worse yet, course materials often do not align with lesson plans. Teachers have to use whatever is available or personally buy them.

Lack of Adequate Appraisal Systems

Developing a test or other assessment instrument requires specialized knowledge and experience. The typical teacher lacks such expertise. Teachers do not ordinarily and routinely have or use tests to determine the number of students who have learned the lessons being taught to meet the district and state learning standards.

Most districts do administer annual achievement and mastery tests, but the school year is almost over when these "mega-tests" are taken, and there is little or no feedback to the teachers or staff for corrective action. The basic assessment goal needs to keep students performing well at grade level throughout the year, not just at the end of it—a feature called quality control.

Lack of Tutoring and Catch-Up Systems

When students fail to learn a lesson and begin to fall behind, they need tutoring or other specific actions with a volunteer, teacher, or a personal computer to catch up. Tutoring is the most effective way to teach and learn. Teachers are expensive, however, so schools need to use volunteers or courseware on an interactive personal computer. If a school has no tutoring or catch-up systems, chances are slim that all students will be at grade level in achievement.

Lack of Time for All Students to Learn

Students need different amounts of time to learn. Currently there is only one specific amount of time allotted to teach a given subject. When the teacher has finished teaching the lesson, the class moves on, ready or not. Some students are bored because they caught on fast. Other students fall behind, get lost, and give up.

Lack of Fixed Staff Responsibility for Student Achievement

As remarked above, schools today are typically run like a series of one-room schoolhouses under a large roof. A task analysis for teachers and principals shows that, when it comes to student achievement, no task has a fixed learning responsibility.

Students learn very little from the least effective teachers and two or three times more from the most effective teachers. Unreliable teaching creates unpredictable learning. This is a fundamental reason for poor student performance—and it has been standard practice in our schools for decades. This systemic problem must be addressed to achieve the goal that all students can be successful learners.

The quality of our public schools directly affects us all as parents, as students, and as citizens. Yet too many children in America are segregated by low expectations, illiteracy, and self-doubt. In a constantly changing world that is demanding increasingly complex skills from its workforce, children are literally being left behind. It doesn't have to be this way.

—George W. Bush, 2001

If a nation expects to be ignorant and free, in a state of civilization, it expects what never was and never will be.

—Thomas Jefferson, 1816

Helping Local Schools Improve Themselves

Today, nearly 70 percent of inner-city fourth-graders are unable to read at a basic level on national reading tests. Our high school seniors trail students in Cyprus and South Africa on international math tests. And nearly a third of our college freshmen need remedial courses before being ready to even begin taking college-level courses.

To quote a White House press release, "Although education is primarily a state and local responsibility, *the federal government is partly at fault for tolerating these abysmal results* [emphasis added]. The federal government currently does not do enough to reward success and sanction failure in our education system."

Federal policy has strongly influenced America's schools since the mid-sixties. And over the past four decades, Congress has created hundreds of programs intended to deal with the problems in education—without first asking whether or not the programs produce results or knowing the impact on local needs. This "program for every problem" solution, as it is sometimes called, is cumulative, so that today there are hundreds of education programs spread across 39 federal agencies and costing $120 billion a year. Yet, the achievement gap between rich and poor and between Anglo and minority is still growing.

In response to such dismal results, some have concluded that there should be no federal involvement in education. Others suggest merely adding new programs into the old system. The summary of priorities listed below is based on the notion that an enterprise works best when responsibility is placed closest to the most important activity of the enterprise (the person on the production line is better able to see and correct problems). Those responsible are given greatest latitude and support and those responsible are held accountable for producing results. The following characterizes the "leave no child behind" education blueprint:

- increases accountability for student performance
- focuses on using what works
- reduces bureaucracy and increases flexibility
- empowers parents

Though these priorities do not address reforms in every federal education program, they do address a general vision for reforming the Elementary and Secondary Education Act (ESEA), and they link federal dollars to specific performance goals to ensure improved results. The seven performance-based titles of the act are:

    I. Improving the academic performance of disadvantaged students
   II. Boosting teacher quality
  III. Moving limited English proficient students to English fluency
  IV. Promoting informed parental choice and innovative programs
   V. Encouraging safe schools for the 21st century in meeting our goals for educational excellence.
  VI. Increasing funding for Impact Aid
 VII. Encouraging freedom and accountability

The following key components are intended to improve the Elementary and Secondary Education Act:

To Close the Achievement Gap:

- *Accountability and high standards* hold states, school districts, and schools accountable for ensuring that all students, including disadvantaged students, meet high academic standards. States must develop a system of sanctions and rewards to hold districts and schools accountable for improving academic achievement.
- *Annual academic assessments* for reading and math will enable parents to know how well their child is doing in school and how good a job the school is doing in educating their child. Annual data will be a vital diagnostic tool for schools to achieve continuous improvement. With adequate time for planning and implementation, each state may select and design assessments of their choosing. In addition, a sample of students in each state will be assessed annually with the National Assessment of Educational Progress (NAEP) fourth- and eighth-grade assessment in reading and math.
- *Schools that fail to educate disadvantaged students* will first receive assistance, and then come under corrective action if they still fail to make progress. If schools fail to make adequate yearly progress for three consecutive years, disadvantaged students may use Title I funds to transfer to a higher-performing public or private school or receive supplemental educational services from a provider of choice.

To Improve Literacy by Putting Reading First:

- *Focus on reading in early grades.* States that establish a comprehensive reading program anchored in scientific research from kindergarten to second grade will be eligible for grants under a new Reading First initiative.
- *Early childhood reading instruction.* States participating in the Reading First program will have the option to receive funding from a new "Early Reading First" program to implement research-based pre-reading methods in pre-school programs, including Head Start centers.

To Expand Flexibility and Reduce Bureaucracy:

- *Title I flexibility* is expected to allow more school-wide programs and combine federal funds with local and state funds to improve the quality of the entire school.
- *Increased funds to schools for technology* will be made available by consolidating E-rate funds and technology grant funds and distributing them to schools through states and local districts on the basis of need. This helps ensure that schools no longer have to submit multiple grant applications and incur the associated administrative burdens to obtain education technology funding.
- *Reducing bureaucracy* will be achieved by consolidating overlapping and duplicative categorical grant programs and sending them to states and school districts.
- *New state and local flexibility options* and a charter option for states and districts committed to accountability and reform is to be created. Under this program, charter states and districts would be freed from categorical program requirements in return for submitting a five-year performance agreement to the secretary of education and being subject to especially rigorous standards of accountability.

To Reward Success and Sanction Failure:

- *Rewards for closing the achievement gap* will be given in high-performing states that narrow the achievement gap and improve overall student achievement.
- *Accountability bonus for states* will be offered where they meet accountability requirements, including establishing annual assessments in grades 3 through 8, within two years of enacting this plan.
- *"No Child Left Behind" school bonuses* will reward successful schools that have made the greatest progress in improving the achievement of disadvantaged students.
- *Consequences for failure* include authorizing the secretary of education to reduce federal funds available to a state for administrative expenses if a state fails to meet its performance objectives and does not demonstrate results in academic achievement.

To Promote Informed Parental Choice:

- *School reports to parents* will enable them to make informed choices about schools for their children; they will have access to school-by-school report cards on student achievement for all groups of students.
- *Charter school* funding will be available to assist charter schools with start-up costs, facilities, and other needs associated with creating high-quality schools.
- *Innovative school choice programs and research programs* will be awarded grants by the secretary of education for innovative efforts to expand parental choice, as well as to conduct research on the effects of school choice.

To Improve Teacher Quality:

- *All students taught by quality teachers* will be achieved by giving states and localities flexibility in using federal funds to focus on improving teacher quality. States are expected to ensure that an effective teacher teaches every child.
- *Funding what works* will be achieved by establishing high standards for professional development to help ensure that federal funds promote research-based, effective classroom practice.
- *Strengthening K–12 math and science education* will be achieved through math and science partnerships for states to work with institutions of higher education to improve instruction and curriculum.

To Make Schools Safer for the 21st Century:

- *Teacher protection* will be improved by empowering teachers to remove violent or persistently disruptive students from the classroom.
- *Promoting school safety* will be accomplished by funding and promoting safety and drug prevention during and after school. States are allowed to give consideration to religious organizations on the same basis as other nongovernmental organizations when awarding grants for after-school programs.
- *Rescuing students from unsafe schools* will provide victims of school-based crimes or students trapped in persistently dangerous

schools with a safe alternative. States must report to parents and the public whether a school is safe.

- *Supporting character education* will be achieved through additional funds and grants to states and districts to train teachers in methods of incorporating character-building lessons and activities into the classroom.

THE *SOLUTIONS FIELDBOOK* AND YOU

The *Solutions Fieldbook* is designed to help states, educators, and schools implement these far-reaching performance-based reforms. It takes more than money and good intentions. It takes brainpower supported by the right tools to help educators make the right decisions at the right time. In summary, the tools include:

- *The Quality Dimension in the School* tools such as the Baldrige and ISO 9000 provide the structure to pursue such far-reaching goals.
- *Customer Relationship Management in Education* tools to build an informed linkage between the parents and their child's school as well as fostering intraschool participation and teamwork.
- *The Balanced Scorecard and Schools tools* to help administrators and teachers evaluate in advance the cost and benefit of actions intended to be taken to improve student or teacher performance and to help provide a yardstick to measure success.
- *Data Warehouse* as tools to provide administrators, teachers, and schools, with the useful and useable data to help make better-informed decisions.
- "Using What Works" as scientifically based source material for taking improvement actions.

At the end of the day the task of improving our local K–12 school falls to us all—administrators, teachers, parents, state education officials, boards of education, and the business community—each and all of us. These tools are presented to help us help ourselves.

---

3. OK, HOW DO WE FIX IT?

Currently, few educators and even fewer school policymakers understand that the *processes* used to run all aspects of the school can be measured but are not being measured. The consequence of poor or no measurement is that when changes in test scores occur, for example, few educators are in position to correctly diagnose the causes. More often than not, the result is a misdiagnosis or no diagnosis at all of cause and effect. It is increasingly common to tag the so-called "quality" of the students (the raw material of the process) as the reason test scores (the end result) are either falling or remain static. This is precisely like blaming the defects in a new car solely on the parts (materials) that are assembled, rather than looking to the assembly process (as the predictor of the end result) of the finished product.

Such a diagnosis, typical of educators, is not a feature of car manufacturing. For instance, in that enterprise leaders do not jump to finger-pointing at the workers but, rather, shift the focus to the examining the processes that govern the worker. And to misdiagnose in the local school has much more serious implications than doing so in manufacturing cars. In schools, it is both harmful and defeatist and generates the fear of accountability on the part of school leadership and teachers.

It is embarrassing, wasteful, and disgraceful that one in four college freshmen in 1995 required at least one remedial reading, writing, or mathematics course. Schools simply must turn to using the right tools to efficiently manage school processes and to effectively measure the outcome of these processes. Only in this way can schools sharply increase the number of prepared students—students that meet agreed-upon performance standards. The continual failure to cure this illness can only result in more and more U.S. high schools graduating young men and women with Third World skills, thus relegating them to a lifetime of potentially earning only Third World wages.

Sound harsh? The fact is that the school systems have been permitted to go along without including the full cost of the school's version of "scrap"—defined as those students who cannot function in today's interconnected global economy society—as part of its full unit cost of educating each student.

Think about it this way for a moment. If one out of three new cars coming off the assembly line process was unable to properly function—that is, would not start when needed, did not meet quality and performance standards—how long would that car factory remain in business? In human terms, scrap is the lack of proficiency to compete for livable wages. Scrap is wasted cost!

4. WHY DID I EVER GO INTO EDUCATION?

Test Yourself

Here's an opening exercise designed to focus not only our minds and intellects but our feelings as well.

Team up with another person and write down his or her responses to the first question. Then, switch roles. Stop after the first question. After discussion, go on to the second and third question.

I. What single event did you enjoy most in the school this past year?

Why?

II. List five (5) meaningful education experiences you've had *in your life*.

1.
2.
3.
4.
5.

Discuss among yourselves what this exercise revealed about yourself and your relationship to the profession of education.

NOTE

1. Jack Bowsher, *Fix Schools First* (Gaithersburg, Md.: Aspen Publishers, 2001), pp. 43–48.

The Tyranny of Chance

5. THE TYRANNY OF CHANCE IN CLASSROOM TEACHING

Students whose families and communities have many economic, social, and cultural advantages come to class with lots of educational assets. On average, they do relatively well on various measures of academic achievement. But students from families and communities with fewer such advantages arrive with fewer educational assets. These students find it difficult to automatically make good use of what schools offer unless the school is prepared to invest extra time and considerable effort with them. As a rule they generally do more poorly on tests and other measures of academic achievement.

Studies show that students from less advantaged circumstances are as bright and curious as those in the advantaged groups. However, they may not have learned to read or to write at home, as is common in more advantaged or dedicated circumstances. They often receive less help at home with schoolwork, especially if parents are less educated. They may lack breakfast, let alone a quiet space in which to read or do homework after school. But these are factors that can be overcome. The obstacle — the prime reason for poor school performance — is that schools lack the know-how for effectively dealing with such background situations.

When students from disadvantaged homes come to school poorly prepared to take advantage of conventional teaching, most schools and teachers are just as unprepared to help them. And it is precisely *here,* at this point, that the lack of reliability in classroom teaching is so destructive.

- The students do not know how to deal with adults and conventional schoolwork.
- The teachers do not know how to organize books, lessons, and conventional school resources to take advantage of the curiosity and intelligence that the student first brings to school.
- This mutual incapacity is crippling for many students. It eventually defeats many teachers.

6. HOW WE ARRIVE AT CONCLUSIONS DETERMINES SCHOOL QUALITY

A major part of the problem of educating students concerns not only educators' view of students or teachers or schools or programs but also, more critically, their all-but-outdated assumptions about school organization. The message of the *Solutions Fieldbook* is to argue that all students can learn, and that all schools can teach them, and that all barriers to reform can be dealt with. But first, we argue, schools need to be organized to make that happen.

In our fieldwork we have found many pockets of remarkable children, teachers, schools, and programs that have chalked up success in the face of formidable odds. But to date we have been unable to produce examples of school *systems* in which *all* children learn. Are such systems an unrealistic goal? Perhaps. But perhaps not as unrealistic as we might wish to believe. If we are really to address the learning needs of all children, then entire school buildings and respective administrative and teaching systems must achieve levels of quality assurance that exceed the experiences of American education to date.

Relying on Chance Is a Form of Cruelty in Education

Chance is a tyranny that sentences great numbers of students to painful deficiency in what they must learn to be successful. Chance wastes scarce resources that are solely committed to education. Chance blocks the path of systematic, organized efforts to improve quality.

Today, too much of education practice in U.S. classrooms is subject to chance. But the good news is that we know a great deal now about the theory and the practice of teaching, learning, and management.

- We are better able to realistically and practically approach the ideal of making every kid a winner.
- We have explored the philosophies, effective tools, and practical methods for waging a war on the tyranny of chance in classroom teaching.
- We can apply what has worked well for more than a decade in business to prescribing the winning prescription in the public schools tomorrow.

7. A MESSAGE TO THE PARENTS

Children have a natural tendency to explore their environment and to do things for themselves. When parents encourage a child to explore the environment, the child develops a strong sense of competency or self-efficacy and a sense of control. Parents can discourage this sense of competency by *not* allowing children to do things for themselves. As the world-renowned psychologist Rudolf Dreikers said,

> Every time you do something for a child that he can do for himself, you are discouraging the child. If you dress children when they can dress themselves, or clean up for them when they can clean up for themselves, you are sending messages of incompetence.

The parents of successful children can be described as "nurturing caregivers" and "teachers." Nurturing caregivers give love, encourage independence, and support the child's goals in school, sports, and hobbies. The emphasis of their nurturing is on commitment, control, and challenge. In that kind of home support setting, the child can experience the world as meaningful, interesting, and challenging.

Loving, caring parents provide the basic conditions for the development of the healthy, hardy person. But love is not enough; parents must also be teachers for their children, as witnessed by the following.

I was raised until age thirteen by my grandmother, Omi. An anti-fascist both prior to and during the time of Hitler, she has always been a very courageous woman who, as a war widow, learned to live without men supporting her. She took care of both my mother and me during the hardest times. When I was six years old, she began reading newspapers and newsmagazines to me, going through them page by page.

—Petra Kelly, founder of the West German Green political party, cited in Berman (1986)

My grandmother has been the most influential person in my life. Articulate and dynamic, she became a leader in both church and community. I am convinced that had opportunities for furthering her education been available, she would have been a powerful force in our society. Fortunately for me, she was not only my mentor but my best friend. She constantly told me that I was somebody and could be or do anything on this earth if I would only study hard and keep faith in God.

—M. Deborah Hyde-Rowan, M.D., one of two black female neurosurgeons in the United States, cited in Berman (1986)

Children learn through the examples of parents, teachers, peers, television heroes, and even fairy-tale characters. But parents play the primary role. Through what they say and what they do, parents teach children how to adapt to the world. It is no surprise to find that robust people have robust parents. Parents of hardy people view life changes as natural and interesting.

Parents of strong people also teach their children to view change as opportunity by teaching them skills for confronting new challenges. Many parents of successful executives taught their children how to read a map and get around in a city. Others emphasized learning new activities, such as music, sports, or crafts.

Nurture and healthy modeling from parents are the foundations of psychological health in the child. In their absence, the child is at risk. Fortunately, another adult can provide the support. The school is a natural setting for the development of healthy personality characteristics because many of the child's challenges and triumphs are experienced at school. The classroom teacher provides nurture and instruction. By promoting programs that help children develop social skills, stress-management skills, and values, the school system can be a force for health and wellness.

8. WHAT HAPPENS IN THE CLASSROOM?

Some years ago, when coauthor Lessinger served as the Associate U.S. Commissioner for Elementary and Secondary Education, he worked with Don Stewart, a pioneer in bringing the idea of malpractice in education to the attention of teachers, administrators, and the general public. Through seminars, workshops, and publications,[1] Stewart successfully raised awareness of classroom practices that characterize the tyranny of chance in education. He posed questions to provoke discussion among school staff to help pinpoint problems on site. Some of this pioneering work is reflected in what follows.

9. THE PRIMARY PURPOSE OF SCHOOLING

Examples of common classroom teaching practices raise troublesome issues of poor practice or even malpractice in schooling. Don Stewart attacked these practices with a collection of "get to the heart of it" topics focused on the most important reason for schooling: "The primary purpose of schooling is the student's successful achievement of *learning standards*" [emphasis supplied].

Topic 1. Do school materials and student readiness match?

- What is the result of having the teacher give the student learning materials knowing full well that many students cannot be taught from these materials?
- Can the teacher justify failing the student for not learning something that the teacher already knew beforehand the student would be unable to do?

*Topic 2. Do the student's readiness for schoolwork
and any remedial efforts match?*

Too often the school enrolls students from so-called "disadvantaged" groups that are known to have many entrance achievement deficits known as cumulative ignorance.

- Can these students achieve successfully or are they doomed for failure from the start?

Topic 3. Why isn't more time devoted at admission time
to helping students define and overcome their skill shortcomings?

Here, the concern goes well beyond the loss of potential earning power if failing grades cause the student to be suspended or drop out early. It deals with the student's loss of self-respect as a result of failure.

- If gaps remain in the student's preparation, such as low grades or having not taken an earlier course, what are the realistic chances for the student's success in this school?

Topic 4. Can the teacher give the student a list of
objectives covering prerequisite material for the new
courses or give the student a test covering this material
in order that the student can determine what he/she needs to know?

- If such a list is not available, what opportunities are there for the student to make up for any lack of prerequisite knowledge or skills?
- Is there assistance to help the student identify what it is he/she should know to take the course?
- Can the student try to learn the prerequisite material on his/her own?

Topic 5. Is social promotion a blessing or a curse?

- Is it responsible for a teacher to allow a student to leave a course or grade level knowing full well that the student has not achieved the required knowledge, understandings, and skills for the next grade?
- Would your doctor tell his patient that if they do not get well by January 27 or June 10 that they might as well quit the treatment and stay sick or die?

Topic 6. If the student got a C (D or F) in a course,
does the student know what a C is worth in that course?
Is it 60 percent, 70 percent, 80 percent, 65 percent, or 75 percent?

- Does the student know what percentage of the course he/she learned in order to earn only a "C"?

Topic 7. Teachers have long known that administrators
look upon giving too many A and B grades in classes
generally as the teacher being an "easy" grader.

- Is it fair to either the student or the teacher if the school administration expects the teacher to use a learning situation in which a certain percentage of students must fail or do poorly?

Topic 8. How do we close the gap
between remedial work and student knowledge?

- Why are students who take a course for a second time because of a low grade required to take the *entire* course over again instead of the 20, 30, 40 percent or more that they did not learn when they took the course the first time?
- Is this done for school convenience?

Topic 9. Time frames are arbitrary units of measure
for most learning. All schools still measure results on the
basis of time such as two years of a language, two years of math,
and one semester of this, two semesters of that, etc. This practice
continues regardless of how much learning has taken place.

- If learning a course is important, then why aren't students kept in certain courses until such time as they have learned whatever it is they need?
- Doesn't using time, rather than learning, as a measure of achievement skirt the issue that different students learn the same materials at different rates of speed?
- In fact, aren't some students ready to leave the course much earlier than others? Aren't they likely to become bored when they have to stay to the end of the course?

Topic 10. When can teaching methods be mistaken for punishment?

- When a teacher uses a classroom learning activity as a form of punishment, can this help convince the student that this kind of learning activity is always punishment?
- Is it punishment to discipline students by having them write phrases or sentences many times, or to write extra essays, or solve extra problems?
- In physical education classes, when students are often made to run around the gym or field and/or to perform certain extra exercises, is this not a punishment?
- Can the teacher unknowingly seriously affect a student's future view of learning because of an archaic and common practice?

Topic 11. There is confusion between
school accreditation and teaching results.

- Why do state and regional associations often give official accreditation to a school because of its facilities, the faculty, library, building size, and teacher credentials?
- Doesn't it seem logical that accreditation needs to take into account whether the necessary learning is taking place within the school?

10. IS PRACTICE TEACHING A TEACHING PRACTICE?

Most of us are familiar with practice teaching. Many of us probably still recall a day or two when a newly minted teacher came to practice teach in our classroom. But what are we really saying when we talk about "practice" in the teaching profession?

The core of a real profession consists of using the knowledge and skill of that profession to get expected results. These methods are called *professional practice.* We know these in medicine, in law, and in engineering, to name just three.

We expect a professional practice of law, a professional practice of medicine, and a professional practice of engineering. Can we really expect even the appearance of reliability in classroom teaching without training teachers in the *good practices* of their profession?

Teachers "practice teach." But teachers are not yet expected to achieve a professional teaching practice. Teachers are not required to acquire an agreed-upon body of methods and procedures. And yet it is *good practice* that gets dependable and durable results.

This is not meant to imply that there are not some teachers who apply good practice diligently and consistently. Indeed, there are a few top-notch examples of good teaching practice in many school districts. But it takes the application of standard operating procedures to become effective and to become the lifeblood of reliable organizations.

11. GOOD PRACTICE, POOR PRACTICE, AND MALPRACTICE IN EDUCATION

- *Good practice* is defined as the professional way, the standard operating procedures, of doing things in the instructional process. Good practice *will* reliably produce an intended student learning outcome or result. Good practice is the legacy of long experience. It is the product of research and development.
- *Poor practice*, on the other hand, means ways of doing things that have unpredictable or chance results. (None of us would care to ride in an airplane that is piloted by a crew that has irregular results. The results we demand include safety and reliability.)
- *Malpractice* reflects ways of doing things that generally produce a *harmful* result or are *illegal*. When we choose a surgeon we expect that the doctor will do no harm. We demand that the doctor's activities be legal, and we anticipate helpful results. Should we expect anything less in schools, of school teaching?

Consider these other examples:

1. In medicine, it is good practice to sterilize a wound. In law, it is good practice to exercise due process. In engineering, it is good practice to build safety factors into a structure.
2. In medicine, it is poor practice to routinely use antibiotics. In law, it is poor practice to release privileged information about a pend-

ing trial. In engineering, it is poor practice to place a part that will require servicing in an inaccessible place.

3. In medicine, it is malpractice to leave a surgical instrument or other harmful materials inside a patient. In law, it is malpractice to force a client to perjure himself. In engineering, it is malpractice to knowingly use a set of materials that do not meet specification.

In education there is only the barest understanding of the notion of good practice, poor practice, and malpractice in the instructional process. In fact, when the classroom door closes, almost any instructional process the teacher uses is protected and free from correction.

Susan Markle[2] shows us how outrageous is the failure to achieve a professional teaching practice:

The idea of a major industrial concern turning out, on a standardized production line, 10 per cent superior products, 20 percent good products, and 50 percent average products, with the remainder classed as disposable is so ludicrous in this age of modern technology that it would hardly bear mentioning were it not for the obvious parallel between this outlandish image and the present situation in education.

Condemned on Two Counts

A profession that cannot distinguish among good practice, poor practice, and malpractice is doomed to remain in a primitive state. All persons in such a field will have difficulty proving their professional credibility. Thus a major obstacle to improving school effectiveness and the status of educators arises from two factors: (1) the failure of educators to adopt the known good practice as standard operating procedure in the classroom, and (2) their failure to establish a management system that supports high-reliability classroom teaching.

12. GOOD PRACTICE MUST SATISFY THESE REALITIES

To begin with, good practice must address the realities of public education. Facing up squarely to realities means that good practice must be effective in an everyday classroom of students.

A teaching practice is not good if it is not effective under all of the following five conditions:

- Where the teacher has a course of study to follow in a fixed period of time
- Where there is limited time for problem-solving tests
- Where extra adult classroom help is generally not available
- Where student diversity is great
- Where student achievement must be graded

These are standard handicaps that good teaching practice must overcome.

13. WHERE IS UNRELIABILITY NOT A PROBLEM?

Genuine accountability can be traced to readily identifiable characteristics of successful schools. The evidence shows that, in student-centered schools, faculty and students share a vision of the purposes of teaching and the commitment to success. Teachers pledge to help all students succeed. In such schools there is teamwork. They use what works as standard operating procedure (SOP) to help students master the standards. The schools encourage lots of contact between teachers and students in class and outside, and they work to develop high morale. They have administrators who operate to support the teaching under board-adopted quality system policies.

In student-centered schools:

1. Students and teachers and parents know the required standards
2. Teacher-made exams are put in line with the standards
3. Curriculum is aligned to the standards
4. Students receive expert instruction
5. Schools offer as much time and teaching as students need to learn
6. "Stakes" in student and teacher success are high, holding the system accountable

The most significant characteristic of all is *expert instruction*.

Defining "Expert Instruction"

In early April 2000, the National Reading Panel released a long-awaited report. The panel consisted of leading reading research scientists, representatives of colleges of education, reading teachers, educational administrators, and parents. The panel, mandated by the Congress in 1997, was formed to give public schools *conclusive guidance* on teaching beginning reading.

The panel examined approximately 100,000 reading research studies published since 1966 and another 15,000 having been published before then. "For the first time, we now have guidance based on evidence from sound scientific research on how best to teach children to read," the director of the panel said.

The panel found that the research conducted to date strongly supports the concept that explicitly and systematically teaching children to manipulate phonemes significantly improves children's reading and spelling abilities. The evidence for this is so clear-cut that they said in unambiguous language that this method should be an important component of all classroom reading instruction.

A similar case for expert instruction can be made for math, speaking, listening, and study skills.

Stakeholders Know Reliable Classroom Teaching When They See It

Parents and others who visit reliable classes, where teachers use a businesslike, student-centered approach to learning, are visibly impressed and enthusiastic.

- They see well-trained teachers conducting lessons in an orderly environment.
- They see students mastering the basics.
- They watch, often in amazement, even pre-kindergarten and kindergarten children who are often termed "at risk," reading at quality levels much like affluent youngsters in the first and second grades.

They know reliable classroom teaching when they see:

- Time is allocated for individual and team teacher lesson planning.

- Students and parents know what the teacher expects to avoid wasted time and hopeless confusion.
- Teachers align teaching to curriculum standards so that subject matter and standards are likely to agree.
- Teachers follow their union contracts that strictly specify the *minutes of teacher time,* using those minutes as a precious commodity for classroom learning.
- Teachers avoid labeling students as slow or bright or lazy and treat each student as an individual.
- Discipline problems are more rare because the teacher masters the "take charge of the workplace" process, so that students have less time to misbehave.
- Student performance improves because teachers motivate students and measure results with real-time feedback and corrective action.
- Teachers use a consistent strategy for instruction and resources selected to avoid vague objectives.
- Lessons are planned, thought-out, well organized, and well paced.
- Teachers follow as standard operating practice what solid research says really works to achieve reliable quality classroom teaching.

In the absence of good practice as outlined above, is it too harsh to use the term "tyranny" to describe the effects of chance caused by unreliable classroom teaching quality?

- When *reliable* quality teaching methods are encouraged and used by the school system, students succeed in the foundation subjects.
- If these processes are ignored, students fail. It's as simple as that.

We know a great deal about what it takes to create and manage a school system to produce reliable classroom teaching. Although there are many well-researched and effective teaching methods and management systems available, there are still far too many useless—even damaging—techniques actually in use. And, shamefully, many reliable quality teaching methods are ignored.

NOTES

1. See especially Don Stewart, *Educational Malpractices* (Westminster, Calif.: SLATE Services, 1971).

2. Philip W. Tiemann, Susan Markle, *Analyzing Instructional Content* (Champaign, Ill.: Stipes Publishing, 1990).

The Mission of the School in the Information Age

14. DEFINING THE MISSION

The mission of the quality school in the 21st century can be viewed in the following terms:

Learning and earning are now inseparable.

A quality educational system is an absolute essential to the economic, political, and social welfare of the United States.

It's now time to think and work smarter.

Demanding that people work harder or do more of what has always been done, in the way it has always been done, cannot produce needed changes or results.

We need to stop driving down the road with our eyes on the rear-view mirror.

The current system is structured and organized to meet the needs of an age and society that no longer exists.

The social and economic transition is well under way; the school system must catch up.

The system must be restructured to meet the needs of a society already in a transition to an enriched cognitive economy and an information age.

Make "This is the way we've always done it around here" famous last words.

The new culture consists of common understandings about the rules, roles, and relationships between and among employees and stakeholders.

Business, parents, citizens, and educators demand better schools.

Educators cannot make the needed changes in public schools alone. The "public" nature of the school makes all citizens legitimate partners to change.

Change must be persistently ground out.

The changes needed in education require long-term commitment to improvement. There is no quick fix.

"It's the economy, stupid."

There is agreement about the purposes of public school in one highly significant area. There is a consensus that students need employability skills for the new economy.

We need schools to meet the needs of a cognitive-rich Information Age economy.

School leaders and policymakers must commit to the transformation of education and understand what this fully means, or it will not occur.

Leave no stone unturned.

Every aspect of the educational process and system must be studied and reconsidered in light of new and different societal expectations.

We must spell out and more clearly define the purposes and required outcomes of public education at the national, state, and local levels. There needs to be a shared understanding among educators and their constituents about the goals and outcomes of the school process.

Facing this new and more demanding challenge may boggle the mind of many educators. After more than two decades of almost unrelenting criticism and pressure, many educators are skeptical, disillusioned, and just plain worn down. It is understandably threatening to some educators to suggest that they now set out to change the system in which they have succeeded both as students themselves and as professionals.

15. HIJACKING CRITICAL ISSUES FOR OTHER PURPOSES

Let's see. Can the fear of terrorism really spur a resurgence of interest in and greater attention to quality? Israel has lived with this awareness since 1948. Great Britain has slept with one eye open for more than 20 years in Northern Ireland. Consider just these few examples of our country's response to an unprecedented threat:

- Airline passengers demand a higher degree of assurance that the plane they plan to travel in is safe. Every step in the process of airline travel will now be under constant scrutiny to help assure the quality of air travel. Security has replaced the meal served aloft as the first measure of quality.
- Health officials are alert for any signs of chemical or biological infestation. Local officials are taking unprecedented steps to safeguard our sources of drinking water. Designer water and safe water must meet the same rigorous standards. Only safe drinking water is quality drinking water.
- Tunnels, bridges, pipelines, and rail and bus lines are stepping up safety precautions in all stages of the process. The essentials of our way of life, which we took for granted yesterday, are now seen as precious and vulnerable.
- Every stage of the process becomes a point of quality control.

The brave New York City firefighters who gave their lives in an attempt to save others on September 11, 2001, were a brutal loss. But with that loss we relearned that quality in all things is like fire *protection* and is fast becoming as critical to our individual and collective safety as fire fighting. Preventing terrorist strikes has put America on the alert as never before in our history.

Today, and for the foreseeable future, the police, the military, and just ordinary citizens are being urged "to pay increasing attention to your surroundings." Every step in our daily process of living is being reexamined in the same way. Every American now feels a heightened sense of responsibility for his or her own safety and the safety of the family, the neighborhood, and the workplace. Every American now has come to understand that every other American is a "customer" when it comes to the need for mutual protection.

Economists commonly use two measures to sum up performance management: efficiency and effectiveness.

- *Efficiency* is the ratio of how much is accomplished as a proportion of the amount of effort expended. It is the ratio of the useful output of the system to the total input into the system. It is how much bang we get for our buck. It is the *quality* or property of being efficient.

- *Effectiveness* defines the intended or expected effect. It means producing or having the capability of producing a desired effect. It measures the extent to which the bang accomplished its intended purpose. It is the *quality* and power of being effective.

In light of the new world that dawned on September 11, 2001, business and school leaders must now make hard choices. Leaders must increasingly look for ways to improve both their operating efficiency and organizational effectiveness or risk further erosion in performance and deteriorating results. In an America confronted with an array of emerging new priorities, coupled with increasingly strained financial resources, there is no longer any middle ground for schools.

16. FRAMING THE ISSUES

We're no longer grasping for something that will break the grinding cycle of substandard school performance. Nor is this about buzzwords like "standards" or "assessments" or scapegoating the schools. It's simply about writing down what our kids need to know and assuring that they learn it in order to become successful wage earners, enlightened citizens, and informed parents.

Standards and assessments are a good start. But they're not all we need. We need two overarching commitments:

1. Agreement on the urgent need for a vastly improved teaching profession
2. Curricula that can actually move American kids to levels of achievement that are commonplace in the rest of the developed world

Regrettably, America's best students come up just average by international standards. The grim reality is that even as our overall achievement inches up, our sons and daughters remain handicapped by an education system that expects too little and routinely rewards substandard performance against even those minimal requirements.

As a powerful example, each year, when nearly three million high school seniors are ready to enter the workforce—where demands only get steeper—it's no longer any surprise that far too many of them simply cannot cut it; they cannot compete!

"Fortunately, the remedy for all of this isn't the least bit vague," says Lou Gerstner, IBM chairman.

> We already know what the steps need to be. First, we need to improve our ability to test and assess student performance. Next, we need to strengthen accountability inside and outside the schools. Finally, we've got to develop, sustain and support a world-class teaching force. For those who think that short list sounds pretty ordinary—good tests, more accountability, and higher quality teachers—we agree. It's not rocket science. No. It's far, far harder!

We really don't have much choice. Either we do something about this outrage or we're the ones standing between all of our children and a fair and equal opportunity to compete in the global economy of the 21st century. A growing chorus in the nation argues for abandoning the public schools and setting up private-sector alternatives. But the answer for the public schools is not about building charter schools or diverting state or federal monies to send more kids to private school.

Life, we have come to learn, is many things. But it's never easy. Neither is education reform. Our public schools can work. They have to! But there are no shortcuts. We have to be strong and focused. We have to try. We have to fix our schools. We also have to be smart about picking our spots and concentrating on a short list of items that will leverage high-impact change. It's about TAT: Testing, Accountability, and Teachers.

Testing

The issue of genuine testing tied to genuine consequences has been a flash point. Opponents screamed that testing is "unfair, demoralizing, and discriminatory." True, bad tests, poorly administered, are all of those things. But now we have wrung the emotion out of this debate, for the most part, and finally gotten down to the business of making sure that tests do what they're supposed to do—test fairly and be objective measures of progress against standards, so that improvement can be targeted where needed. This isn't that hard to understand.

- Schools and parents need to know what the kids are learning.
- Schools and parents need to know, without mystery, what's on the tests.
- We need confidence that following the curriculum assures that kids score well.

Seen clearly by fair-minded people, these factors support high-stakes testing.

Accountability

It isn't about the kids. It's about the system: teachers, principals, administrators, school board members. It's about parents, and business leaders, governmental leaders, and the media. It's also about balance and fairness, and being tough—but doing it right.

Teaching

Once and for all, it's time to stop whining about making teaching both a real profession and more attractive, and *do* it. We can hang our heads. We can moan about teachers' pay. We can say it's too low and call it unfair or we can commit to fixing the problem with competitive salaries, with pay tied to performance, and with pay for expertise. Teaching is a profession and needs to be treated like one. It means fixing the compensation issues and holding teachers accountable for results. It also means providing teachers access to the kinds of tools that are taken for granted in other professions—access to high-quality teaching materials, information tools, and professional development.

We all know there are factions in education that have vested interests in preserving the status quo. They seek to advance their own agendas behind mask-like discrimination. They hide behind the ghost of testing. And they say they speak for the kids. But listen closely! What we hear is a pathetic willingness to sacrifice an entire generation—and deny them their shot at a better chance, a better future, and a better life.

The forces that would perpetuate a legacy of mediocrity in schools are deeply entrenched. They are not likely to back down easily. But if they are allowed to prevail, there's no doubt we'll see a further exodus out of the public school system and American public education will be reduced to what British sociologist Richard Titmuss has labeled "a poor service for poor people."

17. AN ENGINEERING MIND-SET FOR APTITUDE AND RESULTS

The entire approach to aptitude, so ingrained in our public schools that it seems part of the "natural order" of things, is foreign to an "education engineer" assigned to develop solutions. Of course they might not disagree that students differ in aptitude, but they would argue persuasively that aptitude needs to be defined not as the degree of mastery a student may attain within a given course, but rather as a function of the amount of time and the *quality* of the classroom teaching and support system needed to attain full mastery of a learned task.

The engineering characterization of aptitude turns attention away from the routine of sorting students according to how many questions they successfully answer after a completing a course of study. Rather, it sets as a goal for the end of an educational cycle each student's mastery of skills, not merely a fair grade. In other words, *as applied to the acquisition of basic skills*, this definition of aptitude demonstrates that, apart from a very small percentage of students, every student can earn a grade of A.

Obviously some students master a skill such as basic reading quickly, and others will be quite slow. But if the curriculum and use of reliable teaching methods is tailored to these differences, every student can learn to read, calculate, or master the skills essential to a productive life in our society. And when they do master it they deserve an A or, rather, since letter grades are obsolete assumptions, they deserve a certificate of initial mastery describing the skills—an accurate reflection of a *competence warranty* the teacher and the school proudly stands behind.

What matters is not how long a student took to master a particular skill or even the type of teaching received, but the fact that the student now possesses that skill.

What happens when we accept the engineering mind-set definition of aptitude? In place of a fixed program in which each student learns what he can, a goal of basic mastery is set for everyone, whereupon everyone is offered whatever programs are necessary to meet that goal. Instead of (or, if necessary, along with) grades, teachers give diagnostic tests to help them decide which program each student needs. At the end of this process, teachers might award skill warranties instead of, or together with, the increasingly doubtful "diploma." With regard to the basic skills, instead of labeling some students as "losers," educators would start with the assumption that every kid will finish every class as a winner. In this sense, the school treats learning to read and to do essential math not as a race to the top of a mountain but as the ability to get there, one way or another, at a variety of paces.

As long as schools cling to the distorted notion of aptitude, teachers will remain satisfied to grade students on whether they can mount from one level of reading to the next in the average time allowed within the standard pattern of instruction. Too often a student's doing poorly is defined as "low aptitude" or lack of motivation, or the child is labeled as dyslexic, which he or she quite often is not. The school more often has simply not taught the child how to read. Worse yet, the student goes through the rest of life with a "reading problem" that is seldom blamed on the school. Somehow the school usually blames it on an external condition outside of their control, such as economic or social background.

Whether this has become an institutional copout or carried forward with the best of intentions it is a step toward providing special programs for students who are presumed to have special needs.

18. ENDING CHANCE: RELIABILITY IN CLASSROOM TEACHING

Taxpayers pay for schools to employ and manage competent and qualified education professionals. The requirement *starts* with credentials; it doesn't end there. Like newly minted officers from the military service academies, teachers and administrators begin to develop their education skills under the baptism of fire in today's schools. Reliable teaching is every bit as critical a skill for the educator as strategic and tactical prowess is for the military professional.

Second, parents entrust their kids to the public schools. They have every right to expect reliable performance from every teacher and school administrator. It can no longer be considered permissible to allow marginal performance from a profession that is every bit as important to the future of our nation as the military. Schooling is very serious business.

To allow unreliable classroom teaching to continue to persist in even one public school classroom is to betray the trust of parents and the nation and to relegate an entire generation of American schoolchildren to a lifetime of economic and social struggle.

A Means to an End

More and more states now require performance standards and accountability for measuring local public schools and student achievement through publicly reported statewide testing. But accountability and testing programs are not ends in themselves. They are powerful tools that are intended to help educators accomplish the real purpose of education—higher levels of student achievement and more proficient student learning. The two tools are necessary but not sufficient. They are simply two legs of an indispensable three-legged stool. The missing leg is *reliability* in classroom teaching and a performance management system that supports it.

Reliability is delivering what we count on getting *every time* and not just by chance. In our new world, we not only expect airline maintenance to be perfect every time, but we also expect airport screening and security to be effective. We expect our physician to prescribe the right treatment every time. We want our bank to give us the right balance every time. Regrettably, our expectations about service and product dependability are not always met. When they are not met, we are often motivated—sometimes passionately—to try to do something about it. This, too, must become the standard expectation in education.

19. WHO GUARANTEES RELIABLE CLASSROOM PERFORMANCE?

Parents have long concluded that they can't expect good teaching every time or even from time to time. Parents come to learn, if only intuitively, that luck or chance too often rules the quality of classroom teaching. Their concern is obvious when school opens and they wonder which teacher their child will get this time—*the good one or the other one?* The "luck of the draw" is especially distressing when it affects the elementary school foundation subjects of reading, writing, mathematics, and study skills.

While parents may recognize the value of the teacher's knowledge and skills, they most likely do not realize that it is the *system* the teacher works within that is the crucial underwriter—the guarantor of the quality of that classroom teaching. The performance management of the school determines the effectiveness and reliability of each teacher.

It is now evident that a tyranny of chance need no longer rule in the quality of classroom teaching. Teaching can be reliable, as evidenced by the following examples of practices that work:

1. When time is allocated for teacher planning, teachers do plan their lessons.
2. Students know what their teacher expects, and this eliminates wasted time and hopeless student confusion.
3. Teachers choose what to include or ignore, so when reliable teachers align their teaching to curriculum standards and subject matter, the standards are more likely to be met.
4. Reliable teaching is teaching using every minute of the classroom time period effectively and efficiently. Teaching time is what taxpayers pay for with their school tax dollars. Union contracts strictly specify the *minutes of teacher time*. Time is the unrecoverable commodity for classroom learning. Once wasted or used poorly, time cannot be retrieved.
5. Even a casual visit to some classrooms easily shows the efficient and effective use of time. Reliable teaching closes the wide variation from one teacher to another in classroom time devoted to subject matter.
6. In reliably taught classrooms no student is judged to be a low performer. Each is treated as an individual; none are stereotyped as a group. They are called on as often as others and given the same amount of time to answer the questions. Reliable teaching avoids labeling, either directly or indirectly.

7. Discipline problems are rare in classes where the teacher has mastered the "take charge of the workplace" process. Students don't have time to misbehave.

8. When student performance is motivated and accomplishments measured, the rate and quality of student performance improve. Reliable teachers have both skill and desire to motivate and measure adequately.

9. Reliable teaching secures motivation and measurement with real-time feedback and corrective action.

10. Reliable teaching is teaching with a consistent strategy for instruction. Resources are selected according to that strategy. The teaching avoids vague objectives. Lessons are well thought out and well organized. Classroom work is well paced. Teachers regularly check to see how students are doing. If the check shows learning needs, real-time action is taken to serve student learning needs.

Reliable teachers ask the question, "What does solid research say really works in teaching to achieve quality classroom teaching?" They then use what works as standard operating practice, just as doctors use the treatments that are known to work to treat an illness. Using *what works* in classroom teaching practice can end tyranny of chance in classroom teaching. (See appendix.)

20. GROWING A HIGH-RELIABILITY ORGANIZATION

High-reliability organizations (HROs) are those organizations whose products and services we can depend on every time. They do that for us by communicating a clear mission and achievable goals to staff and stakeholders alike and by passionately focusing on seeing that these goals are actually achieved. If they are not achieved, corrective action is immediately taken.

In HRO schools, all of the classrooms teach a given subject with the same clear objectives and use such "teaching actions" known to be effective in getting increasing levels of student accomplishment. School staffs in such organizations show a strong sense of mission in helping *all* students achieve the learning standards reflected by the educational objectives. They communicate, honor, and vigorously pursue the achievement of the standards set out for them in their respective subject fields. HRO schools obsess over the quality of their processes.

Understanding the Inner Workings of Processes and Systems

Picture for a moment any team sport you have played or observed. With just a little thought, you soon find that you know quite a bit about *processes* and *systems* and the essentials required to support reliable quality in classroom teaching.

Which sport you choose doesn't matter much, because any team sport illustrates the importance of executing effective processes and is performed by a system of players effectively using the tools of their game.

Obviously, no process is complete in itself. To succeed we have to look at the system as a whole. In the world of business and education the system includes not only processes (carried out by workers and leaders) but also suppliers and customers. Customers, especially parents and students, have likes and dislikes, wishes and desires, that need to be scrutinized and fed back into the system so that the system can continually improve, always seeking to please its customers with results that exceed their expectations.

Critical to the success of any system, be it in a sport or a school program, is how that system is coached, led, and managed. Performance management cannot get the best from a system just by trying to get every process in the system to compete and getting each element to do its individual best.

Like an orchestra—to use another analogy—a school system must discourage such an individualized approach. If each member of an orchestra tried to show off his or her individual musical ability rather than playing together, the result would be noise. For orchestras and school systems, the goal has to be harmonious mutual benefit. This requires cooperation.

Systems Need Continual Improvement to Thrive

The concept of continual improvement has been around for thousands of years, especially for personal behavior. Around 1922 a French psychotherapist, Emile Coué, won fame and influence in Europe and the United States by teaching that people could heal their own diseases by repeating his continual improvement slogan, "Every day in every way, I'm getting better and better."

About Analysis and Synthesis—The Central Idea in Systems Thinking

To understand the central ideas in system thinking, just watch children with a new game or toy that they want to understand. They naturally use this three-step process:

1. They take it apart.
2. They try to understand the conduct of each part separately.
3. They try to gather together an understanding of the parts into an understanding of the whole.

That is a good description of analysis.

Analysis has been the leading method of Western thinking for more than four hundred years. Coaches, leaders, and managers use analysis to organize sports, business firms, and schools. But we cannot explain the performance of a system solely by analysis. We must also use synthesis.

Instead of only taking things apart and looking at each part separately, we must put them all together and look at them as an integrated and coordinated unit, be it a team, a toy, or an organization like a school that seeks to achieve some purpose. We must also go on to see that particular system in terms of larger ones to which it belongs. We must expand our thinking and consider those elements that are outside of what we control but that influences what the system can do.

Russell L. Ackoff[1] gives an example of the influence of a larger system to which a system belongs. He points out that auto mechanics can take as many English and American cars apart for as long as they like and they will never discover why the English steering wheel is on the right and the American steering wheel is on the left. The reason for the placement of the steering wheels is not in how the cars were assembled; the reason is in the difference between two societies, the expanded roadway systems in which those cars are used.

Analysis deals with *how* each part works; synthesis deals with the *why* the parts work together, not from a mechanical point of view but from a design and function viewpoint. If you had automotive experts pick the world's best parts separately and you assembled those best parts, the cars wouldn't work except by chance. The parts were not designed to fit together. Once we understand that the object must be to manage the system as a whole to achieve the best interaction of the parts, it is easier to see why so much of what we have tried to do in recent years to improve the quality of our public schools could not possibly work in the long run.

Likewise, to improve the American education system, we must have sharper communication, meaningful coordination, and unexcelled cooperation among the processes. Even the best fiddling with the parts won't do.

21. THE HIGH-RELIABILITY ORGANIZATION LEARNS FROM ITS OWN MISTAKES

Mistakes made need to be transformed into lessons learned. Leaders of high-reliability organizations do not fear exposing what isn't working because the active mind-set behind every HRO is continuous improvement. A problem found is never a declaration of failure; it is an opening for inventing and deploying corrective action aimed at making an imperfect process work better. Further, if the corrective action doesn't work, then another corrective action is taken. This is increasingly a performance goal of school leadership.

All high-reliability school organizations follow these principles:

- They routinely analyze all systems and their processes that make up a school system (e.g., classroom instruction, parent communication, transportation, assessment, logistical support, etc.), for discrepancy and to make decisions for improvement based on fact.
- They consciously define the organization's internal and external customers, actively seeking input from both.
- They drive out fear by encouraging its members to risk making mistakes in order to learn more about the system.
- They remove sole reliance on top-down command and control barriers by establishing clear and open lines of two-way communication.

- They educate and retrain teachers and staff on a scheduled basis.
- They thrive on fostering teamwork and interrelationships.

The ISO and Baldrige Help Insure Reliable Quality

Schools are moving toward becoming high-reliability organizations by using the insights, procedures, and tools of two authoritative quality-improvement systems: ISO 9000 Education Criteria and the Malcolm Baldrige National Quality Program Education Criteria for Performance Excellence.

In our book *Healing Public Schools,* we show the strength of using the ISO 9000 quality management standards together with the Baldrige Education Criteria to formulate a *winning prescription* to help heal the chronic illness that has hit America's public schools: unreliable quality in classroom teaching. The Baldrige Education Criteria raise the basic question-and-answer patterns for improved performance management. ISO 9000 standards guide the development of bottom-up solutions through a set of processes for assessment, treatments, and follow-through. The Baldrige program is self-administered within the organization. ISO 9000 is also self-administered and, further, encourages using independent examiners to help the organization evaluate its performance management.

The ISO process guides school staff:

1. To say what they will do for every key system process
2. To write down the goals they intend to pursue so others may review it
3. To do what they have written down
4. To measure the effectiveness of the results
5. To take corrective action through continual review of the processes used on a defined schedule in order to continue making improvements

Both Baldrige and ISO 9000 criteria charge school leadership with developing a quality policy for key operational and teaching processes. The winning prescription requires constant attention to the *how* of school processes. It means asking probing questions, allowing answers to flow freely, describing successive activities, and openly discussing and challenging the tools, techniques, and methods currently being used during the schooling process. The winning prescription starts with a *survey of processes* intended to motivate, plan, and assure classroom reliability.

22. PROCESS IMPROVEMENT IS CONTINUOUS IMPROVEMENT

By its very nature, a process problem is never permanently solved. The problems either become ingrained bad habits that lead to further decline, or they become consciously improved. Once fully committed to taking the winning prescription, the school staff pulls away from solely playing the role of system inspectors. They evolve into system designers. The difference? In the latter role they seek to constantly improve the systems to achieve what school leadership and the school customer require.

At the end of the day, the objective in applying the winning prescription is not to discover defects. It is about uncovering, understanding, and then continually correcting the *processes* that lead to defects. Following the Baldrige and ISO 9000 prescriptions helps to avert undesirable consequences and move school organizations closer to becoming high-reliability organizations.

23. PERFORMANCE MANAGEMENT TOOLS

Performance management tools that steer the *essential processes* of schools—teaching, transportation, food service, maintenance, and so on—will help bring the entire school and classroom teaching to a higher level of efficiency and effectiveness. After all, schools may not be a business, but there should be little disagreement that schools need to be run on a *businesslike* basis.

Measuring school performance in terms of calculating the unit cost—the *cost per prepared student* (a student meeting agreed-upon performance standards at a given time in the school system progress calendar)—is destined to gain rapid popularity. First, taxpayers can no longer be continually expected to shell out more money for poorer results. Already educators are being forced to stand accountable for the costs and benefits to both students and the community. Second, the American public will not continue to accept the wasted unit cost of school dropout rates running 20 percent or more each year and the one-third or more of high school graduates who are ill-prepared to handle a first job that demands basic thinking skills.

Traditionally, only *spending per student* has been the dollar statistic used to show how much the community values its schools. But the spending-per-student dollar figure offers no information whatsoever about how much value the school delivers to each student in its charge or back to the community, the state, and the nation that pays the bills.

Spending per student is the dollar measure of the resources invested in education, but it is still only an accounting measure. It really tells taxpayers and stakeholders nothing at all about the economic *efficiency* or the management and teaching *effectiveness* of the learning processes taking place inside the school.

This situation reminds one of an old joke. A mother is asked, "What is your son studying in college?"

"Oh," she replies with pride, "he's learning to be a chemist—he makes waste material out of money."

Processes Lead the Way

Schools need to wrestle with the importance of continuous processes. At the outset the major stumbling block to school leaders may be the difficulty in grasping the critical consequences of processes. However, only in this way can the school administration and board expect to achieve dependable teaching time in every classroom. And that is precisely what we are looking for.

Most people are in the habit of thinking solely in terms of *things*. We ordinarily think of products and specific elements. Most folks do not think much about the processes or underlying ways in which things—and services—are created and developed.

A process is merely a repeated activity that changes something. Most homemakers know that beating whipping cream with an egg-beater will first produce whipped cream. If the process continues, it eventually changes the cream to butter. Persistence in the vastly more complex processes of schools produces equally substantial changes.

Steadily evaluating and improving all school processes leads to steady improvement in the reliability of classroom teaching time. For example, one of the processes badly in need of continuous improvement is matching instruction to the readiness of the students in a new class. Teachers need to know about students' previous performance and adjust instruction accordingly. Before they reach that point, the system must be set up to make the information available.

Every repeatable school activity in a school district can be—no, in fact, needs to be—viewed as a process of events. In schools, the processes *are* the system. Even resolving parent complaints is as much an education process as is recruitment, orientation, training, or staff development.

The next time one of your parents declares that the #@$% school system has a problem, you can trace the reasons for that angry statement. The problem needing attention is located in one of the school system's processes.

24. DEMING: THE KEY TO UNLOCK PROCESS IMPROVEMENT

A common mistake made by teachers and staff is to think that problems are the property of an individual or of some special event. Viewed more objectively, most problems are not now considered as isolated situations or special causes. They are not disconnected events but are built into the system. System problems persist over time, the consequence of some cause and effect buried deep in the system's unstudied processes. These chronic flaws, if allowed to remain unstudied, eventually reveal themselves in unexpected ways to block the school's desired end result.

W. Edwards Deming gives us guidance. His lifetime of experience on the character of the processes that are entrenched in the system results in a startling statistic. He is often quoted as saying that fully "94 percent of the troubles an organization has can be attributed to system." Only 5 percent are due to what Deming terms "special causes."[2] Special causes are the occasional glitches that follow Murphy's Law— problems that arise because the system made them possible or inevitable. This bottom line provides guidance to quality experts, parents, and educators with a simple and direct fix. Concentrate on the processes, and the end result you want will take care of itself.

The winning prescription, starting with ISO and Baldrige process improvement methods, gets us to pay constant attention to the "what" and "how" of processes. It asks school leaders and teachers to describe the sequential activities they use—often unconsciously—and to *commit to writing* the tools, techniques, and methods used during those schooling process. Education leaders are urged to think of process-improvement directives as a "census of processes" for motivating staff, planning for needs, and assuring reliable quality.

The attention to processes leads us to the desired continuous improvement. We know that, by their very nature, school processes can never be permanently perfected. School processes either become (1) habit forming and eventually deteriorate, or (2) part of our consciousness and steadily improve. Once fully immersed in process quality improvement, school staff backs away from solely playing the role of inspectors. In its place they begin to think as would an architect, engineer, or designer. They seek to identify *system improvements* that create and sustain the results that other staff members, parents, and future employers—the internal and external customers—demand.

The guts of improving system processes are the path to preventing student failure and reducing the need for student remediation. The target is to find the knowledge and insights needed to correct the processes that lead to defects. We now want to eliminate problems *before* they lead to unintended consequences. Put another way, we are increasingly talking fire prevention and less about fire fighting.

NOTES

1. Russell L. Ackoff, *The Design of Social Research* (Chicago: Chicago University Press, 1953), p. 24.

2. W. Edwards Deming, *Out of the Crisis* (Cambridge, Mass.: Massachusetts Institute of Technology Center for Advanced Engineering Study, 1986), p. 315.

Strategic Planning—The Leadership Role

25. AMERICA HAS A PROBLEM—AND IT IS A BIG ONE

In the foreword to *Healing Public Schools,* Leslie Kossoff, a working colleague of W. Edwards Deming for six years, wrote:

> For all our innovation and creativity; for all that we are the driver of the global economy; for all that we have been and continue to be to ourselves and to the world, we have one big problem. As a country we are complacent. And nowhere is that more apparent than in our educational system.
>
> I am not an educator by trade, although I teach both MBA and professional extension courses. My focus on education is based on my experience in organizations in every sector and throughout this country for the last twenty years.
>
> The constant? In every organization we see the impact of the problems in the educational system.
>
> It doesn't matter that for twenty years—since the "Why Johnny Can't Read" uproar—we have seen educational systems at every level and in every community make new claims to how they would change the situation. Johnny *can* read and he *will*—no matter what it takes.
>
> And what it has taken over these past years has taken its toll on everyone involved in every aspect of education: the educators, trying to find a way to bring higher learning—and more important, a love for learning—into the classroom; the administrators, all dealing with constant change in a system that seems to result in the same outcome—too many Johnnys still can't read; the parents, desperate to ensure that their children will be able to succeed in their learning and fit comfortably into this new economy; the children, almost an ongoing lab course of experiments in everything

from changing methodologies to ever-increasing and unrealistic standards to be met.

The constant? That with all that change, nothing has fundamentally changed. The precepts upon which teaching is performed and school districts are administered have stayed fundamentally the same through thick and thin, change after change, new program after new program.

Every one of those programs was to provide the right answer—this time. Yet, ultimately, no one has truly addressed the issues that need to be addressed to ensure that Johnny can read, write, compute and, more than anything else, think. Johnny has to learn how to think.

The Challenge

The problem with education and educators, as with most large organizations, is that they are entrenched. In many ways the education system is the best example of the complacence of this country. We rest on our laurels even as we say we are going to do things differently.

These problems are further exacerbated by the political climate in which decisions are being made. The educators that become politicos—no matter how well trained, well thought, and well intentioned—become victims of the system. Education may be funded by the government but should not be managed by the government.

As with any specialized industry, education should be monitored and overseen by those who truly specialize in the field. It is an area of expertise as much as it is a field of endeavor.

Moreover, those who house the educational organization at every level have a passion for and a belief in what they do. They are truly committed to fulfilling the needs of the students—of assisting in the creation of thinking, sentient beings who will be valuable, contributing adults. They should be allowed to work to their passion, innovate and create within their classrooms, yet always work within a system that is designed to succeed, as well as to create success for its "customers"—the students.

Educators are well aware that the output of their system is the input into society. We all see the results of education as it stands today and it is not acceptable for individuals or for society. In fact, unless and until we directly address the fundamentals of the system we are dooming our society to a future of being an also-ran. We may believe our press at the moment—but moments pass and we will be working from a seriously disadvantaged position in the not too distant future.

Signs, Portents and Industry History

Those who work in industry are already seeing the signs and portents of things to come. Organizations have to provide far more extensive training in basic skills than ever before. The technology industry, while still recruiting in this country, spends untold millions recruiting in what are considered Third World countries for qualified candidates. Worse yet, they are finding more and more candidates in those countries than they do in our own.

Yet we have had the answer to all these questions and challenges for many years. It has been our complacency that kept us from acting, as we need to act.

In the late 1970s America realized that it had a problem with Japan. Suddenly, it seemed, the Japanese had cornered our markets in both automobiles and consumer electronics. We were at war. We were under siege. We were not prepared.

Yet, for anyone who had been paying attention, it was clear since the 1950s that the Japanese were actively and conscientiously working toward creating marketable products. They knew that their products had to be both competitive and attractive to the American audience.

Where they did not have the foresight to innovate new products, they licensed or bought our technology. Where they already had the products, they focused on creating the highest quality they could so that their products could be easily differentiated from ours.

"Made in Japan" quickly moved from an insult to an expression of the highest regard.

Still, we were unprepared.

Our solution? We mobilized. We learned what the Japanese had done and how to apply it to our way of doing business. We adopted and adapted their systems and turned them into our own. We created a quality improvement system and methodology that continues to keep our organizations competitive to this day.

The lessons to be learned from this bit of history are many and varied—and all apply to education as it now stands.

We are at a crossroads—not only for education, but for our country. It is our responsibility to ensure that we look at the fundamentals of how we perform the business of education to ensure that the products and services we create are of the highest order.

"Made in America" should be a point of pride. And what we must make in this country—first and foremost—is the highest caliber citizen and societal contributor possible.

The way that this can be achieved, in part, is to bring *quality* precepts into the educational system. There are no surprises here. We have all been aware for a very long time that the problem exists.

The only question has been, what must we *really* do about it to ensure that it is fixed—and fixed for the long term.

Opportunities Abound

There is no better time to adopt a quality focus and system in education than now. Whether it is because we simply want to solve a long-standing problem or because we have a strong and true vision for the future doesn't matter. The fact is, we have a problem, it does have a workable solution, and we must have a vision for the future if we are to have a future of our own making.

We are also in the luxurious position of having our answers clearly mapped out for us—and successfully, too. This country has over twenty years of experience in the whys and how of quality. We know how to do it and we know how to do it well. Better yet, we even know what the most common mistakes are and how to recognize and avoid them.

We have the answers. Now the only question is, do we have the where-withal?

By nature, I am an optimist. I believe that we can do anything we set our minds to. More important, as a country we have the ability to band together when the chips are down and create miracles—fast and furious.

Well, the chips are down and they are getting lower. Why that works in our favor at this time is that we are all seeing the problem. It is no longer someone else's issue. It has become the country's issue.

Private industry is escalating its work with schools in their areas. Parents and teachers are banding together to better identify how the children's learning problems can be solved. Schools are trying and trying again to get it right.

All of which means that the passion for success in creating the educational system we all want and need exists. We have to harness that passion and all the energy being put into changing the current system and focus on truly affecting the fundamental system. We must question and challenge—again and again. We must look at how our educational organizations are operating and determine *why* they are as they are and *what* needs to be done to make them as we need and want them to be.

We need to use a system already successfully implemented in this country and throughout the world and turn around the educational system just as we would any ailing organization. The talent is there. The will is there. The method is there.

And so, like any organization working assiduously to create strategic and tactical success, we must channel our energies into making the educational system one of which we can all be proud. That way, no matter what the gender or where Johnny might live, which school he or she attends, or what he or she wants to be when grown up, we are all sure that the dreams of the child will be achieved by the adult with grace, skill, and ability—a tribute to him or herself, the country, and society as a whole.

26. PRACTICING FIRE PREVENTION

School managers have gotten very good at putting out fires, so much so that they have lost sight of the need to practice fire prevention.

The one ingredient essential to the success of any organization, whether it be a multinational corporation or a school preparing kids for work in a multinational workplace, is leadership. Peter Drucker reminds us, "If an enterprise fails to perform, we rightly hire not different workers, but a new president." Look for success or failure at the top.

The leadership of the public school district is placed with a board of education. The board has ultimate responsibility, by law, for the conduct of the school organization in its dealings with employees, suppliers, customers, and the public. The most important board responsibility is to assure the quality of the active management. In any discussion of school leadership the board is included as part of top management. Over the long run, and because they choose to support or thwart the school operating executives, the board ultimately determines the success or failure of the school organization.

The process of changing an organization begins with those who make policy and financial decisions. It begins at the top! The first criterion—*leadership*—is an outline of how the top transforms itself and *how* a school system thinks about and performs its services to meet customer needs.

27. CONTINUOUS DOSAGES OF LEADERSHIP

As W. Edwards Deming points out, the quality of classroom teaching isn't unreliable because of Murphy's Law. Quality experts remind us that only 5 percent of the problems in an organization's performance can be blamed on isolated problems or poor workers. Fully 94 percent is a direct consequence of a poorly performing system. And the system is controlled and maintained by the top leadership. Teachers and principals, the frontline employees and mid-level managers in the public schools, working alone, do not have much chance to make changes against a stubborn and tradition-encrusted organization.

The criterion of leadership plays against this David-and-Goliath scenario. The system's leadership has to be strong enough to focus frontline and mid-level persons on a common objective of reaching reliably high quality in the classroom. Such leadership requires a radical shift from a defensive to an offensive strategy. To manage that shift requires managers with courage and security.

With leaders who are facilitators, improvement knowledge can flow up from the bottom as well as down from the top. New skills can be learned by everyone. Leaders must be equal to the major financial decisions that need to be made. Old habits will need to be broken and new ways mastered.

Such a change will predictably result in a period of turmoil. Leaders must demonstrate that they are in control and have a vision of where the school organization is headed. It takes a firm hand at the wheel to keep a school system on course and keep everyone on board.

The actions of the highest-ranking officials in the district should be examined in four dimensions: personal involvement, ability to promote reliable quality in the system, success in integrating staff into the vision and use of good practices, and relationships with the stakeholders.

These criteria recognize that management behavior and actions register a far greater impact on employee behavior than policies, memos, rules, and suggestions. It asks school leaders to look critically at how and if senior administrators are actively and personally involved in quality-related activities. To satisfy this criterion a school leader must be out front as a role model for motivating people, problem solving, and helping improve processes.

Employees need to be *shown,* not just told, that reliable classroom teaching time comes first. The challenge to school leaders is to find ways to make clear this highest priority, so that it influences all school operating procedures and the traditional conventions of public-school life.

Quality activities are time-consuming. They require shifts in personal priorities. The problem is not one of finding more time. Most leaders' schedules are already fully loaded. The challenge is reallocating time to pursue the central purposes of quality.

Senior school administrators play a major role outside the organization. They have the task of making sure that all those in their organization understand the important needs of school stakeholders. Schools need the support from the larger constituencies of public interests to allow the district to prosper.

Leadership asks how leaders communicate reliable quality to employees. It wants to know the other half of the story as well. How do the employees accept and perform the quality message? These criteria seek more than words and promises. They presume the availability of hard data. The school must show that it has created a working feedback loop for quality control to measure its progress in meeting its own goals.

28. LOOKING FORWARD WITH STRATEGIC PLANNING

The strategic planning standard asks school leadership and staff to examine how goals and plans are formulated. How are these strategies used throughout the school and school system? The questions to be answered run along these lines:

- By what process and methods do you develop the improvement strategies and the action plans to fulfill them?
- What specific action steps do you need to take to achieve dependable and durable (i.e., reliable) quality in teaching time?
- How do you get the participation of all administrators, staff, and support persons involved in quality planning and working together on the same broad objectives? How do you involve the board and other stakeholders?
- Specifically, what are the short-term goals? The long-term goals? The plans to assure reliable quality in classroom teaching performance?

When responding to these criteria, school leadership needs to demonstrate a disciplined, process-oriented, customer-driven approach to quality planning. The ideal school organization fuses together its financial, operational, and quality planning to identify and measure reliable teaching time objectives. Financial planning and classroom quality planning are two faces of the same coin.

Quality planning demands rigor and detail, much like that in a budgeting process. Everyone in the school organization, from superintendent and principals, to teachers and custodians, needs to be involved. When this approach is taken and assured, the school and school system takes the necessary actions. It directly links strategic plans (the *what* to be improved) with process capabilities (*how* to improve it).

Schools know their strategic plans are useful when

- All employees thoroughly know the school's short- and long-term quality initiatives and understand where their objectives fit in,
- Valuable data are collected and then used,
- Plans confront and root out failure in all functional areas, including classroom teaching support,
- The school consciously plans its continuous improvement through measurable lines of attack for quality, and
- Episodic and narrowly focused plans are replaced by bold initiatives.

29. STUDENT AND STAKEHOLDER NEEDS

This element examines how the school determines requirements, expectations, and preferences of its students and stakeholders. Also examined is how the school builds relationships with students and stakeholders and determines their satisfaction.

—Baldrige National Quality Program 2002
Education Criteria for Performance Excellence

The student and parent are the school customer. The school must focus on creating a learning organization that understands, cares about, and works for the student and parent. In the school where this customer-centered mission becomes a clear and continuous purpose, the standards are known and the teachers work together to form an aligned instructional program.

When teachers are skilled in the classroom processes, these processes enable them to predict results and act quickly on the impact of their methods. This increases student achievement. Victoria Bernhardt makes a case for the power of reliable methods to defeat the tyranny of chance when she writes:

> Until teachers are able to predict the impact of their actions on students, change their actions based on these predictions, corroborate the effect of these actions with students, and work with peers to build a comprehensive learning organization, any increases in student achievement and changes in the classroom will be temporary.

Through the information and analysis criterion, the school leadership assembles the data to better understand the student population. The student and stakeholder element excites the commitment of the *entire* school to find out and act on: the identification of students in terms of their needs and how they learn best, the impact of processes both those used and those that should be used, and the essential student achievements.

ESSENTIAL STUDENT ACHIEVEMENTS

Definitions of what students must learn come from asking such questions as: What will these students eventually face? What is it going to be like when they get there in the real world? What must we make sure the students can do by the time they get there? Students need to define objectives if they are to have successful careers and an acceptable quality of life.

For a specific career, the learning objectives come from a model of the situation in which the graduate will use the performances he has learned. This is the model of the trade or professional school. But elementary and secondary school education is not employment. Here we find a different situation. Here, the behaviors to be learned are someday to be applied in a wide variety of life situations. Trying to identify and analyze all possible life situations in which students may find themselves is an enormous and impractical task. Therefore, it is necessary for us to turn to a different type of model—a developmental model.

The new model assumes that there are six areas of human behavior capable of being developed. These are not always independent of each other; at times they may overlap or interrelate. The six areas are (1) intellectual, (2) communication, (3) social, (4) emotional, (5) learning, and (6) physical. The school needs to be concerned with organizing learning situations that develop these six behaviors in various ways that also permit them to be used in life outside the school.

INTELLECTUAL DEVELOPMENT

Aptitude and ability testing has identified a large number of talents. Some educators suggest that there are as many as 120 different intellectual abilities. A smaller set of seven or eight have been identified for many years. Among these are the commonly referred-to verbal, comprehension, word fluency, numerical, reasoning, spatial visualization, spatial orientation, and perceptual speed.

We are suggesting that the school can design explicit methods, materials, and procedures for deliberately practicing the abilities required for intellectual development. There is persuasive evidence that this is now feasible.

COMMUNICATION SKILLS DEVELOPMENT

Among the skills a student needs to develop are those of sending, or transmitting, and receiving in a variety of media. A high school graduate should be able to write correctly and clearly, in a form appropriate to the communication, and, if need be, with art and beauty.

The school should try to develop students who can read with high speed—as fast as those who have taken speed-reading courses. The student should be able to read graphs, charts, and tables of data. The student should be able to speak his or her mind clearly and confidently. He should be able to communicate with both verbal and quantitative symbols.

SOCIAL DEVELOPMENT

An enormous range of social skills could be developed into a ladder of objectives. Teachers might begin with the simplest forms of cooperation and peaceful competition between children, move on to forms of courtesy and politeness desirable in social life, to skills of leadership and followership—up to skills required to be effective American citizens. Much of what is now taught in social studies could be taught here.

EMOTIONAL DEVELOPMENT

The emotional injuries or deficiencies that students bring to school inevitably influence their ability to learn. What schools can do, instead of trying to undo damage done elsewhere, is to make sure that they, the schools, do no further harm and offer all students training in managing emotions.

Students can be taught such skills as the socially acceptable ways for releasing aggression, ways of dealing with fear, how to recognize when another person is having an emotional problem, and how to help that person cope with difficult feelings.

SKILL DEVELOPMENT

In a stable society, there is little need for a high degree of skill in learning. There is a finite amount of material to be learned, and it does not change. However, you and the student both know that this is not the kind of world in which we are living. Nor is it the kind of world in which anyone is likely to be living for a long period of time. We have repeatedly stressed that technological change is occurring at such a pace that many people will have to learn at least two different occupations during their working life. It probably goes without saying that the person who can learn most rapidly will have an enormous advantage.

It is possible for the school to teach the student the skills of effective learning and problem solving. Students trained in self-instructional programs that teach them to ask questions make higher scores than other students on science achievement tests and in turn are rated higher in classroom participation.

PHYSICAL DEVELOPMENT

Athletic performance should emphasize using skills to achieve significant purposes. For example, students should be taught sports, such as swimming and tennis, that they can pursue in adult life. They should know how nutrition and exercise affect health. The more active forms of dancing could serve as both athletic and social performances. Of course, there should be instruction in knowledge about the body, its functions, and how to stay healthy.

30. INFORMATION AND ANALYSIS
HELP TO IMPROVE DECISION MAKING

Appropriate and reliable data empower the school in pursuit of its objectives. Absent an effective system of data collection and analysis, school leadership simply cannot know how their teaching time is performing, what progress has been made on their vision, and what needs improving.

Currently, data collection and analysis are the weakest link in public education. It is the rare school or school system that gathers and analyses relevant data about its processes, complaints, and results for the purpose of fostering change and continuous improvement. Most often, data collected is in response to state or legal mandates. Schools need to collect performance data that can be aggregated and looked at over time to spot important trends. It is important to also look for *patterns* in the data, not just data at fixed points in time.

The school that collects and uses reliable data can soon perform frequent evaluations. It can continually validate its data and information bases. It will then actively analyze and use the data to improve its planning, its day-to-day decision making, and its improvement processes. In short, this "winning prescription" element helps foster a school or school district that manages by fact, not by assumption or bias. It is a school and school district that is well on its way to meeting or exceeding world-class benchmarks.

Schools that fall short or would fail on this criterion are easily identified and are found everywhere. They neither collect nor analyze data adequately. They do not even attempt to benchmark those schools that perform better within their same school system. They lack the most rudimentary statistical orientation for quality. Their leadership and management style is strongly reactive. They are "on top of things" and engaged full-time in "stamping out fires." Such situations supply oxygen to the tyranny of chance.

Once again, in the school, the primary focus of data collection and analysis needs to be on *prevention* of student failure and the enhancement of student and teacher mastery. Spending time early on prevention reduces the amount of time, effort, and expense that comes later. For each process, from teaching to safety to school climate, data collection efforts need to focus on key control points. It is up to staff to define those control points as critical junctures where something is likely to go wrong, or where practices or policies are inconsistent.

The prevention-based approach to data collection means designing and implementing a measurement control device at the earliest monitoring point. This provides an early alert so that teachers, parents, and administrators can take corrective action swiftly.

31. FACULTY AND STAFF NEEDS

It comes as no surprise that a healthy and happy employee is more apt to be a productive employee. This credo could well serve as the catch phrase on a *winning prescription* banner. It suitably describes the spirit behind this prescription. It is the school system that defines employee satisfaction. How it uses this definition in practice determines the quality of work life.

Fair treatment procedures, for example, are generally recognized as a key factor. Fairness affirms the employee's right to appeal an issue through a review by higher administrative levels. It provides feedback to administrators and the school board regarding policies and operations as well as statistics for trend analysis.

Proper recognition of employee achievements is essential to the quality process. Recognition reinforces reliable quality objectives. It encourages staff to cultivate creativity above and beyond the expectations of their typical job performance.

It is hard to develop fair reward systems that balance individual and group recognition. Quality winners have approached performance in a variety of ways. Chief among them is employee involvement and empowerment. Employees need to feel a genuine interest in and sense of ownership of their jobs in order to make rewards significant. Indeed, this is a best way to assure that school employees perceive the approach to be fair and meaningful.

Involvement and a sense of ownership are effective tools. First of all, it is superb training. It creates a pool of talent by training the front-line staff of teachers and principals in problem solving and decision making.

Of course, "empowerment" does not mean that employees run the show. Their input counts, but only in a good system that requires tracking and evaluation based on measurements. Questionnaires and interviews can develop data on how employees feel about their work and what is happening on a daily basis, through inquiries about issues such as "listening to my ideas" or "decision-making authority on the job."

Baldrige judges look for evidence of process and continuous improvement in a systematic effort by the school and school system.

They search for increased staff participation in reliable-quality improvement efforts. Every method needs to have its own set of indicators and be tracked to ensure that stated objectives and benchmarks are met. The idea behind all this is pretty straightforward: to monitor the system and to measure its effectiveness. For instance, in forming work teams, school leadership needs to know how many teams have been put into action. With a suggestion system, there could be a measure of the number of suggestions per year and how many were put into process operations.

"Employee involvement" is a major buzz phrase in education, as in business. But how one gets beyond the slogan is the real challenge. There are lots of methods to attract faculty and staff to participate. One of the best is to involve them in teams. The team concept gives groups of workers the chance and authority to identify problems and opportunities. It helps uncover where and why processes go wrong. It collectively develops and tests proposed solutions. It seeks to implement those improvements that show promise of working. Teams give individuals opportunities to help solve problems they could not solve on their own.

The underlying spirit of this *winning prescription* is optimism and experience. Optimism is not naïve but practical. It shows that all employees want to contribute to the schools' success and do good work. Further, it shows that, given the tools, the training, and responsibility, school staffs can respond with intelligence and innovation.

32. PURSUING PERFORMANCE RESULTS

Our focus on continually improving processes is directly related to the solid research-based knowledge that processes are the "royal road" to excellent results. If the school exhibits the expected high-quality characteristics, the school is a reliable school. It is *prevention-based*; uses *appropriate* tools, techniques, and methods; and is *systematic* in its attention to process improvement. Each process system, from classroom instruction to transportation and budgeting to logistical support of teaching, is aligned to its strategic plan and state education standards. The school is now thoroughly process-oriented.

Results neatly summarize the passage from the approach taken, to approach execution, to final outcomes. A well-documented set of results is the sure sign that the school is ready for continuous improvement.

Progress is measured by comparing results with goals. If there are gaps in the trend of results, then the school and its staffs learn why and go on to devise the corrective actions to be taken.

If measurement data show progress and evidence of classroom reliability, the process systems are in control and producing the desired compliance with state and local standards. The spirit of the winning prescription is now invoked to set even more ambitious improvement plans and goals.

Schools want to be selective in presenting data to customers and stakeholders. Data needs to show comparisons, be clear and specific, and explain promising as well as adverse trends. In brief:

- Be selective: Explain clearly which key measures are being used. Narrow the number down to the vital few and summarize the rest.
- Provide comparisons: Without comparisons there are few ways to understand how well or how poorly the school is performing. Use competitive data, benchmarks, and goals as a frame of reference.
- Be clear and specific: Information should be plainly and concisely presented. Explanations should relate to the data. The data do not all have to be numeric. Awards and recommendations are also appropriate.
- Explain both positive and negative trends: Nobody expects everything to be positive. Adverse trends in results need to be explained and corrective actions taken detailed. Carefully documented results spur intelligent planning and action.

Tools and Strategies for Schools

33. PURPOSES FOR TOOLS PRESENTED IN THE FIELDBOOK

Accountability is a nice-sounding term. It conjures up the image of strong leadership and tough management. It has a parental and authoritative ring to it. It makes a president sound profound, an educator seem on the ball, and a politician look involved. But there's more to school accountability than rhetorical pronouncements. It requires measurement tools that are used purposefully and consistently.

The tools presented here are:

- Quality processes for school improvement
- The Balanced Scorecard
- Customer Relationship Management
- Data Warehousing
- The linking of colleges of engineering and colleges of education
- Global quality and school improvement initiatives
- Benchmarking for world-class schools

Educators can use these tools in four aspects of school management:

1. To develop a deeper understanding of the role of using reliable data to achieve student-centered school improvement;
2. To share with education stakeholders some of the promising practices for collecting, analyzing, and using data at the school level;
3. To provide practicing educators with methods and tools that are usable for student-centering the school; and

4. To give all education stakeholders—parents, teachers, administrators, and community members—the courage to tackle student-
centered school improvement, one step at a time.

Five Lessons about Using Data

In May 1998, the Annenberg Institute for School Reform held a col-
loquium on the use of data to help achieve school improvement. The
conference report highlighted five lessons learned about data usage
from schools around the nation:

Two factors are essential to effective accountability: a belief that principals, teachers, and community stakeholders can help improve teaching and learning, and effective use of data to support that effort to improve.

> From the report:
> "Effective accountability efforts are accomplished by people who be-
> lieve that they can improve teaching and learning."
> "Determined educators are resourceful in finding ways to change their
> schools into places where all students learn to high standards."
> "The belief that they can make a difference is bolstered by their effec-
> tive use of data."

A clearly stated purpose and well-planned data collection and analysis
are the cornerstones of an effective accountability effort.

- How do school teachers and administrators make sense of all the
  data?

> From the report:
> "Having a purpose helps people narrow their focus and leads to
> greater involvement and commitment."
> "When faculty, parents, community and students hold a common pur-
> pose, teachers and principals say it is easier to buy into the process."
> "Purpose helps people refine questions and integrate multiple sources
> of data in search of answers to important concerns."

Assessment tools need to be carefully chosen, suitable to the task at hand, and aligned with purpose.

- Tools such as standardized tests are common.
- Teacher Journals are common but not thought of as tools.
- "Home-grown tools" developed by local schools meet their own specific documentation needs.

> From the report:
> *"No one tool works for all assessment needs. It is important to have, gather, and invent a variety of assessment tools for the assessment 'toolbox.'"*

Accountability is difficult for schools to accomplish alone. Schools need to be creative in finding resources to help with planning, coordination, collection, interpretation, and reporting of data.

- Working with someone knowledgeable about accountability from the outset saves time and other valuable resources.
- Such support is available from consultants, state DOE, and educational support groups.

> From the report:
> *"There needs to be recognition that the school is the unit of change and that teachers are the most important players. But the school being in the center of change shouldn't be translated to mean that the school should be responsible for doing it all."*
> *"Outside support is very helpful when schools are taking on new data-collection approaches. Organization and interpretation of data is another area where schools have used outside expertise."*

There are some questions that are simply better than other questions. Questions that ask "which?" are better than questions that ask "how many?"

Effective accountability recognizes the need to engage the larger school community—district and school administrators, teachers, students, parents, and community.

- Increasingly, community members are becoming active school leaders, accepting more and more responsibility for effective teaching and learning at the school.

From the report:
   "By developing partnerships with parents, a reciprocal sense of accountability starts to take shape, with schools responsible to their communities and communities responsible to their schools."
   "Another important ingredient in successful accountability efforts is teachers making on-going connections with parents about their children's progress."

---

34. THE QUALITY DIMENSION IN THE SCHOOL

Quality processes, including Baldrige and ISO 9000, always bring us back to quality control—timely feedback from data with corrective action in real time. Quality is the cornerstone of the continuous improvement processes. Customer satisfaction, the enthusiastic acceptance of parents, teachers, and future employers, is its Holy Grail.

Quality control and the mastery of its language are easily demonstrated through a common room thermostat. We reliably control room temperature by setting the desired temperature (the performance standard of the system). The built-in sensor gives us a reading of the actual temperature (feedback—the assessment of data for the performance standard). Then any difference between the thermostat setting and the room temperature is offset by either warmer air or cooler air (the corrective action in real time).

Quality control (QC) is the function of a reliability system that compares the reality of a situation against a desired standard. It takes place on an ongoing basis, just as the sensor in a thermostat compares the actual and desired temperatures. If there is a gap, QC takes continuous action to achieve what is desired. You can hear and feel the hot or cold air cut on and off as needed in the A/C system.

QC also activates the continuous improvement link between performance standards and its assessment. When the teacher, administrator, and school board systematically apply QC, it results in noticeable changes in the usual staff attitudes toward the results of teaching. This is also the attitude that can be characterized as *disciplined caring.*

If the teaching does not achieve its intended performance standards, the teaching methods and management support are worked on until the student gets it right. In other words, if the student is not successfully prepared, neither the customer (the student and parents) nor the providers (faculty and staff) are blamed. Or, simply stated, it is the job of the teaching system to teach *successfully*. If it does not, the reasons for what isn't working are thoroughly investigated. Then, corrective action is put into place.

Quality Starts with Understanding Systems

A system is a group of elements that are interconnected to accomplish a purpose. Two main ideas give a system its practical power: the definition of its purpose and the relationships of its parts. All systems have a defined purpose. The various parts of the system must always be carefully related to one another or the purposes of the system cannot be achieved. It is easy, for instance, to see the interconnected structure of the sound system components whose purpose it is to deliver quality sound in the home stereo system.

Likewise, each school system is made up of many system components. There is a transportation system for delivering children to and from school, a cafeteria system for feeding them, a safety system for protecting them. There is a governance system, a management system, a public information system, and an employer/employee system, to name some others. Their differences are subtle but essential to understand.

The leadership of the overall school system needs to understand and be able to track the cause and effect of the interaction of each of these systems. It is essential to keep in mind that 95 percent of all problems result from this interconnectedness, which masks the solutions to dilemmas and seldom allows them to become readily apparent. The solutions are most often buried deep within the structure of the overall school system.

Why Do Systems Thinking?

Sometimes, in order to understand the workings of the system, we need to understand the big picture as well as its individual parts. The story of the blind man and the elephant is often used to illustrate this. A blind man is asked to describe what he thinks an elephant looks like. Taking hold of the animal's tail he quickly assumes the elephant looks like a snake. When he holds the elephant's trunk he concludes it must look like a fire hose. Asked to wrap his arms around one of the elephant's legs the blind man exclaims it must look like a giant tree. Then, after being led over to the animal's ear he finally says in exasperation this animal must look like a big leaf. His final conclusion: "It must look like a very strange animal indeed."

Sometimes, in order to understand the workings of the system, we need to understand both the big picture and its individual parts—lest we draw hasty conclusions, like the blind man with the elephant.

Systems thinking is one of the most powerful tools for achieving a high-reliability school. It gives us the means for better understanding how the interaction of people and technology relates to the professional practice of education.

In simple language the systems thinker says: "It's better to see the whole problem than only just a part of it." System thinking aids us in more clearly accepting the wisdom that good teaching practice—as defined and understood—needs to be the prevailing classroom teaching practice.

We already see a system is a group of essentials that have been integrated to accomplish a purpose. An automobile is a system of parts and components that work together to provide us transportation. An autopilot and an airplane form a controlling system for flying at a specified altitude. A warehouse and loading platform are a delivery system for helping move goods into or out of a truck (that eventually travels within a transportation system). An elephant is used as a system for moving large loads in India. A school is a system to produce an educated citizen.

A system may include people as well as physical parts. The stock clerk and office worker are part of the warehouse system. Management is a system of people for allocating resources and regulating the activity of the enterprise. A family is a system for living and raising children.

The notion of a system is very far-reaching. This is what gives it such great practical power. But if systems are so pervasive, why do the concepts and principles of systems not appear more clearly in education practice and literature? The answer seems to lie in the evolution of three circumstances. Up until now,

1. There has never been much call for an understanding of the nature of school systems,
2. There have been few requirements to apply new thinking to complex school problems, and
3. The principles of tackling school systems call for what is often rare introspective thinking on the part of school personnel.

In a primitive society, the existing systems are mostly composed of elements that arise only in nature. Their characteristics are believed to be divinely given and beyond man's ability to understand or control. People simply adjust themselves to the natural systems around them and to their family and tribal customs. They simply adapt to natural systems without feeling compelled to understand them.

In an industrial and technological society, systems dominate life and produce their own forms of stress. They exhibit themselves in economic cycles, political turmoil, recurring financial panics, fluctuating employment, and unstable prices. Social systems suddenly seem far more complex and their behavior sometimes becomes altogether confusing. A search for an orderly structure, for simplistic cause-and-effect relationships, and for less complicated theories to explain system behavior easily gives way to a belief in random, irrational causes and an array of unintended consequences.

Take This to the Bank

The fabric of the systems concept consists of the system's intended purpose and the coordination of its subsystems to achieve some goal, either explicitly defined or implicitly understood. Schools have many purposes. There are elements and functions that form the school system. These various elements need to be professionally managed to see that all of the principal purposes of the school are realized.

The principal job of school administration is to keep each subsystem performing as smoothly as possible in order to facilitate productive results or to avoid unnecessary conflict. Subsystems need to support one another in furthering the overall purposes of the school.

- The school buses must get the students to school safely and on time. They can also provide additional instruction time.
- The food service must meet nutrition needs within a designated time period. It can also be a lab for the health curriculum.
- Classroom teaching must meet standards within the efficient use of time.

While such subsystems operate independently, it is apparent that their effectiveness is greatly improved when each is managed so as to reinforce the performance of the others.

The Instructional System

At the heart of each school system is the teaching/learning system. This may at first seem obvious, but it, too, is composed of subsystems—classroom spaces, students and their parents, teaching materials, and technology. There is the teaching faculty, charged with expertly performing the teaching functions required. Ideally, the proper functions to successfully guide students toward achieving established standards are well known through research and field-testing. Ideally, too, the administrative staff is there to expertly support the teaching function.

Each classroom makes up its own instructional system. When operating successfully, the internal customers, consisting of other teachers and staff, and the external customers, made up of parents and future employers, can readily see that:

1. Mandated standards are the goals to be achieved.
2. Criterion achievement tests measure how well standards are being met.
3. Course content and media used by teachers help students reach standards.
4. The teacher uses suitable (proven) methods in teaching and classroom management.
5. QC methods are used for corrective action if students do not master standards.

To accomplish the learning achievement purposes of a school, it is necessary to keep all school subsystems dependably working together and in sync with one another. Leaders must quickly resolve the clashes with each other. Operating at its best, the quality function helps define the primary forces for helping manage the successful coordination of the separate subsystems within the school.

Many states now mandate school standards for student learning in such areas as language arts, mathematics, science, and social studies. The standards clearly spell out what the student is to know and be able to do in a given subject area. It goes on to define the kind of student work that demonstrates mastery. Today, these standards represent the learning achievement mission of your local school.

One definition of a classroom subsystem could be this: An integrated set of technology (media, methods, materials), and persons (teachers, students, parents, staff) to efficiently and effectively perform the required functions needed to accomplish the learning standards (goals).

By its very nature, systems thinking helps bring about a remarkable change in teacher and administrator attitudes toward the process of instruction. It fosters an *attitude* of reliable teaching that directly opposes a tyranny of chance. It brings about a mind-set of professional responsibility for defining and applying what works.

It is difficult to overstate the spirit represented by this attitude. It may be the single most important change to bring into schooling, for it has the most direct bearing on school performance and system effectiveness. Applying systems thinking creates a shared attitude among all the partners in schooling. This attitude translates into actions. If the instructional subsystem (the teachers, the materials, the equipment, the methods, the time, and any other component that make it up) is not effective (students do not learn what is expected or required), the subsystem is redesigned until it is. Neither parents, nor teachers, nor students, nor economic or social conditions are blamed.

35. THE EFFECTIVE INSTRUCTIONAL SYSTEM

The general functions that make up an effective instructional system have repeatedly been identified in research. The essentials, discussed below, are five interrelated functions, all of equal importance. The instructional path must have a destination—specific learning goals. Teachers must teach, and students must learn. The learning process must be managed to accommodate the students' needs. And quality control must be exercised over all.

The Specification of Desired Learning Results

Learning is a concept that can only be inferred. We can't really see or touch any learning directly. What we see is a change in condition. Your student can now do something that he or she could not do before the learning experience. That something is the purpose of the classroom learning experience.

It has been an ongoing struggle to persuade educators to state the learning targets in such ways that they can be measured objectively. There continues to be the common school practice of stating desired targets in highly abstract terms that lack measurement possibility. We often hear of such learning targets as the development of "understandings." Beliefs and knowledge are stated without spelling out how we can possibly arrive at a reasonable estimate of results. We need to know the extent to which the learner understands, appreciates, knows, accepts, or believes what the classroom learning experience was intended to provide. We are talking about *measurable results.*

There currently exist tools for describing the learning targets of both education and training. The goals of the learning experience need to be spelled out in ways that can be convincingly verified by both the providers and the customers. In this way we can harness the power of system thinking and apply it to reliable classroom teaching.

The Presentation of Knowledge and Performance

Teachers can now employ a variety of teaching technologies, such as reading, lectures, graphic aids, television, films, tape recorders, computers, videotapes, and CD ROMs to serve the student.

In the past, presentations were usually one-way. They flowed from the teacher to the student. Today we have readily available effective two-way or interactive modes. We can look to the work of a learning subsystem—the presentation of knowledge and performance—to improve the classroom learning experience for increased effectiveness and greater efficiency.

The Practice of Knowledge and Performance

The targets of teaching consist of learning the skills and knowledge that are essential for mastering what has been taught. A *classroom objective* is a meaningful unit of work. A completed task is an example of such an objective.

Here is a case in point. Baking a cake and testing for smog control on a car are two objectives. In the classroom it is critical for the teacher to define in advance the knowledge and skills that meet the class-objective. For baking a cake it may be to know the right ingredients and measurements; for smog-checking a car it may be the skill of placing the instruments in the correct places and reading the output instruments. Educators call this knowledge and skill *enabling classroom objectives* because without them your student cannot master the desired learning objective.

To be effective in meeting the objective, the student must practice the task as well as the skills and knowledge components that make it possible. To master any task, a student needs to be provided with adequate practice. Also, it is more cost-effective and less tedious for the student if the teacher provides the student with practice of the enabling skills and knowledge at the same time. This can reduce the amount of time required for the student to master the full performance.

The Management of the Learning Experience

Managing the classroom learning experience refers to those activities needed to keep the student actively engaged in the entire learning experience. Among several recent developments are cooperative learning, newer forms of individualized instruction, and providing incentives tied directly to progress. (See Six Rules for Setting Rules.)

Quality Control

Measuring the student's actual performance serves as the cornerstone of quality control. This information forms the feedback that leads the student and his or her teacher to the needed corrective action. Therefore, the performance data on the student must be as valid, reliable, objective, and detailed as is possible in each classroom-learning situation.

Quality control measures how well the class target has been achieved. It helps to identify and initiate the proper corrective action. It

Six Rules for Setting Rules: Finding the right balance between democracy and order in your classroom
—Laura Clark
Dual Language Middle School, New York City

As I learned quickly in my first couple of years as a teacher, having clear classroom rules that the students buy into can make all the difference. Here are six "rule-setting rules" that worked for me.

1. Decide what will be nonnegotiable for you in the classroom.
   Many teachers work with new groups of students to develop the rules and procedures that will be used in the classroom. However, if you know that you won't be able to live with students getting up to use the bathroom during your daily read aloud, don't leave that issue open for discussion. Set any nonnegotiable rules yourself.
2. Keep the set of rules to a minimum.
   Students are likely to be overwhelmed by a large set of rules and have trouble distinguishing the most important ones. Keeping the number of rules down will boost your chances that students will understand, remember, and be willing to follow them. And of course, the more rules you set, the more rules you will have to consistently enforce.
3. Don't paint yourself into a corner.
   Rules about minutiae can leave too little wiggle room for cases that didn't occur to you when you made the rules. Exhaustive lists of specific "don'ts" can imply that anything not on the list is okay. Instead of a list including "no name calling," "no spitting," and "no hitting." Try a simple "respect others." Don't announce rules on the specifics unless you find it absolutely necessary.
4. Post your rules clearly.
   This is to help *you* remember what you're trying to be consistent about as much as it is to help your students get it right.
5. When a problem arises, remind students of the rule that applies.
   Don't just tell a student that it's not acceptable to go through another student's backpack—remind her of the rule requiring all your students to "respect others."
6. Review the rules on a regular basis—especially when things are going well.
   It is tempting to believe that, once students begin to follow your rules, the classroom will run itself for the rest of the year. Sometimes students just want to see if the rules are still rules. Let them know they still are.

includes feedback plus corrective action. This is a basic advance over common classroom evaluations that merely identify a gap between what was intended and what was achieved and assign a grade of A to F on what has happened.

Quality produces a remarkable change in attitude among those providing education. It fosters an attitude of mutual accountability for results. If the learning experience provided to a student does not achieve what was intended (i.e., if the student did not succeed), the learning experience is redesigned. Thus your student is provided with additional opportunities to be successful. And most importantly, nobody is blamed. It is the system's job to deliver the achievement of standards.

36. TOOLS TO RAISE THE CEILING, NOT LOWER THE FLOOR

Administrators, teachers, and staff must believe every day that they can make a real difference in the life of each student. That's a tall order, but nothing less achieves high-quality education.

In schools serving the most successful higher-income households, expectations for children are at the "excellent" level rather than the "satisfactory" level. In less successful schools, serving lower-income and minority households one may hear belief statements that all students can learn, but actions speak louder than words. While teachers may say and some may even believe this to be so, the lack of a uniformly challenging curriculum that is repeatedly and reliably measured for results casts doubt as to whether there is a genuine belief that all students can really learn at high levels. As much as teachers may try to distance themselves from the self-fulfilling prophecy that students cannot perform at levels established by their state departments of education, there are pained explanations that reflect teacher and staff lack of conviction that they can make a difference in the learning lives of their students.

Clear and Explicit Goals

Data strongly influence the development of agreed-upon goals. While all schools now may have written goals and mission statements, they differ with respect to the real focus and measurements on meeting the stated intentions. Better schools put more attention on academic achievement; other schools focus on attendance and attitude as priority. But in the most successful schools, goals for high-level results are clear, explicit, and measurable.

In too many schools there is more attention to short-term goals in the school improvement plan, and these are not clearly linked to the underlying needs of the school to align curriculum and teaching time with state assessments, even though student improvement on assessment tests is spelled out as a goal. In too many cases teachers are unable to articulate what the mission or goals are for their school. A concern that many teachers express is a lack of standards and sticking by them.

Performance Measurement

Measuring human achievement has a long history, and our earliest records show that it was reached through performance assessment. We still evaluate achievement through performance. Tests are used in music recitals, scores for sports teams, marksmanship, and driver's license exams, written examinations for Civil Service jobs and licensures in insurance and real estate.

Before the advent and widely held use of standardized tests with their true-false questions, paper-and-pencil multiple-choice items, and machine scoring, teachers relied on the direct approach to assessment of student results. Students wrote essays and were asked to spell words, answer questions, solve problems at the blackboard, and make things work. School board members went into the classroom and selected students at random to perform academic tasks. Testing was direct and observable; it was not inferred from a proxy like the so-called objective multiple-choice test.

The Nature of Measurement

Measurement is focused. Measurements have meaning in terms of their designed use. The results are a direct function of the methods and measurements used. To repeat the obvious, things that are not measured are left to chance. Some examples of measurement:

- Land is surveyed to tax and convey it.
- Carpets and curtains are measured for cutting to fit floors and windows.

- Stock shares owned and their market values are measured to pay interest and dividends or to calculate return on investment.
- Distance is measured to aim weapons, charge for airplane tickets, and to conduct the Olympic trials and games.
- Time is measured to schedule work, to study, to play, to serve a prison term, and to mark the start of enforced retirement.

Measurement is a means of direction and agreement. Measurement is always deliberate, not disengaged; it is shaped by societal structure and not independent; it is slanted by intellectual conventions and never unbiased. By not measuring the reliability of teaching, administrators, school boards, and citizens forfeit their influence over achieving results and turn over that control solely to those who perform the process by which the results are produced.

The absence of measures of output in classroom teaching stands in stark contrast to the obsessive measurement of inputs. Schools know to the penny the cost of bus transporting students and the cost of paper and chalk. In business, budgets are measurements intended to control costs, set prices, and yield a margin of profit. In a nonprofit organization, like schools, budgets are simply "permission" to incur costs without measuring responsibility for results.

The school mind-set is primarily centered around *funding costs,* but not *measuring benefits and returns.* The school budgeting process follows the dollar equivalent of Parkinson's Law: Organizational needs expand to consume available funds. Old activities (and new ones) continue as long as funding continues. Budgeting in schools is ongoing, and new development is opportunistic—new activities are added principally by new funding. Improved school performance cannot come about as a consequence of budget measurement.

It should come as no surprise that, in schools and colleges, measurement controls results. College professors who are rated by the number of their publications devote more time to research and less to teaching, more time to writing and less to student conferences. If the measurement of a school or teacher is student performance on a statewide examination, contents of courses tend to be defined by test areas, and methods of teaching tend to include drill in prior years' examinations, in anticipated questions for the current year, and even in actual questions for the current year if these become known in advance.

Measurement and Values

Measurement and values are part of the same system, each being the reciprocal of the other—cause and effect. Looked at another way, these are part of a never-ending circle of plan-do-act-revise. Together they cast the present and forecast the future. When schools classify non-English-speaking children as retarded because of low test scores in English, the test measurements are evidently complying with social values and expectations. Our conventional measurements often create what conventional values demand—essentially winners and losers, successes and failures. If we perceive the creation of losers and failures as counterproductive, we must find measurements to express and implement our perceptions and values. Measuring the reliability of classroom teaching to achieve success for all children in the basic skills is a direct start at making winners.

Using the Right Tools

In recent years the advent of on-line computer-assisted communication between patient and physician databases has been heralded as a major step forward in the treatment of chronic illness. It holds promise of replacing a great deal of the medical care now delivered in person. Sometimes the information itself will do the work of doctors. However, problems might occur, such as inaccurate information, varied opinions, and contradictory information.

This suggests that, although computers and information systems might create more knowledgeable patients who are active participants in their own care, they will not necessarily render the physician unnecessary. The major error of 20th-century medicine is the belief that medicine involves only the application of facts to an objective problem that can be separated from the person.

In public schools, as in medicine, it is *how to solve the problems* that count. To do so, you need to use the right tools to help uncover the underlying reasons for the educational illness. It wouldn't make much sense to put together a team of sharp people and then neglect to give them the right tools do their jobs.

A bright executive would not communicate with a colleague halfway around the world today with a third-class letter, when he could use e-mail. Similarly, none of us would want to be treated in a health-care facility without the proper diagnostic tools. A high-reliability organization has and uses the right tools to do the high-quality job.

The tools used for mining, metalworking, and carpentry are different from those used for hunting, farming, cooking, and making clothes. And the skills and knowledge needed to use these tools correctly are vastly different. The right tools are essential to doing a job well. But in spite of these obvious facts, people are asked to do their jobs almost daily using the wrong tools or no tools at all. It's as though people in an organization are considered capable of creating and building value without tools at all, as though some sort of magic will yield something from nothing.

The fact is that good tools can make us smarter. In fact, we see evidence of this almost every day. There is only so much we can learn and remember. But we have the tools to extend our memories. We invent things that make us smart.

Things that make us smart can also make us dumb. They can entrap us with their seductive powers. Television captures us with thousands of hours of commercials each year. And news is capsulated into easy-to-swallow headline dosages. But do we know any more about what is going on in the world? Tools must fit the task

We humans are thinking, interpreting creatures. The mind tends to seek explanations, to interpret, and to make suggestions. We are active and creative. We seek interaction with others. We change our behavior as we attempt to understand what others expect of us.

Efficient, routine operations are OK for machines but not for people. For thousands of computer users, the body shows the wear and tear of repetitive stress with carpal tunnel syndrome. Similarly the mind can register a syndrome called "burnout," which manifests in the loss of ability to create, innovate, or simply even care about our work.

A worn-out mind can lead to a demoralized teacher, someone who no longer cares about the job or the quality of teaching work being produced. Worse yet, the improper design of a job can lead to an uninspired staff, where mental activity is much reduced. None of this was planned: It is an accidental by-product of this age of increased stress.

This goes a long way toward explaining the angst people feel as they struggle to do the best they can, in often trying circumstances. The experiences prey on people's fears and self-doubts. Teachers are being told that they're inadequate, that they need to become something else to be something better. This advice may be well meant, but then the road to hell is paved with good intentions. Do teachers want to improve classroom performance by becoming someone else? Or do they want to improve their professionalism by improving what they know? The right tools can help.

The power in using the right tools is that they don't ask you to become someone else. They help create an extension of you. With a little time and skill, using the right tool helps you become more than what you are.

Marshall McLuhan in *Understanding Media*[1] tells us that tools are a medium for self-expression. An appreciation of good tools offers us a way to influence the world. We learn to listen differently, to see differently, and to view with a different sense of proportion. Good tools expand our perceptual boundaries. To only see technology and tools as a way to either reduce costs or speed up output is too simplistic. *Technology is a medium for creating productive environments.*

In the high-reliability organization, technology is at its most expressive and powerful in the form of tools—tools that help build more productive and effective environments. This leads directly to the conclusion that the only tools worth having are those tools that help create and enhance value.

Directly and indirectly, the tools people use—and organizations choose—reflect the sort of value they wish to create. Leaders must deal with an organizational reality: The workplace and the schools are places where people interact to create value.

Now we have the means to transform and harden these ideals into a new organizational reality. Ironically, these ideas are modeled on well-established traditions of excellence and innovation. They demand that people reexamine the way they look at tools—and themselves.

The Meaning of Tools

We choose tools to make our personal lives richer, more meaningful, and convenient. Tools can help create the values that we deem important. These same choices need to also be available for making our professional lives richer, more meaningful, and more productive.

People are an extremely complex subject, the most complex ever studied. Each of our actions is the result of multiple interactions, of a lifetime of experiences and knowledge, and of subtle personal relationships. The scientific measurement tools try to strip away the complexities, studying a single variable at a time. But much of what is of value to a person results from the interaction of the parts: When we measure simple, single variables, we miss the "elephant."

Accurate measurement underlies all of science. Without simple, reliable measurements, science would be denied the use of its most powerful tools. By this we mean precise measurement, repeatable experiments under controlled conditions, and mathematical analyses. The problem is that when it comes to measuring human capabilities we are somewhat limited as well as more biased.

Tools for Teamwork

From a practical point of view, tools force us to choose between two schools of thought—experiential and reflective thought. Tools for experiential thought provide us with a wide range of sensory stimulation, with enough information provided to minimize the need for logical deduction. The telephone extends our voice as well as letting us hear spoken words from hundreds or even thousands of miles away. Similarly, tools for reflective thought are needed to support the exploration of ideas. They need to make it easy for us to compare and evaluate, to explore alternatives. For instance, the education criteria of the Baldrige and ISO 9000 criteria provide such guidance. In both cases the tools must be invisible; they must not get in the way.

The typical principal's office is replete with a collection of tools. This school building leader sits behind a desk with a chair for visitors. On the desk stand the ubiquitous tools of the trade—the phone, the calendar, in and out baskets, pencils and pens, paper clips, rubber bands, a stapler, and a letter opener, and the personal computer with a collection of software packages. Not far away stands a family photo as a morale booster. Nearby is a file cabinet and reams of paper. The successful principal has ready access to a secretary and can schedule a conference room when needed.

Individual educators need tools to support their work as well. But there is nothing in the typical school to support *collaboration*. Simple synchronization and cooperation do not necessarily call for much brainpower. Ants cooperate in an impressive variety of tasks and not through any conscious desire to work together. Similarly, birds flying in a V-shaped formation or schools of fish darting this way and that do not result from any knowledge, but rather from individual responses to the situation. Still, it shows how hard-wired behaviors can lead to sophisticated behavior.

Genuine cooperative behavior calls for shared knowledge and a conscious desire to cooperate. Quality collaboration, the kind of effort that has resulted in breakthroughs in science, the arts, and technology, comes about with neither frequency nor intensity. Organizations are simply not structured for collaboration.

Now it is self-evident that tools play a significant role in shaping the way work gets done. Therefore, it is not unreasonable to assume that using proper tools designed to encourage collaborative work could similarly motivate people.

The Tool of Language

Language is a collaborative tool. Indeed, language is at the core of virtually all the tools one finds in the typical office—the phone, the copier, the dictating machine, and the word processor. Without language, these tools are mute. Most people can speak a language fluently. But it takes care, craftsmanship, and sincerity to speak in a way that consistently evokes mutual understanding and commitment. Since people rely on written and spoken language to get what they want, they need tools to make their language effective.

Under these circumstances language is more than a medium of communication. It needs to be the main tool for collaboration. Language augments *collaborative* relationships. To understand and appreciate that, one needs to better understand and appreciate the role of language.

The virtue of good tools is that they don't ask you to become someone else. They invite you to create an extension of yourself. With a little time and skill good tools let you be more than what you are. Tools are a medium for self-expression.

The application of award-winning collaborative tools such as total quality management (TQM), Baldrige Quality Education Criteria, and

ISO 9000 Education Standards is qualitatively different. They are vastly different from the array of tools provided to support individuals in a school building. As well they should be.

37. PARTNERING: SCHOOLS, PARENTS, COMMUNITY, AND BUSINESS

Students learn as much in the streets, from TV, and in their homes as they do in schools. Students need increasing opportunities to apply their learning within their community through internships, community service, establishing student enterprises, and through participating in community-based learning. Similarly, community members and businesspersons need to be in the schools to support and extend student work and learning. Schools cannot do it alone. As the African proverb says (and Senator Clinton's book is titled), "It takes a village [to raise a child]."

Learning communities work collaboratively to make this a reality, not rhetoric. The education partnership is not about "buy-in"—it is about authentic involvement, active participation, shared leadership, and shared decision making. Involving key persons from "outside" is essential to establishing the school as part of a collaborative learning community. None of this is possible without the involvement—right from the start and continuously throughout the change process—of parents and community people.

To create a learning community, one needs to operate systemically:

- To think in the whole rather than in parts—*the lesson of the blind man and the elephant.*
- To think relationships rather than individuals, or separated objects—*it is team play.*
- To think process rather than structure—*it is strategic thinking rather than tactical planning.*
- To think networks rather than hierarchy—*it is teamwork.*
- To think quality rather than quantity—*it is fitness for use as judged by users.*
- To think sufficiency rather than scarcity—*it's thinking and working smarter.*

- To think dynamic balance rather than steady growth—*it is control and breakthrough*.
- To think interdependence rather than autonomy—*it is about winning as a team, not star power*.
- To think cooperation rather than competition—*it uses coopetition as resource conservation*.
- To think approximation rather than absolute truth—*it recognizes patterns of change*.
- To think partnership rather than domination—*it is win-win*.

The foundation of a learning community is collaboration—working together for common goals, partnership, shared leadership, co-evolving and co-learning—rather than competition and power given to only a few.

Gene Maeroff, president of the New York Times Education Foundation and dean of education journalists, put it this way: "In schools, disciplines are as separate as the planets." To date it has been impossible for educators to even imagine the far-reaching possibilities of collaboration.

The focus of the learning community is in having students actively demonstrate understanding, rather than students solely passing written tests as the single sign of knowing. It is learning based on conceptual understanding and the ability to apply knowledge in a variety of contexts. It puts the focus on student learning, rather than the teacher "covering the content." It also means

- Students taking more responsibility for their own learning,
- Learning experiences geared to students' interests and needs,
- Students actively engaged in learning in a variety of groups and contexts, and
- Learning as applied, internalized, and understood.

Collaboration and learning happen within the context of community—a unity that celebrates diversity. Communities are not the arithmetic total of its individual citizens but rather, the interaction among the individuals themselves. It means "concentrating on what happens between the buildings, not the buildings themselves," said community-builder Jim Rouse.

The school reflects the population and background of the larger community. It helps students learn the attitudes, knowledge, and skills that benefit all in their community.

During this transformation "no one knows who will be a dinosaur and who will be a mammal," writes MIT's Lester Thurow.[2] "That depends upon who is the best at adjusting to a new world—something that can only be known with certainty looking backward."

38. THE BALANCED SCORECARD AND SCHOOLS

Ask any school board member, administrator, or teacher, "What is your school district's most valuable asset?" The answer is predictable. "Our people." Every school organization has at least some good people. But if good people are everywhere and that's all it takes, they apparently aren't a competitive advantage.

The correct answer is *good measurements*.

"A good metric," says Robert Kaplan, author of *The Balanced Scorecard*,[3] "is like a laser pen. It fits into the palm of your hand. You can take it with you wherever you go. Inside it is photons, and the photons keep the beam in phase and coherent. That's what good measurements do for you—they keep you in phase and coherent. They do not break up over distances. They keep telling the truth no matter how far out you go" (July 13, 1999, The Masters Forum).

Kaplan's four ground rules for BSC:

1. When is a measurement good?
When it measures what needs to be measured.

2. When is a measurement great?
When it is a powerful tool not just for diagnosis of the recent past (How're we doing?) but beyond that for strategic implementation (Where are we going?).

3. Diagnostic measures are *vital signs*.
They tell you your current status.

4. Strategic measures *go beyond that.*
They describe outcomes (results) and drivers (causes) of long-term value creation.

A good "balanced scorecard" tells everyone in the school organization, in a single page, the story of its entire district strategy:

- Every measure is part of a chain of cause-and-effect linkages.
- All measures eventually link to organizational outcomes.
- A balance exists between outcome measures (financial and student) and performance drivers (values, internal processes, learning and growth).

The key to effective strategy is efficient implementation. *Fortune* magazine estimates that fewer than 10 percent of all strategies that are effectively formulated are later effectively executed. And author Tom Peters considers that figure grossly inflated!

In the early 1990s Robert Kaplan (Harvard Business School) and David Norton (Balanced Scorecard Collaborative) recognized some of the weaknesses and vagaries of long-standing management approaches. The balanced scorecard provides a clear prescription as to what the organization (profit or not-for-profit) needs to measure in order to "balance" the financial and operating perspectives (for schools: purchasing teacher consumables; operating bus service; costs and returns in running the cafeteria; productive classroom teaching time.)

The Balanced Scorecard is a *management system* (not just a measurement system) that enables the organization to clarify its vision and strategy and to translate these into measurable action. These principles apply equally to the State of Washington, where Governor Gary Locke widely uses BSC, business organizations in transition, or the Red Cross, which now seeks to get a better handle on its business practices. For schools, BSC provides feedback around both the internal operating processes and external educational outcomes in order to continuously measure and make decisions to improve strategic performance and results. When fully deployed, the BSC helps transform the district's strategic planning from an academic exercise into the nerve center of the organization.

Kaplan and Norton describe the innovations flowing from BSC this way:

> The balanced scorecard retains traditional financial measures. But financial measures tell the story of past events, an adequate story for industrial

age thinking organizations for which investments in long-term capabilities and customer relationships were not critical for success. These financial measures are inadequate, however, for guiding and evaluating the journey that information age organizations need to make to create future value through investment in customers, suppliers, employees, processes, technology, and innovation.[4]

The BSC asks that the school organization be observed from four viewpoints and to develop metrics, collect data, and analyze such data relative to each of these angles:

- The learning viewpoint
- The business processes viewpoint
- The customer-centric viewpoint
- The financial viewpoint

39. RESPONSE TO OBJECTIONS FOR DEPLOYING THE BALANCED SCORECARD AND QUALITY

A school district that proposes adopting the balanced scorecard approach should be prepared to defend it. Fortunately, that is not hard to do.

Objection 1. The costs outweigh the benefits. What will we find that we didn't already know?

- What is the cost of not proving your value?
- Today, stakeholders expect schools to show evidence of progress.
- Web sites can enable and automate much of this work—easily and inexpensively, compared to the tools available just a few years ago.
- Performance measurement has repeatedly been demonstrated to be a "best practice" in terms of improving the student outcomes.

Objection 2. But some tasks will be labor intensive: metrics definition, software development, data collection.

- It's true that defining metrics is time consuming and has to be done by administrators in their respective areas. But once they are defined, they won't change very often and some of the metrics are generic across all units, such as productive classroom time, customer satisfaction, staff attitudes, etc. Software tools are commonly available to assist in this task.

- Software development efforts should be kept to a minimum. There are now companies that specialize in this kind of software product, but most districts can probably leverage the existing data warehouse to support this system.
- Data collection can be supported using web-based forms. Manual work such as collecting customer data, telephone interviews, etc. can be supported by broadening the work of the existing noninstructional personnel.

Objection 3. We have only limited control over results. Why should we be held accountable for things we can't control?

- A school district's strategic initiative of customer service demands that it take responsibility for mission effectiveness and to improve customer relationships.
- There is no alternative. School customers will understand its limitations if they are in a close partnership with the school.

Objection 4. The results will be used against us.

- The results can also be used for us. What has hurt schools the most is not having any results to show.
- What better way to gain resources from the sponsor than to clearly show them the consequences of the present situation?
- We can't see our own blind spots. We need someone else to point them out to us. The measurements add visibility, even if it is painful.
- If the school excels, it is no longer generally true that a successful organization loses budget.

Objection 5. Management will misuse or misinterpret the results. The process will be gamed.

- That's why quality process improvement calls for several measures. Inspections such as Baldrige assessments or ISO 9000 internal audits are carried out by a variety of dedicated people across the school organization. They want to do a good, honest job.

- The measurements will be validated by an independent team or third party fully experienced in helping schools reach their strategic and learning objectives.
- The main purpose of quality process improvement is not individual performance improvement, but collective organizational performance. Only the team can win. (A separate system is used for individual performance evaluations.)
- Results at the staff levels can be aggregated in such a way that individual employee performance is not reported out. This helps eliminate a source of fear that leads to gaming or failure to produce data.

Objection 6. They will score us by inappropriate or unfair standards.

- Quality process management allows each school to define its own metrics, at least the ones that are pertinent to each mission. This is the only way for the school to define its mission effectiveness.
- Other metrics, like time and customer satisfaction, are generic across all organizations.

Objection 7. It's too complicated. There are too many systems and quality assessment criteria; how will we combine them all (ISO 9001, Baldrige, TQM, strategic initiatives)?

- It is unnecessary to create a complex improvement system. What's needed is a minimum basic set of measurements across various operational perspectives, aligned to the strategic plan, as quality process improvement criteria already prescribe. We do need to develop ISO certifications when appropriate, but the metrics for them need to be kept simple.
- The purpose in undertaking system-wide improvements is to clarify staff situations for senior administrators, not to make the system more complex.

Objection 8. It's too big and ambitious and expensive to deploy a quality performance measurement system in an entire school district. We can't afford such grandiose efforts.

- Agreed. That's why we do *not* propose deployment across an entire school organization *all at once*.

- Rather, we propose to start small, in a school unit, and to develop step-by-step.
- Experience needs to be gained before district-wide deployment is considered. This reduces cost, risk, and disruption.

Objection 9. How will you get everyone to do this?

- We won't!
- We know that one-third of administrators and teachers will welcome quality changes with open arms;
- One-third will sit on the fence to see what will happen; and
- One-third will quietly resist it from the outset.
- This is where administrative leadership earns its salary! Administrators need to concentrate on bringing along the middle third while dispersing the resistant third to other assignments or early retirement.

40. CUSTOMER RELATIONSHIP MANAGEMENT IN EDUCATION

> Quality is never an accident. It is always the result of intelligent effort. It is the will to produce a superior thing.
>
> —John Ruskin

Who Is the School Customer?

This question nags administrators and teachers when they start to think about the process of school change. By following a Customer Relationship Management (CRM) path the school leader can better define the school customer. It's probably helpful to begin by checking the list below for ideas on who fits the C in the school CRM. In education, customers may be:

- Students and prospective students
- Parents and guardians
- Alumni
- Faculty, administrative staff, and other employees
- Citizens

- Stakeholders in education
- Media contacts
- Businesses as potential school partners
- Businesses as future employers of the school's students
- Suppliers
- Government agencies
- Other educational institutions

Words like *competition*, *efficiency*, and *customer trust* don't usually conjure up the image of school buildings, yellow buses, teachers, and students. But the same forces that have sparked large-scale changes in the world of business—the Internet, globalization, the New Economy—have also left their mark on education.

Home schooling has had an enormous competitive impact. Combined with the number of students in charter schools, the impact on conventional schooling is indeed considerable, and growing. For the first time, the business world and the education sector face the same challenges and are increasingly being held to the same standards. As a result, schools need to turn to the same strategies as businesses—Customer Relationship Management (CRM)—to accomplish the same types of objectives.

Breaking Down Barriers, Building Up Relationships

Faced with ever-increasing pressures of taxpayers demanding more "bang for [their school tax] buck," education organizations have spent more time and effort to improve back-office operational processes, such as payroll, purchasing, and budget management. Now, the time has come for the school organizations to break down departmental barriers and concentrate on building up personal relationships. To do so, they need to change "front-office" practices—the way they provide services, promote and present them, and collaborate with others.

That's where CRM comes in. CRM is part technology solution, part process redefinition; CRM connects the front and back office, using analytical capabilities to help the school organization effectively manage all of its relationships. Automation figures significantly in this strategy, as does distribution of intelligent knowledge (data) and integration of school-wide technology. The result is collaboration, not compartmentalization. Service, support, and communication models are always proactive, never merely responsive. The payoff?

- Efficiency rises, in turn driving costs down and quality of service up.
- Customer services are more directed and insightful, and partnerships become more productive.
- The customer comes away from interacting with such a school organization with greater satisfaction.
- These changes increase the trust among the school's internal and external customer base.

New Challenges Need a Proven Approach

Customer benefits make a world of difference, whether you make widgets, teach math or English, or govern a nation. The ability to reduce costs, improve service, and increase trust is crucial for the education organization—especially now.

Educators mistakenly assume that competition does not apply to them and such "mundane" matters exist solely in the business world.

Schools vigorously compete for funding, faculty, and students. Just look at the turnover and shortage of teachers and earlier discussions on competitive factors. Local and state governments aggressively compete for families and businesses that carefully judge the quality of schools when considering relocating to a new area. And everyone competes for skilled employees—and for scarce funding.

Such increased competitive pressures demand that the school organization distinguish itself. CRM helps the schools do so by concentrating the entire staff on improving service delivery and targeting customer satisfaction.

Budget accountability also defines the new "Customer Age" for schools. Sharp customers know the cost of schooling, and they know that they are the ones paying the bill. Customers expect the school to operate efficiently, not just because it will relieve their frustration but also because it controls costs.

Here, CRM helps provide timely and reassuring answers. Processes are redefined and standardized; time-consuming tasks are automated;

and knowledge is centralized. As a result, school employees are more productive—and increasingly cost-effective. CRM Internet applications help reduce expenses while building greater collaboration and trust.

The Institute for Electronic Government (an IBM affiliate) estimates that federal, state, and local governments could save nearly 70 percent by providing services on-line rather than via traditional, over-the-counter methods. Today, it is has become increasingly common to access blank forms on line and return them completed via the Internet. Add to this the time and cost savings the customer receives from having ready access to and using these tools, and the return on investment is even more compelling.

What Is CRM Not?

Without clearly defining what is meant by *customer relationship*, a school can hardly be expected to develop CRM tools to build and enhance its customer relationships. And since CRM is a fairly new concept, few people can give a clear and workable definition. So it is useful to look at what CRM is not. Rose Palmer at PeopleSoft[5] has done much work in this field.

First, CRM is not one-to-one services. So far, customer relationship management does not fit conventional marketing theory, so CRM application developers have had to find some new theory to promote their products. One-to-one marketing fell in place as the first logical choice. However, this thinking is misleading with respect to the use of CRM. No doubt, one-to-one marketing is about customer relationship. But this is only *one* possible relationship. More importantly, this one-to-one relationship with customers is incorrect.

First, it is harmful as an operational way of thinking. Human beings tend to think in the aggregate. When we see a tree, we see it as a tree in a forest. When we see a student, we see him or her as *one* of the students. When we know the needs of a student, we are able to aggregate such information to determine if other students have the same needs and if we should meet them (if they are not individual or special needs). There are many statistical techniques to help aggregate such information. However, one-to-one services would try to treat each student separately. It would force teachers and administrators to think and treat students individually even though they are from the same segment. So in a one-to-one school enterprise, teachers would be trained to isolate students individually and to treat *each* student differently. By definition we know this is does not apply in practical terms.

Next, CRM is not personalization. Strictly speaking, personalization is also not one-to-one marketing, although people often use these two concepts interchangeably. Here's an example. The Amazon.com personal book recommendations illustrate that most personalization applications are actually market segment targeting. If I bought a book on Dante's *Divine Comedy*, I belong to one segment and all others belong to other segments.

Personalization sounds hot because it is . . . personal. To personalize or not to personalize? Before such a decision is made, we need to know the dangers that await us.

Finally, CRM is not database applications. Did we manage to manage customer relationships before we had use of the computer? The database applications used in CRM are only a *tool* to help the school administrator and teacher manage student and customer relationship more effectively. But they are not CRM itself.

Can CRM Really Help Build Customer Relations?

Most people worry about the potential damage of its current customer relationship after bringing customer relationship management tools on-line. They're rightly concerned about the infringement of customer privacy by CRM tools.

The best way to head off problems of this kind is for the district to identify its stakeholder relationships.

When education leaders *define* the most important relationships among the internal school customers (teacher to teacher, staff to staff, support persons to educators, etc.) and between the school and its external customer, school leaders will be off to a strong CRM start.

41. DATA WAREHOUSES

A data warehouse (DW), or more accurately, an "information warehouse," is a *subject-oriented* database designed with *enterprise-wide access* in mind. The enterprise can be defined as a school, as well as a district, a county, a state, or a business. The DW provides tools to satisfy the information needs of managers at all organizational levels—not just for complex data queries, but as a *general facility* for getting quick, accurate, and often insightful information. A data warehouse is designed and intended so its users can easily recognize the information they want and then access that information for use in making better decisions, using simple tools.

The information gleaned from the DW is intended to be as ubiquitous in performance managing the school and classroom as reading the dials on your automobile dashboard is to determine distance traveled, rate of speed, condition of the vehicle, and so forth. The DW blends technologies, including relational and multidimensional databases, graphical user interfaces, and more. Data in the DW differs from operational systems data in that it is *read-only;* this means that it cannot be modified. Operational systems create, update, and delete production data that "feed" into the data warehouse. The principal reason for developing a DW is to integrate operational data from various sources into a single and consistent warehouse that can support analysis and proper decision making within the defined school enterprise.

For school enterprises that believe information is a valuable resource, the DW is analogous to a physical warehouse.

- Operational systems create data "parts" that are loaded into and stored in the warehouse.
- Some of those parts are summarized into information "components" and stored in the warehouse.
- DW users make requests and are delivered "products" that are created from the components and parts stored in the warehouse.

DW has become one of the most popular and stable industry trends—for good reason. A well-defined and thought-out DW, properly implemented, is a valuable performance management tool.

Summarizing the Benefits of a Data Warehouse

- *Cost-effective decision making.* A data warehouse allows for simplification. It eliminates staff and computer resources ordinarily required to support data queries and reports against operational and production databases. This offers significant savings by eliminating the resource drain on district IT systems when executing long-running complex queries and reports.

- *Better enterprise intelligence.* Increased quality and flexibility of school analysis results from the multitiered data structures of a data warehouse that support data ranging from detailed performance level to high-level summaries. Guaranteed data accuracy and reliability result from ensuring that a data warehouse contains only "trusted" data.
- *Improved customer service.* The school enterprise can maintain better relationships with all classes of customers by linking customer data via a single data warehouse.
- *Process reengineering.* Allows unlimited analysis of school information, often providing fresh insights into school processes that may yield breakthrough ideas for reengineering such processes. The act of defining the requirements for a data warehouse almost always results in better school goals and measures.
- *Information system reengineering.* A data warehouse based upon district-wide data requirements, provides a cost-effective means of establishing both data standardization and school system interoperability.

A Data Warehouse Primer

The following information is based on the work of W. H. Inmon, the father of the data warehouse concept.[6]

Current Detail

The heart of a data warehouse is its current detail. It is the place where the bulk of data resides. Current detail comes directly from operational systems—i.e., district consolidation of individual schools—and may be stored as raw data or as an aggregation of raw data. Current detail, organized by subject area, represents the *entire* school enterprise, rather than a given application.

Current detail is the lowest level of data granularity (ranging from coarse to fine grain) in the data warehouse. Every data entry in current detail is a snapshot, at a moment in time, representing the instance when the data are accurate. Current detail is typically two to five years old. Current detail is refreshed as often as necessary to support district requirements.

System of Record

A system of record is the source of the best or "most correct" data that feed the data warehouse. The "most correct" data are those that are most timely, complete, and accurate and conform best to the data warehouse. The "most correct" data usually come from closest to the source of the information—teachers, principals, etc. In other cases, a system of record may be one containing previously summarized data.

Integration and Transformation Programs

Even the "most correct" operational data cannot usually be copied, as is, into a data warehouse. Raw operational data are virtually unintelligible to most end users. Operational data seldom conform to the logical, subject-oriented structure of a data warehouse. Further, different operational systems represent data differently, use different codes for the same thing, squeeze multiple pieces of information into one field, and more. Operational data can also come from many different physical sources: old centralized computer files, nonrelational databases, indexed flat files, even proprietary tape and card-based systems. Thus, operational data must be cleaned up, edited, and reformatted before being loaded into a data warehouse.

As operational data bits and pieces pass from their original systems of record to a data warehouse, integration and transformation programs convert them from application-specific data into *enterprise-wide* data. These integration and transformation programs perform functions such as:

- Reformatting, recalculating, or modifying key structures
- Adding time elements
- Identifying default values
- Supplying logic to choose between multiple data sources
- Summarizing, tallying, and merging data from multiple sources

When either operational or data warehouse environments change, integration and transformation programs are modified to reflect that change.

Summarized Data

Lightly summarized data are the hallmark of a data warehouse. All school enterprise elements (department, school, district, specialized function, etc.) have different information requirements. Effective data warehouse design provides for customized, lightly summarized data for every enterprise element. A district-wide element may have access to both detailed and summarized data, but there will be much less than the total stored in current detail.

Highly summarized data are primarily for district-wide administrators. Highly summarized data can come from either the lightly summarized data used by district-wide elements or from current detail. Data volume at this level is much less than at other levels and represents an eclectic collection supporting a wide variety of data needs and interests. In addition to access to highly summarized data, generally administrators are given the ability to access increasing levels of detail through what is commonly called a "drill down" process. As the term implies, the user digs deeper for the desired information.

Archives

Data warehouse archives contain old data (normally over two years old) of significant, continuing interest and value to the school district. There is usually a massive amount of data stored in the data warehouse archives that has a low incidence of access. Archive data are most often used for forecasting and trend analysis, such as student registrations and geographical distributions. Although archive data may be stored with the same level of detail as current data, it is more likely that archive data are aggregated as they are archived. Archives include both old data (in raw or summarized form) and metadata that describe the old data's characteristics.

Metadata

One of the most important parts of a data warehouse is its metadata—or data about data. Also called data warehouse *architecture*, metadata is integral to all levels of the data warehouse, but exists and functions in a different dimension from other warehouse data. Metadata used by data warehouse developers to manage and control data warehouse creation and maintenance reside outside the data warehouse. Metadata for data warehouse users is part of the data warehouse itself and are available to control access and analysis of the data warehouse. To a data warehouse user, metadata are like a "card catalog" to the subjects contained in the data warehouse.

Data Warehouse Structure

A data warehouse may have any of several structures:

- *Physical Data Warehouse*—A physical database in which all the data for the data warehouse are stored, along with metadata and processing logic for scrubbing, organizing, packaging, and processing the detail data.
- *Logical Data Warehouse*—Also contains metadata including district-wide rules and processing logic for scrubbing, organizing, packaging, and processing the data, but does *not* contain actual data. Instead it contains the information necessary to *access* the data wherever they reside.
- *Data Mart*—A subset of a district-wide data warehouse. Typically it supports an enterprise element (department, school, specialty function, etc.). As part of an iterative data warehouse development process, an enterprise builds a *series* of physical data marts over time and *links* them via an enterprise-wide logical data warehouse or feeds them from a single physical warehouse.

Data Warehouse Development

There are three popular "approaches" for data warehouse—two of which are bad.

1. "Data Dump"—All enterprise data are replicated or made available with no attempt made to "scrub" or even categorize the data. It's like *dumping* all the contents in a physical warehouse in the middle of the floor and asking people to pick out what they need.

2. "Magic Window"—Data are accessible from wherever they are throughout the enterprise, again without ensuring data quality. It's like a big sack in which there are rubies and emeralds and gold nuggets and broken glass and rat droppings and poisonous snakes. At some point you quit putting your hand in the bag.

3. "Strategic Data Warehouse"—This stores enterprise-wide data based upon the organization's requirements!

Computer-based tools provide the flexibility and capability to easily develop a school-wide, strategic data warehouse.

42. CASE STUDY: WAYS TO PERFORM COMPLEX QUERIES

A Web site, which can be accessed from the Education Data Partnership home page at www.ed-data.k12.ca.us, provides fiscal data on all of California's one thousand elementary, unified, and high school districts. Users can see how federal, state, and local funds allocated to their district compare with those allocated to other districts and to the state as a whole. They can select and search variables and the range of each variable, and they can output a variety of reports. Using the query tool, education professionals can locate districts that are similar to their own in particular respects. These districts can then serve as references when the educators argue their case for additional funding. The site uses pull-down menus as a means of drilling down to whatever information is needed.

Lower Unit Costs and Better Decision Making

The California Department of Education (CDE) expects the primary users of the site will be education professionals who deal with fiscal information. The districts are required by CDE to submit the information, but the state has not thus far done a good job of managing the data and putting it in a place where these professionals can get at it.

Prior to making the data available to the school districts, many schools and districts had to join various associations and pay membership fees. The associations would come to CDE to get the data, which, as public information, would then be provided for a nominal fee. Then, the association would develop the data and charge the districts for the reports, which were based originally on data that the districts them-selves had submitted. Essentially, districts spent money to get their own data back. Now, CDE is giving the districts direct access to the data, helping them cut costs and providing information to more people, lead-ing to better decisions and to a higher quality of education.

Easier Access and Reporting

With the Internet and its own Web site, the CDE is now better pre-pared to handle queries from education professionals and calls from the news media about the status of various education programs. University students and research groups ask for data for their analyses. Businesses who sell to the education market are also interested in this data so they can follow trends in education programs and better position their prod-uct or service offerings. Even construction companies take advantage of data on funding for new schools to pinpoint upcoming building op-portunities.

Soon, CDE expects to provide school-level data that parents can use at school board meetings. There is also a wealth of data on teachers' education, pay levels, and benefits. Both the teachers' unions and the school districts need these data to make intelligent decisions.[7]

In the private sector, enterprise-wide systems integrate data networks to better deliver services and products to their customers. These enterprise-wide systems are often referred to as "customer centric" because they can provide information "responsively" to customers from synchronized data-bases. When a customer calls, the vendor can respond with real-time in-formation unique to that customer. This type of delivery system illustrates the awesome power of customer relationship management. It not only im-proves the customer centric functionality of the organization's networks; it also enhances the services, manages the relationship, allows for mean-ingful segmentation, and provides unique treatment of each customer.

In the public sector, and especially in school systems, it is now pos-sible to mirror this type of functionality within the district's informa-tion technology (IT) structure. New tools tailored to school districts, cities, and counties are being developed and implemented. Such sys-tems may come to be called citizen relationship management. Because citizens are also on our list of customers, they have come to expect 24/7 service and interactive delivery systems. All government entities, including schools, need to begin responding to this expectation.

Using Technology

School districts and city, county, and state governments are also being affected by the one-to-one trend. The possibility of treating each citizen differently is now here. There are many tools available to help. Some are designed specifically for the public sector to provide improved information services to citizens, making it easier for citizens to fill out forms, get answers to questions, and be informed on controversial public projects.

Technology can help enhance communication with citizens. The first step may be the use of a database for building a mailing list with intelligence. Starting with a current mailing list, the database would address various interests, such as agriculture, traffic, utilities, technology, cultural arts, and development. Unique outreach messages can be sent to segments, as various topics need to be addressed. Additional interests could be added as necessary. Sorting alphabetically and by category, geographic areas, and level of interest is now possible. Such a database can also note preferences on how *each* individual prefers to receive information, either by mail, e-mail, fax, or phone. Studies show an increase in response to messages sent through a person's preferred channel of communicating.

In addition, a project database allows recording a history of the individual's interaction with the process, noting such events as meetings, documents sent, and telephone and e-mail records. Anyone who has done business in the public sector immediately understands the value of ensuring that the right people receive the right information from the agency and that there is a record of it.

The next step is a Web site dedicated to the organization's current issues or projects and its processes. (Consider, for example, a Web site notice regarding a change in student dress code policy that once would have been sent home with a mimeographed notice.) Web pages linked to the district's home page can clarify why and how the issue is being handled, along with schedules of related events such as public meetings. The site can refer readers to key reports and studies and can be set up to receive comments from its public. Stakeholders can communicate directly with the right persons or department or have a forum where questions can be asked as the process unfolds. In addition, if there are maps involved, various mapping concepts could be posted and made readily available to everybody involved in the process.

Combined, the database and the Web site help reinforce traditional forms of outreach, such as notification mailings, feedback reports, surveying, important documents in draft and final stages, and any legally required notices.

Examples of Participation

In Santa Rosa, California, the city's Geyser Pipeline Project *Data Instincts* is responsible for public information and notification to areas potentially impacted by this unique public project that will pump millions of gallons of treated reclaimed water to geothermal wells, 42 miles away. Through their Web site and custom databases, detailed information is made available to those potentially affected.

The Monterey County, California, General Plan Update *Data Instincts* is responsible for public information and notification to areas potentially affected by the project.

The St. Johns County (Florida) School District Strategic Plan, two years in the making, involved a significant cross section of the school stakeholder community. Plans are under way to evaluate Customer Relationship Management (CRM) tools to extend the scope of citizen contact.

These projects use unique databases configured especially for them. The databases contain information on those who have an interest or are potentially impacted by such important projects, noting what meetings to attend, what documents are sent, and important e-mail and telephone communications.

43. THE SPIRIT OF ORGANIZATIONAL CHANGE

Ready. Fire. Aim! There is a psychological dimension of data usage and benchmarking (see below) because billions of dollars are wasted on ambitious efforts to alter patterns and practices in businesses, hospitals, and schools. Most of these initiatives start with a bang and shortly sputter, ending with things pretty much the way they were. The energy created in the beginning is lost or misplaced somewhere along the way. The cause of this sad track record is now becoming clearer.

If we approach change in a human enterprise solely from a technical mind-set, assuming that simply changing strategy or restructuring roles or data usage is going to do the trick, we're probably doomed to fail. In such cases everything we try will be quickly absorbed by the very cultural patterns and practices we want to change.

On the other hand, if we think about changing behavior as a spiritual undertaking, a different set of opportunities present themselves. First of all, we use a different vocabulary and embrace different, less familiar, assumptions. Secondly, we pose new questions that are routine in other aspects of our lives but rarely thought about in business or schools. Questions like:

- How can we beef up our schools' spirit?
- How can our work be uplifted by more spirit?
- How can we move our people to a new commitment to student success or revive the enthusiasm they once had ?
- How can we reclaim the spiritual underpinnings of the origins of public schooling to create new sources of energy to sustain the demanding journey change requires?

In a prophetic paragraph quoted for many generations, John Adams wrote:

I must study politics and war that my sons may have the liberty to study mathematics and philosophy. My sons ought to study mathematics and philosophy, geography, natural history, naval architecture, navigation, commerce, and agriculture in order to give their children a right to study paintings, poetry, music, architecture, statuary, tapestry, and porcelain.

We know how modern people create spiritual energy. In church, or synagogue, or mosque, spirit is beckoned through myths, stories, scripture, liturgy, music, and ritual. It should be possible to tap such energy in a school system.

The solution, at least as a first step, is to recognize that ours is a spiritually, as well as a technically, driven world. Such consciousness fits our knowledge that the path to genuine power also requires the recognition of the nonphysical dimensions of the human being.

Of course, explaining how spirit works in an organization is a tough task. But here is an example that might help us. Spirit is like going to the bank to open a safety-deposit box. It takes two keys to open it, your key and the bank's. Leaders of change understand that spirit applies to fundamental matters, to what counts most for us, and that it cannot be kept apart from other aspects of our lives. We need both keys.

Spirit, as we have come to understand it, defies rigorous definition. The spirit of a holiday like Thanksgiving, for example, shines brilliantly once each year. It inspires people to experience the magic of the season. It creates plentiful if only a temporary supply of ego energy. As the spirit rises, the world looks and feels different: more sunny and confident. When spirit is removed, only the basic outward appearance remains—the energy slips away.

Spirit moves us beyond failure. It helps us strive toward setting new goals, developing new attitudes, and achieving new accomplishments. We cannot live and work in a school totally driven by efficiency, productivity, and materialism. One only needs to look at the drive and remarkable comeback of three-time Tour de France winner Lance Armstrong, whose testicular cancer had spread to his lungs and brain. Just a few years earlier, Armstrong was given less than a 50–50 chance to live. But here he was in 2001, driven by his indomitable spirit, triumphing once again and wearing the winner's yellow jersey.

Must we look for our daily motivation from other sources? Not really. Sure, spirit has some credibility problems. Yet, despite all this, the term "spirit" regularly weaves itself into our everyday conversation and experiences. Lindbergh flew "The Spirit of St. Louis" solo to Paris. The American Revolution is immortalized in "The Spirit of '76." We use expressions like "Keep the spirit," "The spirit is willing but the flesh is weak," "team spirit," "esprit de corps," "school spirit," "His spirits are up." In the wake of the September 11, 2001, atrocity, it was the indomitable spirit of Americans in general, and New Yorkers in particular, that immediately shone through.

We Need to Work at It

Spirit can be either a constructive or destructive force. Positive spirit spawns hope, ego energy, and confidence—a belief in one's self—a can-do mind-set. But it's easy to spot what happens when an organization's spirit goes sour.

Negative spirit is the root of hopelessness. It saps energy, shatters hope, and drags down performance. If an organization is plagued by unhealthy spirit, what can be done? Consider what happens to a sports team that spirals down into a prolonged slump. It takes us to the point at which tinkering with input and structural features of the organization will not get us to where we need to go.

What's needed to break out of the slump? It takes bold, risk-taking leaders that are willing to leave the safety of the status quo—to sail uncharted waters in the quest of finding new spirit. Otherwise, our schools, like the sports team, will continue to lose both faith in themselves and the public's confidence in their ability to help students meet the skill demands of intense 21st-century competition.

Low-Performing Schools

A central piece in state and district accountability systems, mandated by ESEA Title I, is the establishment of procedures and standards (measurements) for defining and identifying low-performing schools. For example:

- Maryland established a school performance index to determine if a school is meeting state expectations. To meet standards schools must maintain a 94 percent attendance rate, have 70 percent of students scoring at the satisfactory level on the state assessment, and have no more than a 3 percent high school dropout rate.
- In New York, at least 90 percent of students in each school are expected to score at or above state benchmarks. In addition, no school's dropout rate should exceed 5 percent. Schools that fail to achieve minimum performance standards risk having their registration placed under review.
- The Kentucky Instructional Results Information System (KIRIS) establishes a baseline starting point and academic goals for each school

in the state. The state has projected goals for student performance through the year 2010. Schools that exceed the goals are eligible for financial awards, and schools that fall behind are designated "in decline." The lowest-performing schools, designated as "schools in crisis," are those whose performance declines by more than 5 percent of their baseline for two consecutive assessment cycles.

- The Texas Education Agency annually collects data on its more than one thousand school districts and 3.7 million students. In conjunction with results from the Texas Assessment of Academic Skills (TAAS), Texas disaggregates student performance data and measures not only a school's progress but also student performance across a range of racial/ethnic and income groups. In order to make adequate yearly progress, Texas schools must obtain an "acceptable" rating from the state's accountability system—a rating that requires at least 40 percent of all students and student groups to pass each section of the TAAS, a dropout rate of no more than 6 percent, and an attendance rate of at least 94 percent. These standards increase each year.

- San Francisco Unified School District uses nine performance indicators to identify low-performing schools, including the percentage of students who score below the 25th percentile on the district assessment; the numbers of suspensions, dropouts, and student absences in schools; the percentage of teachers who are long-term substitutes; and the number of students requesting open enrollment transfers out of certain schools.

As part of this emphasis on accountability, data gathered from state and district assessments are informing the public about school performance. Eighteen states, including Florida, Oklahoma, Maryland, Texas, and Wisconsin, distribute school "report cards" that display information about student learning in every school in the state. These report cards are helping stakeholders judge how well schools are achieving their long-range goals and how schools measure up to other schools with similar student populations. For example:

- The New York State Education Department issues a "report card" for every school each year. These report cards allow for comparisons of student achievement results across a cohort of similar schools based on the age range served by the school, the resource capacity of the district, and the economic need of the school's students.

- The Charlotte-Mecklenburg (North Carolina) school system distributes easy-to-read student learning goals to parents at the beginning of the school year. The district follows up with school report cards on student attendance and performance that are distributed to parents and every household in the district and are published in the newspaper.

The establishment of state and local systems of accountability has been important for leveraging change in low-performing schools. In many cases, being publicly identified as low performing has been a necessary impetus for change. But it is only the first step on the road to improvement. Turning around low-performing schools requires tough choices and a focus on strategies that will improve curriculum, teaching, and learning.

Real school transformation demands changes in the relationships among adults within schools and between educators and parents, school and community leaders, unions, district officials, and partners at all levels of government. School reform requires a willingness to learn, to alter old practices, and to act in new ways.

NOTES

1. Marshall McLuhan, *Understanding Media* (Cambridge, Mass.: MIT Press, 1994).

2. Lester C. Thurow, *Building Wealth: The New Rules for Individuals, Companies, and Nations in a Knowledge-Based Economy* (New York: HarperCollins, 2000).

3. Robert Kaplan, *The Balanced Scorecard: Translating Strategy into Action* (Boston, Mass.: Harvard Business School Press, 1996).

4. Ibid.

5. Rose Palmer, PeopleSoft.

6. W. H. Inmon, *Building the Data Warehouse* (New York: Wiley, 2002).

7. IBM Business Intelligence Web site, www-3.ibm.com/software/data/bi, 2 August 2001.

Money and Schools

44. SCHOOL FINANCE ISSUES

The central issue in school finance is about performance managing school processes. First, money fuels all essential schooling processes. While the following studies shed new light on the financing of schools, educators need to keep in mind that, first and foremost, efficient and effective management of school processes is what delivers proficient students.

Two widely respected publications look at school-funding issues from different perspectives:

- *Making Money Matter: Financing America's Schools,* from the National Academy of Science's (NAS) Committee on Education Finance, advocates a new approach called "funding adequacy."
- A policy briefing by Allan Odden, *Creating School Finance Policies That Facilitate New Goals,* sums up three publications by researchers at the Office of Education Research and Improvement [OERI] Center for Policy Research in Education [CPRE]. It looks at school financing from this new perspective.

NAS reminds us that since *Brown v. Board of Education* equity in funding still remains the primary focus of policymakers and lawmakers. A number of innovative ways have been devised to try equalizing the amount of funds going to children in different school districts. Few would argue that glaring inequities exist in the dollars spent on children from affluent areas versus children from poverty areas. This issue is of most concern in urban schools, where some of the largest and most persistent pockets of poverty exist.

THE BIG YELLOW BUS

Brown v. Board of Education spawned the nationwide effort to erase the separate but equal doctrine. And at last count some 440,000 school buses take 24 million children to and from school every day, traveling more than 4 billion miles each year. Those rides cost nearly $10 billion every year, reports the *National School Transportation Association*, a trade organization for school bus contractors. Of course, not all bus transportation is intended to foster school integration. But how much of that $10 billion has been looked at as a cost-benefit trade-off to potentially improve student-centered learning?

45. EVERY SCHOOL SYSTEM HAS A PURPOSE

The purposes may be extravagant and general, as is often described in college of education textbooks and vigorously argued for in local school budgets. Components of the school system must be both carefully managed and measured to accomplish its purposes.

Today, through the state and federal mandates for accountability, the purpose of the school system is more clearly spelled out: It is student-centered results. Applying systems thinking and cost-benefit analysis can guide educators to better understand and measure the components that must be smoothly integrated in order to accomplish the purposes of the school system.

Most of us recognize that a system comprises a group of components that are intended to run smoothly to accomplish a purpose. The general idea is illustrated in the human body, its circulatory or the digestive system, or in transportation, such as the interstate highway system or the air controller systems operating at each of the nation's airports.

The power of systems thinking springs from two main ideas:

- The idea of purpose
- The idea of coordination of the parts to achieve the system's purpose

Systems have purposes, and once they are clearly stated and focused, the individual components that compose the system can then be carefully aimed toward accomplishing its purposes and properly measured.

We visited two schools to benchmark the cost-benefit use of television as a classroom instructional medium for the Spanish language program. In the first school visited, an excellent system was in place and ready for use. Both television and classroom teachers had clear goals for the teaching. Both groups met regularly to work out problems that arose from time to time. There were teachers' manuals and student workbooks by which the classroom could support television instruction with extra practice. The principal had a list of formative evaluation criteria to ensure that the quality was built in before the instruction began.

To benchmark best practice, we visited another school. The second school, teaching the same language experience through television, functioned bit-by-bit; it was a typical non-system. A summative evaluation showed that most of the students not only did not learn successfully, they actually learned to hate the subject of Spanish.

Classroom teaching worked like this. For three successive years in the project, and for three times a week, the teacher turned on the television set and kept the class quiet for 30 minutes. The students watched the program, which was all in Spanish and incomprehensible to all but a few who had that background. At the end of the TV program, the set was turned off and the teacher proceeded to teach something else. Spanish was perceived as a dull program most students could not understand. This eventually translated into "I hate Spanish."

To put the systems concept and cost-benefit analysis into practical use in a classroom teaching:

1. A set of valid and clearly stated objectives is prepared to directly reflect the purpose of the classroom teaching.
2. A criterion test to measure the achievement of the objectives is obtained.
3. The content required to make possible the students' mastery of the objectives is set in appropriate media (textbook passages, computer programs, photographs, etc.), with the teacher applying the appropriate principles of learning and student management.
4. The approach is studied and measured through review of test results.
5. Corrective actions are put in place.

On the basis of such actions, all teachers pursuing the same purposes are given the benefit of what has been learned.

46. SCHOOLS RUN ON MONEY

Property owners pay school taxes. States collect tax revenues. Some states earmark lottery money to help pay the costs of K–12 schools. The federal government targets dollars to specific programs aimed at realizing some larger social purpose. All of this money, tens of millions of dollars each year, is distributed to the local school district based on a *per-pupil* calculation.

Even with such an impressive hierarchy of money handling, few know the *real cost* of educating an American student. Worse yet, schools lack an education-industry standard of quality to measure the true cost of public schooling. They either don't have the tools, or don't use the tools they have, that are currently available to performance manage the processes of schools.

While 99 percent of adult Americans can read, in the sense they can decode words, nearly half of adult Americans are *functionally* illiterate; they are unable to read well enough to manage daily living effectively and perform work tasks calling for reading skills beyond the basic level.

Schools are charged with preparing young people to function as responsible citizens and productive employees in a world in which people are bombarded 24 hours a day with raw data and unprocessed information. Today, the ability to synthesize facts and to give proper meaning to those facts is as necessary for citizenship as it is for holding a good job in the modern workplace.

St. Johns County (Florida) School District Superintendent Hugh Balboni has taken the bull by the horns to find solutions to this chronic problem. He offers a money-back guarantee to any employer in his area if a graduate from one of his high schools lacks the requisite skills to perform his or her first job. Balboni will take the student back and retrain him or her at school district expense. It takes serious money to correct such shortcomings, and Balboni knows that the "customer" defines quality. We are reminded of a marketing truism; dog food is not good if the dogs won't eat it.

The actions of Superintendent Balboni are a good example of imposing a market discipline in education. In many ways the most promising element of market discipline for schools is cost control. The true power of markets is to bring down the costs of production and the delivery of goods and services, encouraging and rewarding efficiency.

Forget expenditures. Cost is the litmus test of measuring schools. Unit costs in health care offer an analogy. The discipline of market forces has already begun to overturn some of the inefficient workings of the health-care profession and in just three years.

MAYBE THIS WILL GET YOUR ATTENTION!

The annual cost of producing a *proficient* fourth-grader in Connecticut schools ranges from $8,317 in Simsbury to $67,684 in Hartford, according to the *1998 Connecticut Public Schools Guide* published by the Hartford-based CPEC Foundation.

Troubling? That's right. It costs $67,684 a year to achieve *one classroom-capable* Hartford fourth-grader. That's more than twice the cost of sending a graduate student to Harvard, Princeton, or MIT for one year. And Hartford's cost experience is closer to the rule than the exception in today's chronic school poor-performance mess.

As it stands today, schools have no metric—no way of properly measuring results—that also allows anyone to say with confidence that schools are spending too much, too little, or just the right amount. In terms of market discipline, schools are strongly encouraged to optimize—to do what they are good at, to learn to do better, and to set goals that are both high and realistic. To do so is the only practical way to have the schools and their staffs reap the rewards of a clearer sense of accountability.

---

47. THE STUBBORNNESS OF SCHOOL-FUNDING THINKING

Because of the intractability of equalizing funding, attention has finally shifted to studying how to *equalize the effective educational experience* for all children. The National Academy of Science (NAS) argues for the more effective use of education dollars within the emerging concept of funding adequacy.

- This is an *outcome-oriented view* of funding.
- It forces schools to focus on *educational achievement* and *how much money is needed* to reach a defined academic goal, such as the agreed-upon performance standards reflected in the mandatory testing programs.
- It is a *cost-benefit* formula.

Funding adequacy is such a new idea that implementing it represents a radical departure and different experience in different school locations because of many unknowns.

- First, there is at present no standard definition of "adequate education" for education policymakers to build a financial system around.
- Second, there is no clear idea what amount of funding is necessary to reach a goal once it has been defined.
- Third, other problems include how much additional funding is necessary for disadvantaged children and children with disabilities.

Researchers believe the *process* of reaching funding adequacy involves these three things:

1. Investing in the capacity of the education system
2. Promoting performance by ensuring the incentive system to recognize achievement
3. Bringing schools and parents into the process by empowering them to help make funding decisions

The NAS report is gaining notice because it calls for more research into charter schools and voucher systems, rather than inter-district and intra-district choice programs, to improve poor-performing schools. Because existing voucher efforts are small in scale and cannot provide adequate data on the results of the program, it calls for a "large and ambitious" research program that includes the participation of private schools.

To aid in these and other reform efforts, better and more focused education research is identified as being needed especially in the following three areas:

1. Capacity building, including developing and retaining well-prepared teachers
2. Incentives designed to motivate higher teacher performance
3. The voucher program

The NAS study further calls for more integration of special education because the previous distinctions have "compromised educational effectiveness."

The study also refers to a "perceived" crisis in urban education. It is startling and says much about a continuing head-in-the-sand view of school improvement when a prestigious group meets in Washington, D.C., with that urban school system right under its nose, and still refers to the urban education crisis as "perceived."

The Center for Policy Research in Education (CPRE) brief is based on three studies; *Improving State School Finance Systems: New Realities Create Need to Re-Engineer School Finance Structures, School Finance Systems: Aging Structures in Need of Renovation*, and *School Based Financing in North America.*

The composite study advocates statewide policy initiatives because states provide between 30 to 100 percent of school funding. The new financial structure would be based on *adequate funding linked to educational standards* and would involve four elements:

1. A base spending level considered adequate for the average child to reach high standards
2. Consideration given to those groups of students who require additional resources above the base to achieve standards
3. An adjustment for area economic factors
4. Yearly inflation rates to be factored into annual allotments

48. THE RIGHT METRICS: SPENDING PER PROFICIENT STUDENT

Working independently, the CPEC Foundation has included in its latest guide to Connecticut schools the statistic, "spending per proficient student." (*Capable, skilled, qualified*, and *expert* are a few synonyms for *proficient*.)

Research Analyst Susan W. Beckman calculates the new metrics by dividing each school's spending per student by the percentage of students in that school who meet or exceeded state goals on the Connecticut Mastery Test for fourth-grade mathematics, reading, and writing.

Although spending per Connecticut fourth-grade student varies by less than a factor of two, from $5,874 in Union to $10,909 in Greenwich, spending per *proficient* student varies by a factor of over seven, from $8,317 in Simsbury to the shameful sum of $67,684 in Hartford.

Even when comparing towns or districts with similar wealth and family education background in the same region, large differences in cost per proficient student in Connecticut are noted: for example, $8,767 in Union, $11,958 in Coventry, and $20,673 in Scotland.

Forty states now require that schools be graded and their scores be made available to the public, but none has yet gone far enough! To guarantee a solution, each state must begin to calculate and publish the extensive comparative information provided by the CPEC Connecticut *Guide.* There, municipalities are grouped into six regions to help educators and stakeholders compare their results with neighboring communities. It also provides information on demographics, school enrollments, and average teacher salaries.

As newspapers and commercial publishers become aware of the magnitude of wasteful unit costs as uncovered in Connecticut schools and the effective solution-prone power of calculating and comparing school districts by the cost-per-proficient-student metric, the public can expect these sources to rapidly start to fill the information void. This focus on measurable school results will only further ratchet up the pressure on schools for greater accountability, especially in light of the competing schooling options now available.

49. THE HIDDEN COSTS OF HOME SCHOOLING

K–12 public schools no longer enjoy a monopoly. Once they almost did, and administrators and teachers tend to operate as though they still do. It's true that state laws mandate school attendance up to a designated age. But only to that extent may public schooling be viewed as the sole source of childhood education.

Today there is an intense contest for each student's mind—TV, peers, and family pressures, to name only a few, compete for attention and acknowledgment. After all is said and done, isn't that what the schools are competing for—the student's attention and to develop the student's mind? To merely have his or her body sitting in a classroom is not enough.

Currently a warm student body, registered in school, is all that it takes for the school to secure from various sources the dollars for *per-student* funding. The truant officer, now renamed "attendance officer," pays his or her own way by helping keep kids in school, but what are they doing there?

Schools, like other nonprofit organizations, need money, and lots of it, to lubricate the wheels of its array of services. It may be that school policymakers and leaders have become desensitized to the vast amounts of money needed and where the money comes from (and how hard it is for people to come by it) and the educational purposes for which educational funding has been entrusted to them.

It may help sensitize school policymakers and leaders to note the resurgence of home schooling. According to the U.S. Department of Education (USDOE) *Home Schooling in the United States: 1999*, at least 850,000 students now learn at home; almost double the 345,000 of 1994. Some educators feel the number may actually be closer to double the study results. An estimate of 4 percent of the entire K–12 student population means more kids learning at home than are currently enrolled in all the public schools of ten states combined: Alaska, Delaware, Hawaii, Montana, New Hampshire, North Dakota, Rhode Island, South Dakota, Vermont, and Wyoming. This home-schooling number exceeds the half million kids enrolled in such highly publicized efforts as charter schools and the mere 65,000 receiving vouchers.

Home schooling has moved from a romantic notion to big business. The home-schooling trend, which is expected to continue its 11-percent-a-year growth trajectory, means that the school districts that are intended to serve these students will continue to "dollar-hemorrhage" badly; millions of dollars in per-pupil funding will continue to be bled away. Two examples drive home the point:[1]

- Maricopa County, Arizona, has lost $35 million in per-student funding in 1999 as some 7,000 students (1.4 percent of school-age kids) switched to home schooling.
- Florida had 41,128 children (1.7 percent) learning at home in 1999—up from just 10,039 in 1991–1992 and representing a loss of nearly $130 million to local school budgets.

As the late Senator Everett Dirksen is remembered for saying, "A billion here, a billion there, and pretty soon you're talking about real money." These are serious dollars. (An expanded discussion of quality process improvement in K-12 schools to head off a financial catastrophe is covered in *Healing Public Schools*, ScarecrowEducation Press, 2001.)

Almost three-quarters of home-schooling families say they do so because they are worried about the *quality* of their children's education, according to the USDOE study findings.

In Florida, a 2001 report showed a quarter of home-schooling families doing so for religious reasons. The 1999 USDOE study found 38.4 percent do so for religious reasons; 25.6 percent because they feel school is a poor learning environment; 48.9 percent because they feel they can give their child a better education at home.

A NOTABLE TURN OF EVENTS

No less a personage than Bill Bennett, former U.S. Secretary of Education, talks of the home-schooling trend as "the revolution of common sense."[2] Bennett is now traveling the country promoting *K12*, his Web-based, for-profit home-schooling service. It is as though former Joint Chiefs of Staff Chairman Colin Powell promoted the abandonment of the U.S. Army and the assembly of local militia units in its place.

The next wave in home schooling may be building in California and Texas, where school districts are forming strategic alliances with home-schooling families by allowing their home-schooled kids to sign up for science lab classes or sports.

NOTES

1. *Time*, 27 August 2001.
2. Ibid.

50. WHERE WERE YOU WHEN
THEY HIT THE WORLD TRADE CENTER?

Can anyone still remember what he or she was doing on Monday, September 10, 2001? Was it urgent enough to override the next day's events in shaping thinking and action?

Just a few weeks earlier, Washington debated what to do with all of our projected and ongoing prosperity. Tax refund checks were in the mail. States were basking in the glow of fiscal surplus. Proponents of improving the quality and performance management of business and education enterprises were being rebuffed by the "business as usual" mind-set.

But September 11, 2001, turned all that upside down and with it, the tidy and prosperous world Americans had come to know and had expected to continue indefinitely. In a few dramatic moments, the shock of a new reality hit us here at home—as we saw with our own eyes that we were no longer insulated from global terrorism. And, with this one act, all of our deeply entrenched priorities changed in a flash. Only now, and for the foreseeable future, we will gradually, but deliberately, take stock of what this all means and adjust to the new normalcy.

President Bush prepares us for a protracted campaign against global terrorism unlike any other defense effort in world history. Defense Secretary Rumsfeld reminds us that it could last longer than the Cold War, which lasted 50 years—half a century. And Henry Kissinger tells us in unstatesmanlike language that "the terrorists will learn they picked on the wrong guys this time."

The U.S. Treasury quickly readied a modern version of war bonds, not seen since World War II, to help finance this expected long-term war. The city of New York issued its first billion dollars in Reconstruction Bonds, which was oversubscribed. And the antiterrorist campaign is expected to take more money—lots more money.

Throughout the country, state and local governments, school districts, and all sizes of business enterprise are frantically rerunning their budget numbers, trying to determine how to meet their respective public obligations or stay in business profitably.

If American business and education are serious about thriving in this new environment, they will need first to recognize that the new conflict has already begun to realign forces in the world. Like the 50-year Cold War, this one, while it lasts, will exert a gravitational pull on everything. It will determine who our friends are, revise our priorities, and test the elasticity of our ideals. It will influence which departments are suddenly overenrolled in colleges and who the bad guys are in our movies. It is already siphoning away charity from a hundred important, but suddenly less important, causes. It is turning grade-school fire drills into the modern equivalent of World War II and Nuclear Age duck-and-cover exercises. It is already providing a new, opportunistic national-interest spin for lobbyists peddling everything from corporate tax cuts to medical research to farm subsidies. It has belatedly started to reshape our lumbering military and our neglected intelligence services. In a flash it took the missile-defense shield off of the table and replaced it with the need for agility and shrewdness and daring.

The new campaign will determine which foreign leaders and which issues occupy the president's attention. For instance, not long after George W. Bush took office, President Vicente Fox of Mexico campaigned for a more porous border between the U.S. and Mexico. Not much chance of that now.

Look again. Russian President Vladimir Putin is now a soul mate in the battle against terrorism. The common fear of terrorism is beginning to drive us together, much as the fear of nuclear annihilation did. This common interest even finally got the United States to pay a major portion of its long-past-due United Nations assessments.

51. IT'S BEEN CHANGING FOR A WHILE NOW

At one time an American student looking over his or her classmates would be looking at his or her eventual competition for jobs after school. In a global economy, that student can expect to compete for economic survival with students being schooled today in Asia, Latin America, Europe, and other parts of the globe. More than ever, there is an iron link between what we know and can learn and how well we can earn our daily bread.

American educators need to increase the percentage of young people entering the workforce with *new economy skills*. In addition, the majority of the present workforce needs to "rethink" and "retool" its skills—in order to hold its own in the global economy.

Today's information-rich economy has led to a new pattern of jobs while, at the same time, making obsolete many typical job categories. There is clear evidence of the need for more highly skilled but fewer production workers; fewer middle managers; more electronic information workers; and increasing numbers of "smart worker teams." Bulletin 2472, titled *Employment Outlook: 1994–2005: Job Quality and Other Aspects of Projected Employment Growth,* published by the U.S. Bureau of Labor Statistics, said:

- Occupations that will have the highest percentage growth are tied to health, computers, electronics, counseling, records technicians— all jobs calling for highly knowledgeable and skilled workers.
- Jobs requiring an associate degree from a community college will grow faster than average. Jobs for those with master's degrees from a college will grow the most, almost 28 percent.
- A bachelor's degree or more will be required in nearly 6 million new jobs.
- High-paying jobs will grow faster than low-paying jobs. Sixty percent of new jobs will offer above average wages.
- Almost one million additional persons are expected to join the ranks of the self-employed.

In the industrial economy of the 20th century, capital meant bank accounts, shares of stock, assembly lines, and physical assets. In the information economy of the 21st century, capital means *human* capital:

the skill, talent, knowledge, and commitment of people, and their optimal use on the job.

It is a transition from brawn to brains. It is an era of thinking for a living and not merely knowing how to answer questions and take orders.

Global Economic Perspective

Opponents of full U.S. participation in the global economy often try promoting fear. They cite loss of jobs, empty factories, and bread and soup lines, circa 1929. On the other hand, supporters of this new form of vigorous competition look forward to the challenge of the global economy with the confidence and with the judgment that the U.S. firms and workers can not only regain the lead in the global economy but also go on to help shape its future.

There will be consequences if we fully proceed into the new economy. There will be consequences if we fail to proceed. The message will be either that America is ready for the 21st century or that America has lost its vision and its will to compete. This is the kind of choice that confronts us today. It will have an impact on generations to come; it will send a clear message to our neighbors in the global village.

America is already being tested in the challenges of a post-Taliban Afghanistan. Those who are embroiled in ancient disputes in the Middle East and the Asian subcontinent continue to test us.

Just as we have been repeatedly warned that the war on terrorism is a long-term struggle, we must know, too, that active participation in the global economy is not a one-shot deal; it is not a single decision made at one point in history. It is a gradual process, with pivotal choices made years or even decades apart. Simultaneous international cooperation, along with zealous competitive participation in the global economy, is our best, and perhaps only, hope for sustaining a strong domestic economy and creating world-class paying jobs for Americans. Investing in the future comes down to creating the highest-skilled, best-trained, and most productive workforce in the world.

Measuring Wealth

Wealth is measured differently in different periods in history. In the 16th, 17th, and 18th centuries, capital was measured by the amount of *land* one owned. In the 19th and 20th centuries, ownership of *physical capital*—factories, equipment, and energy power—was the principal measure of wealth. The earlier period is known as the agricultural age, the latter the industrial age. In the 21st century we live, learn, and work in the knowledge and information age, where wealth is measured by the most advantageous use of human skill and brainpower—*human capital*.

Understanding the importance and differences between *physical capital* and *human capital* in each of these historic periods is essential.

- In an agricultural economy, land is the physical capital; physical strength and endurance are the prime labor asset.
- In the industrial economy, corporations require a steady supply of relatively low-skill labor to operate its machines, factories, and the energy to run them.
- In a knowledge and information economy, a high-performance employer succeeds to the extent that its workforce consists of people who can think, use information, make decisions, and take responsibility for their and their company's success. This is the pragmatic side of human capital.

52. ORGANIZATIONAL LEADERSHIP IS DIFFERENT

The organizational processes and leadership best suited for the 21st-century information age is also a far cry from those that dominated the 20th-century industrial age. Leadership is no longer the exclusive domain of the CEO or the school superintendent. In an educational organization, the teacher now comes to share the leadership role with the principal and superintendent, in carrying out the many dimensions and sweeping intentions of quality.

This partnership will come to promote a new sense of ownership among teachers and staff. It will foster the vital commitments so necessary to a new understanding of quality. Those who gain a sense of ownership in their work will come to see themselves as responsible for its quality. The leadership who manages the enterprise, be it a business or school district, helps creates the new system, and only leadership can alter it. These are the persons who ensure that the system pursues continuous improvement of its processes and its people.

But transitions take time. More than anything else, however, transition takes dedication to an idea. It doesn't matter much how long it takes. It isn't some ultimate goal that counts; it's the path to improvement that yields the results.

Consider this paradox in medicine. Physicians care, but their medicine is uncaring. When young medical students enter school, they are full of enthusiasm for taking care of people. They are deeply interested in patients' stories of illness and medical care. They are solicitous of patients. By time they finish three years of medical school, plus their internships, they may often become cynical.

It is the structure and culture of the health-care organization within which they eventually practice that greatly influence their future effectiveness as doctors. Working in a city-owned hospital, treating knife and gunshot wounds in the emergency room on a Saturday night, is all together different from practicing medicine at the Mayo Clinic. But in both cases, the organization gears itself to meeting the needs of its patients. It tries to treat each patient as though he or she is the only patient it has.

A school cannot, and most likely will not, become a high-reliability organization (HRO) on its own. If history is any lesson, school leaders need to be shown and prodded along the paths of transformation and into the necessary process changes. It's not that easy to modify school culture and to rethink the school mission. But it can be done. It is being done right now.

53. A NEW IDEA BROUGHT TO LIFE: AMERICAN KAIZEN

The American legal system operates under the overarching constitutional framework of due process. Here we refer to *substantive* due process as opposed to simply *procedural* due process. Here we are concerned with fundamental rights, as opposed to just legal technicalities.

There exists a set of universal concepts and practices either unknown, neglected, or misunderstood by both educators and the public. But when properly applied, they can help solve our present learning achievement problems in our schools.

Taken together, the principles of *due care, due diligence,* and *due regard* offer a powerful means toward reaching desired results. This is the personal caring for each student that is so sorely needed for reliable quality classroom teaching.

At present, law mandates this framework as a protection of the employment rights for public-school teachers. Interestingly, the same mandated framework formed the principles for the guided learning experiences that were successfully used to train virtually all American workers to produce the war materials for World War II. Today, if properly working in our schools, this framework would provide a proven process for continuous development of human skill, knowledge, and attitude—for every kid to become a winner in school.

When widely understood and properly practiced to improve learning in our schools, this framework can become a powerful tool of American economic advantage. It could give every kid a leg up when ready to enter the fiercely competitive yet collaborative global workplace.

Here, we call upon the concept of "American Kaizen" as a leading candidate to help the school. *Kaizen* is ingrained in Japanese culture and is the term for pursuing the discipline of "continuous improvement." What follows is a brief account of the legal framework for the use of a *model standard operating procedure* for guiding reliable classroom teaching.

Framework for American Kaizen

In repeated court opinions substantive due process, which is the foundation of due care in common law, is found to consist of these five elements:

1. Known *expectations* of what is required to be achieved
2. Documented *assistance* in meeting the expectations
3. Timely knowledge of *results*
4. Feedback from the results to construct necessary *corrective action*
5. *Many chances* to be successful through repetition of all the previous elements

It bears repeating that knowing what's expected, getting assistance, knowing the results, taking corrective action, and having repeated chances are the "stuff" of the Guided Learning Experience. These are the five essentials of due care.

There are two other ideas needed for you to be faithful to the *spirit* of substantive due process. They are due diligence and due regard.

- *Due diligence* is the obligation for you to be aware of problems and dangers *before* they occur. It mandates that you be proactive to prevent problems.
- *Due regard* represents the caring spirit of substantive due process. It means *respect for every person with no strings, no requirements, no reservations attached because of gender, race, age, physical or mental handicap, religion or ethnicity.*

Due regard reflects the common law's insistence on fundamental fairness. It hardens American Kaizen into a discipline of caring.

Through the elements of due care (Guided Learning Experience), due diligence (prevention of problems), and due regard (respect and caring for each person), American Kaizen gives us a system of caring in which:

1. You know what is expected and have an opportunity to influence what is expected. The step is called KOE *(Knowledge of Expectations)*.
2. You are given proactive assistance to successfully meet each expectation, such as meeting standards. This proviso is KOA *(Knowledge of Assistance)*.
3. You are given timely feedback, so you know how well you are meeting expectations. Timely knowledge of results is the basic principle for mastery of a skill, attitude, or knowledge. The element is KOR *(Knowledge of Results)*.
4. You are guided to successful learning through the joint development of a corrective action plan matched to expectations not yet satisfactorily met. This element is KOCA *(Knowledge of Corrective Action)*.
5. You are given multiple chances to succeed. A reasonable person knows that it takes time to master new skills, attitudes, and knowledge. The element is KOMC *(Knowledge of Many Chances)*.

For those wishing to or required to help people learn, American Kaizen provides an authoritative process approach.

54. FIRST DAY OF SCHOOL:
FROM THE BUSINESS WORLD INTO THE CLASSROOM

The following contribution came from Jane A. Lockett, Principal, IBM Education Services. Jane passed along to us this story from an associate of hers who began a teaching career after retiring from many years in business:

> As I entered the teacher's lounge, I was reminded about the educational humor I'd heard during my practice teaching assignment. Then a colleague remarked, "School would be great if it wasn't for the kids!" Laughter resonated throughout the room. I entered the room and they looked at me. I was a bit different from the rest of the faculty. I was coming into the classroom after 11 years in the business world. I was an outsider. I was qualified and certified, but I had done other things rather than spend 20 years in the classroom. Nevertheless, I smiled, walked to the coffeepot, poured my cup, in a mug that had been on sight since the 1960's. It read, "Make love, not war." And then I retreated to my classroom.
>
> Unlocking the door, I was greeted with educational "state of the art technology." Unfortunately, state of the art in the classroom is about 10 years late. There were 3 Apple II computers, with outboard 5-1/4 floppy drives. (The media specialist told me proudly, "We never throw anything away.") I had a PC on my desk, attached to the Internet and a telephone with no speaker functions.
>
> What did I need to do my job that was missing? When I compare it with the business world, a great deal.
>
> I was driven to produce in the business world; billings, signings, revenue, expense controls, customer satisfaction, performance reviews by my peers, employees and management. If I needed software applications to achieve my objectives it was given to me. In education, I was given a spreadsheet, word processor and storyboarding software.
>
> Let's see, what were my objectives in the high school business classroom?
>
> MISSION: To provide a quality education for all students in a safe and positive setting.
>
> To achieve this mission I need the following information from the educational system:

- Attendance tracking and enrollment daily software,
- A grade book,
- Remote wireless tools to capture those fleeting student "eureka" moments that I could document their unique, individual successes; real time grading through observation,
- Discipline history software,
- Health data for each student, so I could tell if that starry look in Sammy's eyes were a result of his anti-seizure medicine and not smoking pot during his lunch break, and
- A historic business intelligence system, a data warehouse. An information system where I could see his history from head start to high school. I need to analyze data and get historical reports about the educational strengths and weakness of my kids, just like I used to with my clients.

During my interview with the district recruiter, I was told to stop dreaming. "This is a public school, not a business." I wondered if the recruiter understood that the public school system is one of the largest employers in the county, the largest provider of food, transportation, health services and social services, in addition to teaching and learning. Public schools have the third largest business budget in the county.

Anyway, the recruiter said he couldn't even imagine that type of information being provided to teachers. Real time reporting on history of each child. It now takes him weeks to get reports and then they are usually not valid.

Why did I have access to the Internet? When I discussed using it to teach, I was told, I needed it to do research and provide the students with real time learning based upon the most current information. Of course, I did not have an attachment to project my computer screen; basic Business 101 seemed to be missing in my classroom. Back in the 1960s, when I was in high school, my algebra teacher proudly used a projection device to demonstrate large group instruction, but that tool was missing. I had an isolated computer, hooked up to the Web, and a network that I could use for small groups of kids, but not the option to use it for the entire classroom of 30 kids.

Oh, well, I will make the best of it. I want excellence, but it's the lowest common denominator theory that is pervasive in the schools. It is the pervasive attitude of negligence: "What makes you think you should have the best? We never have the best in this profession. Get used to it."

So, why am I here?

I was here to teach, and help my kids learn. My motto, "You are here to learn and nothing will interfere with my teaching and nothing will interfere with your learning. FOCUS, FOCUS, FOCUS! That worked in the business world." Will it work in the classroom?

Jane Lockett, a former teacher herself and author of two textbooks, takes up the argument:

> What can we do to help my friend and all of her colleagues achieve their mission of teaching and learning? Can it be so simple as to provide better, student-focused information? Information about their students, information about their educational histories, information that demonstrates the uniqueness of each and every student, what they know, and what they need to learn?

She goes on, "We provide this type of decision-making information every day in business settings in order to empower every employee to make better-informed decisions. It is a single view of information to support all aspects of student learning provided in real time to teachers when they ask for it. It's already a reality in business. We can make the same reality happen in schools."

55. IF NOT NOW, WHEN?

There are three compelling reasons to support the *why now* that we have identified:

1. Unlike many approaches to solving the well-publicized problems of public education, the prescription for improvement is built on the fact that most Americans want to reform the existing public schools, not support schemes for abandoning or excessively tinkering with them.
2. In line with what the most accurate polling results tell us, we directly deal with the most urgent question on people's minds, "*How* do we go about improving and strengthening the existing public schools?"
3. We tackle what we now know is the single most distressing challenge in all public schools, the *unreliability* in the quality of classroom teaching from one classroom to another, from semester to semester, and from school year to school year. We directly concentrate on this *tyranny of chance* and show how it can be overcome.

What the American People Care About When Asked

"The notion that the public is dissatisfied with its public schools is based on myth instead of fact," says the 2000 Phi Delta Kappa/Gallup poll summary.[1] "Respondents continue to indicate a high level of satisfaction with their local schools, a level of satisfaction that this year approaches its all-time high among the parents whose children attend those schools."

Supporters of the public schools found other promising news. The report shows a "turning away from high-stakes testing; the leveling off and the downward trend in support for choice involving private or church-related schools; the fact that lack of financial support has jumped into first place as the biggest problem; the preference for balance in the curriculum over a focus on 'the basics'; and the clear support for public schools that is evident throughout the poll."

From Gallup again, "Public satisfaction is also evident in the fact that 59 percent of Americans believe that *reforming the existing system of public schools* [emphasis added], rather than seeking an alternative system, is the best way to bring about school improvement."

Setting aside the popular political arguments of the day, our *Solutions Fieldbook* bottom line is supported by the results of the Gallup researchers: "When given the specific choice, 75 percent [of respondents] would improve and strengthen existing public schools while just 22 percent would opt for vouchers, the alternative most frequently mentioned by public school critics."

Financial resources will always be limited, but zeal for school improvement will continue unabated. This leaves the unanswered question as simply: *How do we go about improving and strengthening the existing public schools?* In the post–September 11 budget crunch and increasing demands for monies that compete with the needs of schools, the question becomes: *How do schools, administrators, and teachers learn to do more with less?*

The 2000 Gallup Report goes on further: "Today's accountability efforts are directed toward the schools' role in improving achievement. The parents have a greater effect than the schools, teachers, or students themselves on student achievement." It goes on to clarify the public's inertia, concluding "These findings may go a long way toward explaining why the public does not seem inclined to blame the public schools when students have difficulty achieving satisfactory levels of learning."

We would strongly argue with any conclusions that encourage letting the public schools "off the hook." We repeat that it is precisely because the public schools do not currently have in place reliable quality process systems that the public schools do not, will not, and cannot hold themselves to increasingly higher standards of performance mandated by their states. This fact is buried underneath poor student achievement, poor student behavior, and inadequate school leadership.

For example, with limited human and financial resources, the movement for charter schools—along with vouchers, a leading choice for many reformers—may in fact further distract us from concentrating on solving the larger school improvement equation. Most parents have neither read nor heard about such schools. Most parents surveyed oppose freeing charter school operations from state regulations, especially in matters related to curriculum. The public strongly believes that any charter school must be accountable to state standards in the same way other public schools are accountable.

When all else fails, the public and its political leaders (or are they really "front-running followers"?) watch where polls lead them and then jump out in front of the crowd and turn to the quick fix.

Topping the school improvement agenda is lack of financial support, followed by lack of discipline, overcrowding, violence, and drugs.

Not surprisingly, money is named as the number one problem. Over the years educators have done a wonderful job of selling their inability to get the job done unless they have more money. Each year schools are doled out more money, and the results seem to get more discouraging. If money was all there was to it, we could buy our way out of the school mess in a flash. But billions of dollars spent each year have not helped improve the situation and, in fact, may have had the unintentional consequence of making the job even harder. It's as though we first treat a sprained ankle with a cane, then with crutches, then use a wheelchair. The sequence only steers the patient with the sprained ankle straight for bed.

What the public defines as the purposes of the public schools mirrors what it expects from its schools. Gallup reports, "The public sees the most important purposes [of the public schools] as preparing students to become responsible citizens and helping people to become *econom-*

ically self-sufficient [emphasis added]. These are purposes that are frequently mentioned as reasons why public schools were first created."

Faced with difficult choices, the public chooses public schools providing a *balanced* education over solely teaching the basic subjects. Moreover, seeking a more *pragmatic* view of purpose, *"The public chooses preparing students for college or work over preparing them for effective citizenship."* [Emphasis added]. It grades extracurricular activities as supplements to academic subjects.

A majority of the public believes that all students have the ability to attain high levels of learning. "The most important finding in this area is the strong public consensus that most students achieve only a small part of their full academic potential in school."

We place testing in the context of *teach what you say you are going to teach and then measure it.* Increased emphasis on using of standardized tests is not supported by Gallup's findings. The public sees class work and homework as significantly more important than tests in measuring student achievement. They would not use standardized tests to determine what students have learned, but *to determine the kind of instruction they need* [emphasis added].

The public squarely affirms the principle of local control. They would like to see:

- Less federal influence
- State government have somewhat less influence
- More decisions made by students, parents, and teachers

In addition, they

- View local boards of education as having the right amount or too little say in decisions that affect the local schools,
- Seem reasonably satisfied with the role of principals and superintendents, and
- Are less ambivalent about the role of local teacher unions.

This is indeed a mixed bag. By now it seems obvious that these principles may have worked well in simpler times but now there is need to update and more sharply focus the goals of our schools. The United

States. may lead the globe in guns, ships, planes, and food production and have a strong economy and a high standard of living, but:

- We need to prepare students for 21st-century world-class job competition.
- We need to energize the nation so it no longer accepts lagging U.S. educational results when compared with other industrialized nations.
- We do not now stack up very well when it comes to preparing students to effectively compete in a new information-driven economic world.

How we gain school improvement while holding fast to our American values of local school control underpins our recommendations.

Why Now?

A 90-year-old man decides to go back to school and take a course in mathematics.

One of his contemporaries asks him, "You're going to learn mathematics at your age? Why now?"

The old man answers, "If not now, when?"

56. THE COURTS: PARENTS ARE RUNNING OUT OF PATIENCE

In America we eventually deal with long-standing frustrations and attempt to solve our major problems by calling in the lawyers, and the field of education is no different. Malpractice suits in which competencies are at issue are the newest tort area of education. Once this door opens wider, an avalanche of litigation can be expected to follow. If every student who is failing to master the survival skills of an information-based workplace society should decide to bring suit against his or her school district and its teachers for educational malpractice, the country's courtrooms would be overwhelmed.

The San Francisco Case

The first of the major competency malpractice cases was *Peter W. v. San Francisco Unified School Dis*trict (60 C.A. 3d 814, 131 Cal. Rptr.

854, 1976). Peter W. graduated from the San Francisco schools with a high school diploma. California statutes require that high school graduates read at a level above the eighth grade. Allegedly Peter W. could not survive in the workplace society, because he lacked reading or writing ability, and he sued the San Francisco Public Schools on five counts, claiming that the district:

1. "Negligently and carelessly" failed to apprehend his reading disabilities.
2. "Negligently and carelessly" assigned him to classes in which he could not read "the books and other materials."
3. "Negligently and carelessly" allowed him "to pass and advance from a course or grade level" with knowledge that he had not achieved either its completion or the skills necessary for him to succeed or benefit from subsequent courses.
4. "Negligently and carelessly" assigned him to classes in which the instructors were unqualified or which were not "geared" to his reading level, and,
5. "Negligently and carelessly" permitted him to graduate from high school although he was "unable to read above the eighth-grade level, as required by Education Code 8573 . . . thereby depriving him of additional instruction in reading and other academic skills."

Peter W. was seeking two sets of damages. First, he sought general damages because of his "permanent disability and inability to gain meaningful employment." In parallel, he sought specific damages to compensate him for the cost of tutoring to correct the injury that the San Francisco schools had inflicted upon him.

The California Court of Appeals affirmed the superior court's dismissal of the suit against the school district.

The New York Case

Less than two years after *Peter W.,* the second important competency malpractice case was decided three thousand miles away. The New York Supreme Court, Appellate Division, also ruled against a pupil alleging educational malpractice in *Donohue v. Copiague Union Free*

School District (407 N.Y.S. 874 2d, 64 A.D. 2d 29, 1978). In this case Edward Donohue sought $5,000,000 in damages, making two allegations. First, his attorneys claimed that the public schools failed to

> . . . teach the several and varied subjects to plaintiff, ascertain his learning capacity and ability, and correctly and properly test him for such capacity in order to evaluate his ability to comprehend the subject matters of the various courses and have sufficient understanding and comprehension of subject matters in said courses as to be able to achieve sufficient passing grades in said subject matters, and therefore, qualify for a Certificate of Graduation.

Since Edward Donohue did not have basic skills in reading and writing, the suit claimed that the school system breached its "duty of care" because it

> gave to the plaintiff passing grades and/or minimal or failing grades in various subjects; failed to evaluate the plaintiff's mental ability and capacity to comprehend the subjects being taught to him at said school; failed to take proper means and precautions that they reasonably should have taken under the circumstances; failed to interview, discuss, evaluate and/or psychologically test the plaintiff in order to ascertain his ability to comprehend and understand such subject matter; failed to provide adequate school facilities, teachers, administrators, psychologists, and other personnel trained to take the necessary steps in testing and evaluation processes insofar as the plaintiff is concerned in order to ascertain the learning capacity, intelligence, and intellectual absorption on the part of the plaintiff, failed to hire proper personnel . . .; failed to teach the plaintiff in such a manner so that he could reasonably understand what was necessary under the circumstances so that he could cope with the various subjects . . . ; failed to properly supervise the plaintiff; [and] failed to advise his parents of the difficulty and necessity to call in psychiatric help.

The New York court, using the *Peter W.* case as precedent, also claimed that public policy does not allow the judiciary to become embroiled in education affairs.

The Illinois Case

A teacher-dismissal case with implications for the competency malpractice area is *Gilliland v. Board of Education* (365 N.E. 2d 322,

1977). An Illinois school board dismissed a tenured elementary teacher because she had

> ruined the students' attitudes toward school, had not established effective student/teacher rapport, constantly harassed students, habitually left her students unattended and gave unreasonable and irregular homework assignments.

With more and more states implementing minimal competency tests as prerequisites for receiving a diploma, there is only one thing certain in the future. Pupil suits to recover damages as a result of educational malpractice have laid the groundwork for more and more attempts.

The Texas Case

A January 7, 2000, decision by a federal district judge in Texas is decisive in this litigation area. The following excerpt from a recent publication[2] presents the case:

> Who should issue driver's licenses to teenagers? Should it be the driving instructors who are responsible for teaching teens to drive? Or should it be an impartial examiner who tests each teen to see if he or she has the skills and knowledge needed to drive?
>
> Most people agree that using an examiner is the better way of making sure that a driver's license isn't given to teens who can't read traffic signs and don't know the rules of the road.
>
> U.S. District Court Judge Edward C. Prado, in an important and closely watched Texas case, handed down a similarly commonsense decision in January 2000. The case asked: Who should be responsible for issuing high school diplomas? A student's teachers, who may give the student passing grades in all classes? Or the Texas Education Agency (TEA), which may flunk the same student for not possessing a minimum set of academic skills?
>
> Judge Prado gave the nod to the state, not to the teachers, upholding the right of TEA to make the award of the high school diploma conditional on passing a competency test.
>
> "In spite of projected disparities in passing rates [of different ethnic groups], the TEA determined that objective measures of mastery should be imposed in order to eliminate what it perceived to be inconsistent and

possibly subjective teacher evaluations of students," wrote Judge Prado, noting that the state agency presented evidence of subjective teacher evaluations. The problem with subjective teacher evaluations, Prado noted, is that they "can work to disadvantage minority students by allowing inflated grades to mask gaps in learning."

"Texans want a high school diploma to mean something," explained Texas Education Commissioner Jim Nelson.

Education officials in several states had anxiously awaited the outcome of this case. Many already have developed or are developing similar high-stakes graduation tests. Nineteen states have tests required for graduation. At this writing, another eight have plans to put them into place. The court ruling preserves the Texas school accountability system, where the state holds educators accountable for student learning, attendance, and dropout.

The use of the TAAS test to deny high school diplomas was challenged by the Mexican-American Legal Defense and Education Fund (MALDEF). They argued that the test was discriminatory simply because the failure rate for African-Americans and Hispanics was higher than for whites. MALDEF claimed the test had "an impermissible adverse impact on minority students in Texas" and violated their right to due process.

A case was brought on behalf of nine students who did not pass the TAAS exit-level examination prior to their scheduled graduation dates. They requested that their respective school districts issue their diplomas. The court denied their request.

MALDEF presented an argument frequently made by apologists for the poor performance of urban public schools—that the state could not hold students accountable for acquiring any knowledge unless it guarantees that all students are given an equal opportunity to learn. According to MALDEF, it is unfair to penalize minority students by denying them a high school diploma when their school district has not provided them with the same opportunity to learn that white students have. Teacher assessments, not TAAS test results, should be the main criteria for awarding diplomas, argued MALDEF

Judge Prado *rejected* this argument. He recognized that minorities were under-represented in advanced placement courses and in gifted-and-talented programs, and that non-certified teachers disproportionately taught minority students. He went on to find:

> The Plaintiffs presented insufficient evidence to support a finding that minority students do not have a reasonable opportunity to learn the material covered in the TAAS examination, whether because of unequal education in the past or the current residual effects of an unequal system.

Prado went on to say that the TAAS test accomplishes exactly what it sets out to accomplish, which is "to provide an objective assessment of whether students have mastered a discrete set of skills and knowledge." Since the state has linked the test to the state curriculum, "the Court finds that all Texas students have an equal opportunity to learn the items presented on the TAAS test, which is the issue before the Court."

While acknowledging that the TAAS test "does adversely affect minority students in significant numbers," Prado ruled that there was an "educational necessity" for the test. The plaintiffs, he determined, had failed to identify equally effective alternatives. He also concluded that there had been no violation of due process rights, since the TEA provided adequate notice of the consequences of the exam and ensured that the exam is strongly correlated to material actually taught in the classroom. "The system is not perfect, but the Court cannot say that it is unconstitutional," wrote Prado.

The Likely Future Scenario

More malpractice suits for educational incompetence will be equally needless but likely. Very simply, recognizing a cause of action in negligence to recover for "educational malpractice" would eventually require the courts to oversee the administration of a state's public school system. Thus far, courts have held that state public policy recognizes no cause of action for educational malpractice.

However, the New York court also felt that the process of education is a two-step process. First, there must be teaching. Second, there must be learning. The court was not willing to conclude that when a pupil does not learn it is automatically the fault of the teacher. The New York court put it this way: "The failure to learn does not bespeak a failure to teach. It is not alleged that the plaintiff's classmates, who were exposed to the identical classroom instruction, also failed to learn."

The court placed a certain amount of fault on the student himself and on the parents as well: "The grades on the plaintiff's periodic report cards gave notice both to his parents and himself that he had failed in two or more subjects, thus meeting the definition of an 'underachiever' provided in the regulations of the Commissioner of Education (8 NY-CRR 203.1/2). Having this knowledge, the plaintiff could properly have demanded the special testing and evaluation directed by the statute."

But since neither the student nor the parents requested special help, the court felt it could not blame the failure to learn on the school system or its teachers.

The one vital difference between the *Peter W.* and the *Donohue* decisions is this. The New York Supreme Court, Appellate Division, did *not* completely rule out future education malpractice suits. The court suggested that if more than a single individual suffers injury as a result of educational malpractice, a negligence suit might be successful. Wrote the Court:

> This determination does not mean that educators are not ethically and legally responsible for providing a meaningful public education for the youth of our State. Quite the contrary, all teachers and other officials of our schools bear an important public trust and may be held to answer for the failure to faithfully perform their duties. It doesn't mean, however, that they may not be sued for damages by an individual student for an alleged failure to reach certain educational objectives.

57. DEMING FRAMEWORK FOR SCHOOL IMPROVEMENT

Having demonstrated its effectiveness for half a century, the Deming quality management principles now serve us exceedingly well in learning how to apply quality criteria to public schools. Dr. Deming himself provided the following guideposts:

Constancy of Purpose:

- Meeting or exceeding customer needs commits the total organization.
- Everyone in the organization looks for continuous improvement of product and services, research and education, and innovation.
- Constancy of purpose helps everyone work together to move the organization, school or school district in a single direction with a long-term focus.

Continuous Improvement:

- The total organization commits to ongoing improvement.
- It looks for refinement of products, services, and processes as the means of satisfying the customer.

- The status quo is never good enough. All processes are under study at all times.
- Improvement occurs through both step-by-step change and through carefully evaluated innovation.

Comprehensive Perspective:

- The organization is viewed as a system of inter-connected components.
- Constancy of purpose is achieved when all the components of the system work toward the same aim. This is system optimization.
- All share responsibility for the final product or service.

Customer-Driven Service:

- Quality improvement involves finding out what the customer wants and satisfying that customer time and again.
- Determining the needs and desires of the customer is an ongoing effort because customer needs and desires change with time.
- Systems are designed to deliver what the customer wants without hassle.

School and District Culture:

- The understandings that people in the school and district share about how things work in the district are its culture.
- Culture represents the basic mindset, attitudes, and values of the community.

Counting for Quality:

- Everyone in the school analyzes, understands, and solves quality improvement problems using statistical methods and problem-solving processes.
- Use of the most important tools, brainpower and rational thinking, needs to be encouraged.

Decentralized Decision Making:

- Quality improvement decision making is decentralized within the total system to empower those closest to the point of improvement.

- An integral part of decentralization is internal communication.
- Roles, responsibilities, and relationships are affected by decentralization.

Collegial Leadership:

- Barriers between people and departments are eliminated.
- Teamwork and cooperation is encouraged so that employees can focus on the purpose of quality improvement.
- Knowledge, resources, ideas, and solutions are pooled to solve problems.

Another Angle on the Need for School Quality

As many have said in different ways, the demographic, economic, social, and cultural realities of the 21st century require a new and different system of education.

Once American schools led the way. They were once the engines of upward mobility in America and—to mix metaphors—the doorway to economic success. They readied individuals to go on to serve our society. A century ago, America had the best-educated workforce in the world. Americans were first to exploit the technologies of Europe (just as Japan and other Asian nations have done with the West during the last half of the 20th century). But now, with the exception of graduate schools emphasizing such areas as math, science, and business, American education currently lags badly behind other developed nations.

In many respects, American schools have been victims of their own success. More importantly, our schools have brought about a deep respect for education among our citizens. No people prize and admire education more than do Americans. It is the sum and substance of the American dream. But the better educated Americans became, the more they expected of education, and because they expected too much, disappointment was inevitable. Our schools, in fact, did successfully produce a nation of workers and citizens sufficiently educated for the demands of an earlier day.

Today, America's thorniest social problem is not unemployment but too many *unemployables*. "The gap between haves and have-nots is increasingly a chasm between 'knows' and 'know-nots,'" writes former

Harvard Business Review editor Bernard Avishai in *The Wall Street Journal*.[3]

The modern economy requires broadly and deeply educated workers who can effectively communicate with coworkers and customers. They need both verbal and writing skills. Workers need to know how to solve problems and innovate. They need to be able to think critically and analytically. They must meet the public and deal with complex electronic technologies. These workers must be alert and presentable and have a well-developed "work ethic." And, most important, these workers need to be prepared to continue learning over their entire working lives.

Each year, American business is forced to hire more than one million entry-level workers who cannot read, write, or count. The cost of training such workers recently exceeded $200 billion each year. No longer can we afford to write off the children who have not learned to read or write. Yet, today's high schools are graduating 700,000 functionally illiterate young people *each year*. And still another 700,000 drop out of high school each year.

Imagine any enterprise surviving that says that it cannot compete because the world around it has changed. Enterprises that fail to change are enterprises that fail. And so it is with the public schools. Of necessity, the public schools need to take into account social and cultural trends just as they need to feature changes in the nature of the work.

Absent an educated workforce, American business cannot hope to compete in a global economy. American business cares about education because business must care. The reason is not rooted in humanity or self-sacrifice. It takes educated workers for employers to achieve the required economic return on investment and to reach the "bottom line." People create the wealth of the new economy. Educated people create more wealth faster.

American education is falling behind at a faster clip for the simplest of reasons. The public schools are fundamentally out of step with the larger social and economic realities of the global economy. Public schools, like all government enterprises, are woefully slow to change. They have not kept pace with the changing economic and social landscape of America.

The problem is stark. Too many students lack even the minimal skills needed to meet the demands of the current economy, let alone those of the future. A torrent of business studies show that as many as 60 percent of high school graduates cannot handle an entry-level job.

And a growing number of American companies report they are experiencing even more problems. As manufacturing processes have become more automated and other business activities have advanced in complexity, the level of reading, writing, and mathematics skills needed to make it in the workplace has also risen. Too many worker deficiencies in these basic skills of the Information Age are proving to be a barrier to companies seeking to bring about new techniques and competitive strategies.

58. CASE STUDIES IN ENGINEERING AND EDUCATION COLLABORATION

Pennsylvania State University

For Akhlesh Lakhtakia, professor of engineering science and mechanics at Penn State, the need for effective science and technical education in public schools hit home when he watched his daughter in elementary school. "When my daughter started going to school, I noticed she wasn't being challenged in science." He became concerned that his daughter would rule out a career in science and engineering at a very young age. "When a child is eight or nine years old, that's when decisions take place. A child is ready to receive complicated ideas, so long as they feel involved."

His concerns prompted Professor Lakhtakia to collaborate with the College of Education, teaming up with Tom Dana, associate professor of science education, Vince Lunetta, professor of science education, Mehmet Tasar, doctoral candidate in science education, Johanna Ramos, graduate assistant in the College of Engineering, and Joe Taylor, a doctoral candidate in science education.

Together they developed a new course, ENGR/SCIED 497F, designed to teach education majors about engineering before they get to the classroom. According to Lakhtakia, the class is supposed help future teachers become comfortable with engineering principles and practices, give them increased confidence in teaching their own students, and allow them to cultivate the children's curiosity of the natural world.

This course is a long-term investment with an impact spanning the next 30 to 35 years. The future teachers who take such a course will, in turn, have access to and teach thousands of kids in that time.

To quote Lakhtakia, "Educating our citizenry is an important mission of universities—not just educating experts. We need to establish both a depth and a breadth of science experience in our society. This course is one of many things we should do to make our citizens well-informed, rational consumers, and to give those with interests in science the foundation that can take them, and us, to new frontiers."[4]

University of Colorado at Boulder

The College of Engineering and Applied Science offers specialized workshops and other programs to assist K–12 teachers in bringing science and engineering concepts into their classrooms through hands-on activities that will stimulate the curiosity of young students. Programs include:

- Space Education: Citizen Explorer Project offering classroom activities for teachers as part of its latest NASA-funded project.
- Engineering in Everyday Life integrates theoretical engineering concepts with fun classroom applications that teachers can take back into their classrooms.
- Graduate Teaching Fellows send engineering students into local classrooms at the elementary, middle, and high school levels to assist teachers in hands-on science and engineering education.[5]

University of Pennsylvania

New Tools for Teaching: Blackboard Pilot Project

Over 2,000 Penn students tried out new tools for teaching and learning in the fall of 1999. A dozen engineering courses and a dozen arts and sciences courses are experimenting with Blackboard Course info, an easy-to-use Web application that helps professors meet their teaching needs. "It makes course management a snap," said Bioengineering Professor Mitchell Litt. "I can post all course information, assignments, quizzes, from home via internet."

The largest single course in the pilot program is ECON 1, with enrollment close to 950 in all the sections. Courses from the Graduate School of Education, Dental Medicine, Nursing and Veterinary Medicine are expected to join the pilot program during the fall. Blackboard Course info provides on-line quizzes, on-line homework hand-in, group file sharing areas, chat areas, and much more. Students are automatically loaded into the system based on their registration.

"This isn't a technology project. It's a collaboration among some of Penn's best teachers to find ways to become better teachers and for Penn students to become better, more empowered learners," said James O'Donnell, Vice Provost for Information Systems & Computing and Professor of Classics and co-chair of the New Tools for Teaching committee. Helen Anderson, Senior Director of Computing and Educational Technology Services at the School of Engineering and Applied Science and the other committee co-chair said, "Committee members from school and centers across the university are participating in the ongoing effort to provide top quality support for teaching and learning at Penn."[6]

The Challenge to Public Education

Educational engineering is linked to school administration, for which it is a method, and to basic research, on which it depends for knowledge. Its main function, however, is to mediate between the school and the sources of innovation.

In discussions dealing with how to combat the almost inevitable movement of an organization toward elaborateness, rigidity, and massiveness and away from simplicity, flexibility, and manageable size, John Gardner, a veteran of the worlds of the university, the foundation, the federal bureaucracy, and the voluntary association, observed that a classic bureaucracy can manage to renew itself by calling in a variety of outside servicing organizations. He points out that corporations routinely call on lawyers, auditors, management consultants, and many other specialists who work for a variety of firms in turn. Although their names appear only on contracts, not on the organization chart, few corporations could exist without them, In fact, Gardner points out:

> The remarkable range of such professional and technical services that are
> available, plus the flexibility of the contractual relationship, gives the

modern organization a wide range of choice in shaping its own future. Within limits, top management can put its finger on almost any function within the organization and decree that henceforth that function will be performed by an outside organization on contract. For the organization that wishes to maintain the maneuverability so essential to renewal, this offers priceless opportunities.

—John Gardner[7]

Can such wisdom be applied to public education? By now the need for renewal in the schools should be clear. It remains for administrators, teachers, and stakeholders to take advantage of the opportunities extended by understanding and applying the engineering frame of reference as a newly developed process of school improvement.

School Performance Management Through Engineering Thinking

Articles in administrative management seldom integrate the technical and psychological aspects of school management into a comprehensive picture of the educator-manager role. Such compartmentalization highlights the differences and hides the common threads that underlie both engineering and school management. For the teacher it is helpful to keep in mind:

- The engineer often sees the administrator and teacher as superficial and lacking intellectual rigor and depth, even though the typical educator deals with systems of far greater complexity each day than the engineer could dream of designing.
- Conversely, the administrator and teacher look upon the technical person as narrow and lacking interest in people and social problems, even though the engineer always designs his technical systems on the basis of a body of knowledge, attitude, and theory that helps people live a richer, fuller, safer life. Bridges, roads, planes, cars, traffic signals, safety belts, and on and on are designed first and foremost with people's needs in mind.

Such insights can help the future teacher or administrator to better understand the complexity of the social systems they work within.

We tend to see engineering and school management resting on different foundations—engineering on physics and school management on economics—whereas school management, economics, and much of engineering share common foundations in feedback, system behavior, and psychology.

A new era in preparing teachers and administrators for the growing demands of K–12 schooling builds on the foundations created by its predecessors. At the same time, engineering has in the past five decades provided a basis for a new, general insight into the dynamics of the school as a complex social system. We might consider administrative education and classroom management of the future as "school enterprise engineering." If so, here are five contributions that engineering thinking can help bring to school enterprise (administrative) engineering.

1. The concept of understanding and improving the workings of the school as a system
2. The principle of using feedback control and data to manage the school organization and classroom
3. The distinction between policy making (change) and decision making (static) performance management
4. The lower cost of electronic communication to strengthen teacher and administrator knowledge
5. The substitution of tools for data reinforcement in place of pure feeling and intuition to reach better analytic solutions

Engineering thinking can be an effective "change agent" to hasten improvements in our school systems. To do so, such thinking must help clarify the enduring goals and objectives of education and the school organization. This approach will give more attention to the surrounding system as a whole rather than looking upon it as an array of isolated parts to be controlled. Engineering thinking brings to school organizations the courage to experiment with promising new approaches based on a foundation of design for performance improvement.

59. THE GHOST OF DR. SEMMELWEISS

The image of Ignaz Semmelweiss haunts America's schools and classrooms. At the turn of the century, Semmelweiss was an important and

well-respected medical doctor in Vienna. As a solid science professional of his day, he studied the reported birth and death statistics. He
took special note of the higher incidence of death among women in
childbirth that were attended by physicians than among those women
attended only by a midwife.

Being intrigued, astonished, and curious, the doctor decided to study
the reasons why this might be happening. He found that the physicians
did not use as common practice the thorough washing of their hands or
the washing of their equipment when they treated more than one
woman.

When the data he collected became sufficiently large to allow him to
make valid predictions, he went to his medical society to share his findings. He alerted his fellow doctors to the dangers of their lack of hand-
washing practices.

Understandably, his fellow physicians and former friends were, at
first, very skeptical. When he continued to insist that they adopt as
standard practice rigorous hand washing, they voted almost unani-
mously to remove him from the medical society. Further, they discred-
ited him publicly and ruined his reputation as a physician. He died a
pauper in disgrace.

Today, a statue stands in his honor in the Vienna medical society
headquarters. Medical doctors in Vienna, as well as all other doctors,
now routinely use as standard operating procedure the good practice of
washing their hands and instruments thoroughly before working with a
patient.

A patient going to a doctor in Vienna, Austria, or Vienna, Virginia,
need not wonder or even be concerned about the reliability of his or her
doctor to use as standard operating practice in the office or hospital
what the profession now accepts as good practice. Practitioners teach
proper hand washing during orientation to all new health-care employees and daily whenever the need arises. Hand washing is considered serious business, and proper practice is enforced. We now know that hand
washing is important in the home, in schools, and in the workplace, as
well as in hospitals. It is the number one prevention against the spread
of infection.

With respect to accepting the best that research has to offer, school
teaching is a carbon copy of the doctors' mind-set in the Vienna Medical

Society when Dr. Semmelweiss made his presentations. Tested, scientifically based teaching practices compete regularly in schools with untested, unscientifically based teaching practices. Worse yet, even when the teaching practices in use are proven to be useless or even harmful for learning, they continue to be used. Customers—the students and the parents, as well as other stakeholders of this day—cannot assume that any particular teachers or schools know about or use good practice in teaching and learning as their standard operating practice.

Currently school teaching is an unreliable profession. No parent sending a child to any school in any state can honestly be assured by school administrators that that child's teacher will (1) know her subject, (2) know how best to teach it, or (3) know how best to lead and manage the classroom so that all children get maximum benefit.

It is the ghost of Dr. Semmelweiss that haunts America's schools and classrooms today. When it comes to receiving reliable quality classroom teaching, parents, students and those who care deeply about the quality of schools live under the control of a tyranny of chance. Someday, we need to put the ghost of Dr. Semmelweiss to rest in his job of haunting American education. Given what we now know about how to insure and assure reliability in classroom teaching, continuing to accept unreliability is a disgrace.

NOTES

1. Phi Delta Kappa /Gallup poll summary.

2. George A. Clowes, "Texas Academic Standards Upheld," *School Reform News*, vol. 4, no. 3 (March 2000).

3. *The Wall Street Journal,* 29 July 1996.

4. From the Penn State College of Engineering Web site, 30 July 2001.

5. From the University of Colorado at Boulder Web site, 27 July 2001.

6. From the University of Pennsylvania Web site, "New Tools," 13 September 1999) www.seas.upenn.edu/newtools

7. John Gardner, *Self-Renewal* (New York: Norton, 1995).

Benchmarking Reliable Schools

60. BENCHMARKING PRINCIPLES FOR RELIABLE SCHOOLS

The job of every school is to continually improve the learning experience of each student, to assume responsibility for student learning, to assess student performance against rising achievement standards, and to assure students are readied to perform quality work in the 21st century.

We created the Benchmarking Principles for Schools to help guide education leaders and teachers toward measuring their progress. The principles focus on goals. They are intended to help faculty measure effectiveness. They are adapted from the 2002 Baldrige National Quality Program Criteria for Education. Each benchmark principle identifies expectations for growth and establishes a tool for school self-appraisal.

To pursue reliable quality in schools ushers in a new era of caring. By applying Baldrige Education Criteria, the reliable quality school comes into being. The hallmark of this school is found in its using evaluation and accountability. The education benchmark principles are intended to bring relevant principles and metrics of performance management into schools.

The principles to measure *system-wide* school improvement consist of seven interrelated factors of systemic change: (1) Information and Analysis, (2) Leadership, (3) Student Achievement, (4) Quality Planning, (5) Professional Development, (6) Partnership Development, and (7) Continuous Improvement and Evaluation.

In our approach, reliable quality schools would measure their progress three times each school year to see their progress. This would give them motivation to keep improving. Equally important, the measurement process brings the staff together to reinforce their shared vision and to plan for other continuous improvement steps for the school. This process strengthens the belief that improvement is continuous and ongoing.

Benchmark Principles are not static. The principles themselves can help school leaders and stakeholders learn more about school change and the most effective ways to nourish it.

61. POSSIBILITIES FOR IMPROVING EDUCATION

In adapting to new demands for better results and greater accountability, schools need to take advantage of the benefits of more research on learning, as three U.S. presidents have noted in their special messages on educational reform. But we must not defer action, or the means to support it, until the day when we may finally understand fully the mystery of the learning process.

School leaders already know a great deal more than they are willing— or able—to put into practice. Careful studies and voluminous reports generated by billions of federal, state, and private-sector dollars spent on education research have given educators many examples of proven opportunities to improve school performance:

1. Elementary schools where children have more choice of study,
2. Schools where older students tutor younger ones,
3. Schools in which each student sets his own pace in prescribed instruction,
4. Work-study schools that link education and the world outside,
5. Schools with emphasis on learning outside the classroom,
6. Schools where parents and community actively participate in planning, and
7. Parallel programs so students may choose alternatives to reach similar goals.

Each example is responsive and more satisfying than in institutions still using rigid and conventional formats to meet the needs of students and teachers.

Benchmarking is still unique to schooling. Carried forward correctly, the process almost always induces culture shock, making the subject of change a pressing matter to tackle. In schools, as in all organizations, change happens when there is an activist, a promoter, a believer, and a true sponsor of change.

The first step, the benchmarking breakthrough, comes when followers see that change is both desirable and feasible and school leadership is behind it. The climate has to be right, just as it is in biology. Every school system has a cemetery full of dead projects. Each change effort was once alive and warmly promoted by some enthusiast. But remember, we are not speaking about projects in this discussion of tools. We are speaking of using decision tools to help improve processes.

We have carefully set forth in *Healing Public Schools* the cycle of plan-do-act-measure as a clinical methodology. Skepticism has become so rampant that many educators (and stakeholders) are wary of *all* proposed improvements, no matter how reasonable and necessary.

The greatest obstacle to change, whether it be via benchmarking others' "best practices" or following quality process improvement criteria, is more psychological than technical. No proposed solution and no set of tools, no matter how strong the supporting evidence, can be adopted and nurtured until school leaders overcome one widespread malady in school life: the *desensitization* of teachers, administrators, and school board members to chronic school problems.

62. CONDUCTING THE BENCHMARKING SITE VISIT

It's necessary to do more than collect information by phone or survey. Schools need to conduct site visits. This is primary research and first-hand feedback. It is on-the-ground information. While site visits are the most time-consuming and expensive method of information gathering, they do provide the highest quality of information. You can witness firsthand work processes, methods, and practices in action. But before you set out on your visit, here are nine guidelines excerpted from *Benchmarking for Best Practices* [1] to help your site-visit teams be more effective. It is helpful to keep in mind that the persons you are going to meet and the institution you plan to benchmark will become your partners in this venture.

1. Learn about the partner you are going to visit. Collect information in advance to help the benchmarking team understand the partner's processes.
2. Prepare your questions in advance to guide and structure your team's visit.
3. Prepare the benchmarking partner for your team's visit. Send questions ahead of time and set an agenda.
4. Use the questionnaire to structure your visit and discussions.
5. Travel in pairs or small groups during the site tour.
6. Arrange for follow-up conversation should there be additional questions.
7. Conduct a post-session debriefing to discuss the team's observations and ideas.
8. Prepare a trip report summarizing site-visit findings and conclusions.
9. Send a thank-you note and confirm the accuracy of site-visit notes describing the benchmarking partner's operations.

All of this preparation is worthwhile when you consider the value of effectively benchmarking best practices. For every student failing to be well enough prepared to earn a living or share in the benefits and obligations of American citizenship, *all of us* pay a price in more taxes, greater social unrest, increased crime, and a general vulnerability in a ferociously competitive global economy. At the end of the day, the student is deprived of the realistic chance to reach his or her full potential.

"Insiders" must no longer be allowed to live comfortably with unattended chronic school problems. Perhaps, when "outsiders" finally *see* these chronic problems for the first time, they may finally be shocked into action, since they have thus far not been rendered shockproof.

63. BENCHMARK: GOOD RESEARCH

There are, literally, thousands of studies dealing with school effects on student learning. We have read hundreds of them. No doubt one could find good research that we did not include with this book. Good schools do lots of good things at the same time. Often these actions are mutually reinforcing. Therefore, it is difficult to isolate the distinct contributions of particular policies and practices.

The literature is also full of case studies that describe the interdependence of the characteristics of effective schools. Despite the limitations of education research, there appears to be substantial consensus among those who study schools about the consequences of certain policies and practices for student learning. There is less agreement about particular instructional strategies, curricula, and learning resources.

Almost all good benchmarking studies illustrate the effectiveness of widely differing schools and the importance of context in determining the impact of any one school's policies and practices. Thus, much of what we conclude may seem unsurprising. At the same time, what we find in the research is much less often found in schools. Policies and practices likely to improve student learning might be more widely used if they more neatly fit into the pattern of good schools that dominates popular thinking.

One reason why school effectiveness research has had less impact than it might have had is that it rides alongside of, rather than within, the thinking of many educators, policymakers, civic leaders, and parents. While likely to criticize many proposals for school improvement as "too theoretical," almost all stakeholders carry around with them assumptions—call them "mental models"—and general explanations relating to education. These become the window through which they explain what they see and hear. Most often such embedded theories and "facts" influence what people learn and choose to do.

Benchmark: Reliable Teaching and School Effectiveness

Research-based principles have important consequences for teaching and learning. For example, they explain why (1) effective instruction must actively engage students in problem solving that is meaningful to them, (2) what students can learn is shaped by what they already know and believe, (3) why teaching that is unresponsive to student differences is likely to be unproductive, and (4) why schools need to engage the full range of influences on student learning. Teachers influence student learning in many ways. A review of research on alternative explanations for student achievement conducted for the U.S. Department of Education in the mid-1980s concluded:

> In virtually every instance in which researchers have examined the factors that account for student performance, teachers prove to have a greater impact than programs. This is true for average students and exceptional students, for normal classrooms and special classrooms. Teachers allocate and manage the students' time, set and communicate standards and expectations for student performance, and, in a multitude of other ways, enhance or impede what students learn.

Benchmark: Processes That Drive Performance

Organizations are ways of putting together, concentrating, and making easier collective human behavior. Some elements of an organization are more vital to what makes them successful or effective than others. If these vital processes do not work well, other elements of the organization can be expected to be relatively ineffective. School organizational processes need to be sharpened when one or more of the following conditions exist:

- When the relationship between core activities and goal attainment is uncertain. For example, teaching becomes less reliable when the effects of particular instructional practices depend on circumstances the practitioners cannot know about or even affect.
- When the task to be performed varies greatly and must be modified in response to its observed effects. For example, students vary in readiness to learn from day to day and from subject to subject in ways difficult to predict.
- When the desired outcomes are multiple, diffuse, and difficult to measure. What do we mean, for example, when we claim to "prepare students for democratic citizenship"?

Therefore, the processes needed for school organizational effectiveness depend on (a) flexibility and adaptability, (b) the quality of information about the tasks to be performed and the probable consequences of alternatives to perform such tasks, and (c) the competencies, judgment, and collaborative skills of the persons responsible for the core activities.

Benchmark: Essentials of Effective Schools

To put it simply, school effectiveness is determined by what students learn in school. And solid evidence of student learning and productivity is the criterion by which school effectiveness needs to be measured. While advocates for school reform have developed models and long lists to identify conditions, structures, policies, programs, and practices associated with student learning, there appear to be five types of inter-related school-level influences that most powerfully affect student learning:

1. Teacher motivation and capabilities related to effective teaching
2. School-level conditions that support collaborative problem solving
3. Shared values, beliefs, and professional standards of the school
4. School resources that affect student opportunities to learn in school
5. School policies and practices that affect student readiness to learn

So does it all come down to leadership when we talk school effectiveness? Almost every study of achieving more effective schools starts with the importance of leadership. Leaders look first and foremost at the processes used in the school to define and achieve its strategic objectives.

64. BENCHMARKING CASE STUDIES

The Job That Couldn't Be Done:
Guilford County Schools, Greensboro, N.C.

Results of an international mathematics and science exam released by Boston College ranked Guilford County, North Carolina, students above Massachusetts, Connecticut, Pennsylvania, Maryland, South Carolina, and other schools in North Carolina in both mathematics and science achievement. The 1999 Third International Mathematics and Science Study (TIMSS) concentrated on the mathematics and science achievement of eighth-grade students.

Guilford County Schools' students scored 27 points above the international average in mathematics and 46 points higher than the international average in science. Guilford County eighth-graders scored 12 points above the U.S. average in mathematics and 19 points above the U.S. average in science.

"We are very pleased that the study revealed that our students stack up exceedingly well with students from across the country and around the world," said Dr. Terry Grier, superintendent of schools. "The scores are even more revealing when you compare our spending and population characteristics of those with similar demographics."

The United States scored in the middle of the pack of 38 participating countries. The top-scoring U.S. school systems were in predominantly white areas, with a high rate of per-pupil expenditures.

The 1999 data revealed that 37 percent of Guilford County Schools' participants were from families who are eligible to receive free or reduced-price meals, classifying them as low-income. The top-scoring U.S. systems had only 14 percent of their participants from low-income families. The Benchmarking Study, which assessed eighth-grade students' knowledge of mathematics and science, provides an in-depth look at the achievement of districts and states that participated.[2]

Twenty-seven states, districts, and consortia of districts participated in the TIMSS 1999 Benchmarking Study. They are:

States	Districts and Consortia
Connecticut	Academy School District #20, Colorado Springs, Colo.
Idaho	Chicago Public Schools, Ill.
Illinois	Michigan Invitational Group, Mich.
Indiana	Delaware Science Coalition, Del.
Maryland	First in the World Consortium, Ill.
Massachusetts	Fremont/Lincoln/West Side Public Schools, Neb.
Michigan	Guilford County, N.C.
Missouri	Jersey City Public Schools, N.J.
North Carolina	Miami-Dade County Public Schools, Fla.
Oregon	Montgomery County, Md.
Pennsylvania	Naperville Community Unit School District #203, Ill.
South Carolina	Project SMART Consortium, Ohio
Texas	Rochester City School District, N.Y.
	SW Pennsylvania Regional Math and Science Collaborative, Pa.

U.S. Schools Accept Singapore Math Books

Thanks to the Third International Mathematics and Science Study, one of Singapore's most talked-about exports these days is neither the computer equipment from its factories nor the rubber from its plantations. It is its math textbooks. Elementary and middle school students in this 247-square-mile Southeast Asian nation ranked first in the world on the math portions of the TIMSS assessments, which were given in 1994 and 1995. To earn that title, Singaporeans outpaced their counterparts in 39 other countries, including such educational powerhouses as Japan and Taiwan. They also outscored students in Belgium, Canada, France, Hong Kong, and Switzerland. And they beat the United States!

Now, scattered groups of U.S. educators are hoping the textbooks from that island nation in part hold the secret to Singaporean students' notable success. Sales of the books, published in English, have multiplied since 1998, according to their sole U.S. distributor. It has filled orders for "several thousand" of the paperbacks so far in school year 2000–2001. And the volumes are going to a wide range of educators, including home-schoolers, private school operators, and public schools from Colorado to Maryland.

Early Algebra

Printed primarily in black and white, "early algebra" books from Singapore contain none of the colorful, eye-popping graphics that publishers incorporate into many American textbooks to grab and hold students' attention. But admirers of these straightforward math books praise them for their clear, simple text, their novel problem-solving approaches, and the complex, multi-step problems they give students, beginning in the first grade. Students are introduced to algebra concepts early through word problems that seem more at home in high school texts. But, rather than use algebraic equations to solve the problems, the books present *pictorial strategies* that are easily grasped by elementary-level pupils.

"There is a great insistence on full understanding, and an avoidance of mindless rituals that lead to a solution," said Yoram Sagher, a mathematics professor at the University of Illinois at Chicago. Between his university math education duties, Mr. Sagher crisscrosses the country teaching practicing teachers how to put the texts from Singapore to best use. The Gabriella and Paul Rosenbaum Foundation, a Chicago-based family philanthropy that promotes math achievement, finances many of those sessions. Whether due to the textbooks or not, students in the program, known as the Ingenuity Project, have gone on to receive honors in local and national mathematics competitions. Two ninth-graders, in fact, scored in the top 1 percent on a national mathematics competition in February 2000.

Schools in Chicago, Montgomery County, Md., and Paterson, N.J., are also piloting the books for more heterogeneous student population, including some children who find school a struggle. One bonus for students using these books is that they are thinner and lighter than most American-made math texts. A drawback is that the books are riddled with unfamiliar names, British-flavored spellings and terms, and metric measurements.

Like the math texts published by Saxon Publishers, a small Marion, Oklahoma, firm, the Singapore text may buck the current American trends in mathematics education and local or national standards for teaching the subject. Though Singaporeans speak a mix of languages, more than 90 percent of the 4.2 million residents of the former British colony are literate. The central Ministry of Education develops textbooks in every subject, and students pay a fee to use them. Singaporean parents, like parents in other Southeast Asian countries, also typically supplement their children's learning with after-school tutoring sessions.[3]

65. CASE STUDY: BENCHMARKING THE COMER SCHOOL IMPROVEMENT PROCESS

The goal of the Comer School Improvement Process is to assure that *all* students are successful in learning the essential curriculum. This process is the outcome of a model that was developed through the collaborative efforts of Dr. James Comer, with his Yale Child Study Center staff, and the New Haven Public School System. It addresses the negative impact of change, social stratification, and conflict and distrust between home and school. Documented results of the implemented process dramatically demonstrate improved student attendance and achievement, as well as a new bonding between parents, teachers, and students.

The Comer School Improvement Process focuses on the knowledge of behavioral and social sciences as applied to every aspect of the school program. Central to this process is the belief that all students can learn and that all the adults involved do their learning best when it is the result of collaborative participation. This approach focuses on high expectations for students, a team approach to identifying student and school needs, and parent involvement in school goal-setting and planning.

The Comer School Improvement Process requires schools to accept the fact that students enter school at different points along a developmental continuum. Staff, parents, and the school community are actively involved in and committed to an instructional program that recognizes that, although students enter school with different backgrounds and experience, all can be successful when the school accepts them at their current level of development and guides their growth in an appropriate manner.

Components and Effectiveness Indicators

The Comer School Improvement Process is designed to work in all schools. The process, however, may develop differently because of the unique needs of a school and its students. This systems-level, prevention approach is used to plan and manage all activities within the school in a way that promotes desirable staff and parent functioning and, as a consequence, desirable student learning and behavior. It is the *process model* that allows the school to review its goals and methods and to identify problems and opportunities in a "no-fault" atmosphere. It seeks to develop creative ways of dealing with problems and to implement intervention using the collective good judgment of school staff and parents. The program is carried out through regularly scheduled meetings of its major components: a district steering committee, the school management team (SMT) and home/school services team (HSST), the parent program, and the comprehensive school plan.

District Steering Committee

The Comer School Improvement Process is monitored by a district steering committee consisting of district-level staff, building-level administrators, instructional staff, and parents. The committee provides support and direction in the key areas of planning, prioritizing, monitoring, and evaluation. The steering committee meets regularly with a predetermined agenda. Summary minutes are provided.

The School Management Team

A key program component is the building-level governance and management body commonly referred to as the school management team (SMT). The principal or other identified chairperson leads this group. It must be representative of the teachers, administrators, and other employee groups within the school, as well as parents and other members of the school community. A representative from the home/school services team and the parent organization are also to be included. The school management team is to meet regularly and include an agenda that is distributed in advance of the meeting. Members are responsible for communicating information and recommendations to their constituents. In order to encourage broad participation, various subcommittees need to be formed to work on projects and to deal with issues that affect the overall functioning of the school. The SMT sets out

- To establish policy guidelines for all aspects of the school program;
- To respond directly to problems and/or opportunities, or delegate this responsibility to other groups or individuals who will report back;
- To carry out systematic school planning related to social climate, academics, and staff development, and public relations;
- To promote effective resource utilization, coordination, and program implementation;
- To work closely with parents to plan an annual school calendar that integrates social, academic, and staff development functions; and

- To monitor program activities and other activities related to the on-going management of the school and its programs.

The comprehensive school plan is to be developed by the SMT. Through this plan the SMT provides yearlong direction and focus to the school in its effort to fulfill its mission. The comprehensive school plan is monitored and adjusted through SMT meetings. It is aligned with the district's comprehensive plan and places specific emphasis on academic and social development, school climate, public relations, and staff development.

1. The SMT consists of representatives from all groups within the school community, i.e., parents, grade-level teachers, administrators, and instructional and classified support staff.
2. General operating procedures are developed and adhered to by the SMT. These include identification of a chairperson or facilitator, established meeting times, procedures for agenda development, and dissemination of the minutes.
3. The SMT establishes standing subcommittees as needed that allow all staff members within the building to participate.
4. Additional SMT meetings can be established as the need arises.
5. SMT representatives report to their constituents and gather input for SMT process.
6. All school planning and decision making is funneled through the SMT process.
7. The comprehensive school plan (CSP) is monitored by the SMT on a monthly basis.
8. A structured problem-solving approach is used to address school problems.
9. A SMT meeting is characterized by straight, descriptive talk that is nonjudgmental (i.e., solutions talk). Participants do not hedge in identifying problems. They work creatively to solve them.

Home/School Services Team (HSST)

The principal or designee leads this group. It works in a diagnostic/prescriptive and preventive fashion. It provides ongoing consultation and services to teachers and to the school management team in matters that pertain to child development. It meets on a regular basis to

- Facilitate parent and school interaction;
- Develop and recommend to the school management team programs and activities that contribute to positive school climate and promote student success;
- Consult with classroom teachers to assist them in responding to students in a way which promotes growth and development;
- Assist classroom teachers in developing strategies that prevent minor problems from becoming major ones;
- Establish individualized programs for children with special needs, which may involve the utilization of services outside of the school;
- Make recommendations for building-level policy changes designed to prevent problems;
- Assist all staff members in bridging the gap between exceptional student education and regular classroom activities; and
- Recommend to the school management team in-service activities for staff and parents related to child development, human relations, and other home/school issues.

The HSST's composition and working methods extend throughout the school system.

1. The HSST is composed of the principal, counselor, curriculum resource teacher, social worker, psychologist, ESE representative, public health nurse, and other appropriate building-level support staff.
2. The HSST views parents as partners in developing programs for individual students and for the general student population. Consequently, it provides ways in which parents can give input and provide support for interventions and strategies.
3. The HSST develops preventive strategies that modify the school setting in a way that creates optimum conditions for teaching and learning, and develops into class support rather than pull outs.
4. The HSST uses a diagnostic/prescriptive model that is designed to provide interventions for individual students.

5. The HSST recommends and advises the school management Team in matters related to child development, human relations, home/school services and appropriate in-service needs.
6. The HSST develops a process to meet the individual needs of children and promotes student success by utilizing school-based services, school district services, and services provided by the community.

Parent Program

The Comer School Improvement Process views the parent program as the cornerstone for success in developing a school environment that stimulates the total development of its students. Parents are expected to select representatives from their group to serve on the SMT; participate in activities initiated by the parent-teacher general membership group and SMT; review the school plan developed by the SMT; and support the efforts of the school to assist students in their overall development. Parent involvement is critical to the overall workings of the program.

1. The school has a parent-teacher organization (PTA/PTO/Booster Group) that meets with the principal on a monthly basis to discuss relevant issues.
2. The agenda for each meeting is developed in consultation with the principal and is discussed prior to each meeting by the principal and representatives from the executive board of the parent-teacher organization.
3. The minutes of each PTO meeting are distributed to parents and teachers.
4. Parents regularly attend school-sponsored programs.
5. Parents assist in the planning of child-centered programs and activities.
6. Parents volunteer in the school on a day-to-day basis in instructional support positions.
7. Parent representative(s) serve on the SMT and act as a liaison between this group and the parent-teacher organization executive board.

8. The home/school services facilitator serves as a liaison between parents and the school.

9. Parent involvement is reflective of the demographics of the student population.

Comprehensive School Plan   The comprehensive school plan is the document by which the Comer School Improvement Process defines the specific goals and school needs on a yearly basis. The goals are established in four areas: academic, social, public relations, and staff development. Members of the school management team (SMT), using input from their constituents, develop the comprehensive school plan, coordinating and integrating all activities of the school for the entire year. The SMT monitors the school plan on a regular basis to evaluate, assess, and/or modify the components as deemed necessary.

The academic area specifically outlines which subjects are to be targeted to maximize student achievement, what outcomes are projected, and a timeline for completing instructional objectives. The social area lists any social activities that will be held during the year, indicating in what way these activities relate directly to the assessed needs of the school population. The public relations part of the plan seeks to bring support to the process through continued public exposure to school activities. Through staff development, the comprehensive school plan addresses the needs of the school staff for inservice activities to successfully support the implementation of the process.

The comprehensive school plan, utilizing the four components as described, gives the school a vehicle to continually update and monitor the development of the Comer School Improvement Process.

1. The plan addresses academic, staff development, social, and public relations aspects of the school's operations. Yearlong programs are developed in each of these four areas and monitored by the SMT on a monthly basis

2. The comprehensive school plan is distributed to all staff members and an abbreviated version is sent home to parents.

3. A mid-year appraisal of the comprehensive school plan is conducted by the SMT. Revisions are made if they are seen by the team to be necessary.
4. A comprehensive evaluation of the impact of the plan is made. Results are communicated to staff and parents. Data are used in generating a plan for the following school year.
5. The objectives within the plan are in harmony with the district's comprehensive plan.

Guiding Principles of the Comer Program

In order to meet the demands of an increasingly complex society, all children must experience a high level of personal development. We must efficiently and effectively use our collective energies and resources to prepare them to enter into the adult world as confident and competent individuals. Hence, schools must endeavor to build working relationships that allow the young to solve the problems that impede their development. By creating a desirable climate or ethos, schools provide models of appropriate human behavior that children can identify with, imitate, and internalize as they grow and fully develop academically and socially. These conditions must be generated and nurtured through a process of positive interactions among parents, staff, and students. The school management team, home/school services team, and parent program provide the structure or framework through which the process takes place.

The principal is a key figure in that he/she leads this undertaking and sets the model of appropriate behavior. As teachers, parents, and support staff serve on the respective teams, they assume some responsibility for exhibiting the behaviors that move the school toward a climate characterized by collaboration, trust, problem solving, and the recognition of all as important partners in the education of children.

The assumption is that virtually any human problem can be solved if people are willing to meet on a consistent basis, explore and develop solutions without placing blame, develop interventions, and expend the energy necessary to implement and monitor interventions. Hard work and dedication, along with a passionate belief in human growth and potential, must characterize the school improvement effort. The specific goals are described below:

High Expectations

Educators and parents hold high expectations with regard to educational accomplishments and social development of students by building positive interpersonal relationships and by modeling respect for academic achievement. Educators and parents work together to create optimum conditions for student learning and social development.

Child-Centered, Collaborative Decision Making

All decisions in the school are based on the developmental and performance needs of students. Input from parents, teachers, and appropriate school personnel is essential. In all committee work done under the auspices of the SMT, the group shall develop a consensus rather than a "majority rule" vote in arriving at its decisions and recommendations. During meetings participants make a conscious attempt to focus on problem solving rather than placing blame. Within the Comer School Improvement Process problems are seen as opportunities to tap the creativity and resourcefulness of the group, rather than as crises that immobilize the movement of the school.

Positive, Productive Relationships

The quality of the relationships between adults within the school community directly influences the social development of students. Healthy relationships between adults provide models for student to identify with, imitate, and internalize. Hence, it is important for educators and parents to work together to identify and solve problems that could adversely impact the overall school climate and student development.

Parental Involvement

Parental involvement promotes accountability—parent to staff and staff to parents. The involvement of parents reduces behavior problems and increases support for academic learning. Parents and school staff share the responsibility for developing children in the key developmental pathways (cognitive, social, psychological, moral, and speech and language).

The first level of parental involvement is in broad-based activities for a large number of parents, such as social events. At the second level, parents volunteer in the school on a day-to-day basis in instructional and support positions. At the third level parent representatives participate in the SMT.

Planning and Coordination

The planning and introduction of new programs should be facilitated through the school management team. Planning should be conducted from a systems perspective. Any program development or modification should first consider how such change would impact the total system or school community. Planning and coordination should prevent program duplication, fragmentation, and wasted energy and resources and create a sense of direction and purpose.

Effective Material and Resources Allocation

Schools must make maximum and efficient use of people, material, and other resources. Equitable distribution of the same is also essential.

An Individualized Instructional Methodology

The instructional program should contain activities, experiences, and content that allow students to develop academically and socially regardless of their background. It should be stimulating and should have personal meaning and utility for students. Children bring different needs and styles of learning to their respective schools. Professional educators must accommodate these needs and styles by using the most appropriate research-based techniques that will encourage each student to reach his/her highest academic potential.

Relevant Curriculum

The school's curriculum must give each child the opportunity to acquire a well-rounded basic education. There is an emphasis on the processes of reading comprehension, language development, written communication, problem solving, and creative expression at each grade level, as well as the core content knowledge of mathematics, social studies, science, and the arts. The curriculum should provide activities that promote creativity, self-expression, and higher-order thinking. Additionally, it should provide for social development and the acquisition for life management skills.

Frequent Monitoring of Instruction

An effective evaluation system is one which is timely, diagnostic, and prescriptive and gives students immediate and specific feedback regarding their performances. Tests and other forms of evaluation should be used to assist parents and students identify strengths and weaknesses, and to plan strategies for remediation or enrichment. The school accepts the responsibility for informing parents in a timely fashion as to the academic progress of students.

Effective Staff Development

Staff development programs should be based on what is needed to accomplish the goals set forth in the comprehensive school plan. Staff development should be a collaborative effort between appropriate individuals at the central office level, working with the principal, faculty, staff, and parents at the building level.

Standards of Effectiveness

There is a written statement guiding the principles and goals of the Comer School Improvement Process school.

Quality Indicators
1. A copy of the statement is available.
2. The statement is consistent with the school district's philosophy.
3. The statement has been developed cooperatively, with contributions from groups within the school community.
4. The statement reflects staff consensus.

5. Staff members can:
   a. Articulate the belief and goals
   b. State specific instructions, and co-instructional activities directed toward meeting those beliefs and goals
   c. Cite assessment procedures that monitor student performance
6. The state's goals are used in planning the school's educational objectives and activities.
7. The statement is reviewed at least annually.

Curriculum

The curriculum is used in planning the instructional program. The district curriculum is adjusted to meet individual school needs if indicated. It is adjusted without reducing standards and expectations.

1. The curriculum specifies all areas of learning that are taught in the school.
2. The established learning objectives are appropriate for the growth level of the individual child.
3. Academic performance objectives are aligned with those that are in the compendium of the norm-referenced test, and any state-mandated mastery test that is used by the school district.
4. The principal, teachers, and parents are to address the psychological, emotional, and social development needs of students and cooperatively develop a social development curriculum.
5. All teachers work together to create a continuum of learning.
6. The instructional program includes experiences that provide children with basic skills necessary to function effectively in our society.
7. Communication skills of reading, writing, speaking, and listening are developed through meaningful, integrated activities.
8. Mathematics instruction emphasizes concept development and problem solving through manipulative-based activity and real-life situations.
9. Science instruction integrates the development of science concepts with the process of scientific investigation and utilizes an inquiry approach to the study of the natural and physical world.

10. Social studies instruction includes study of the interrelationship of peoples and cultures to the historical, geographic, political, and economic factors in the environment. Map and globe skills are developed through meaningful activities in this study.
11. Computer literacy is developed through opportunities for students to use the computer as an instructional tool.

Staff Relationships

Shared governance that recognizes the principal as the key in determining the school's quality, focus, and direction characterizes the Comer School Improvement Process.

1. The principal conveys high expectations for students, staff, and self.
2. The principal is able to communicate effectively with all segments of the school and community, and welcomes communications from these groups.
3. The principal encourages leadership by students, teachers, parents, and community members.
4. Teachers use instructional techniques that are relevant to the curricular objectives and to research-based principles of learning.
5. Teachers use formal and informal evaluation techniques and instruments to measure the curriculum's success.

Budgetary Matters

Adequate financial and material resources support the curriculum.

1. Budget allocations are sufficient to meet the needs generated by the curriculum.
2. Appropriate and relevant materials are available for each student.
3. The school makes use of appropriate resources from other educational institutions, parents, business, industry, and service clubs.
4. The school management team recommends the expenditure of funds available to accomplish the school's mission.

Teachers' Roles

1. Teachers plan and provide effective instruction to accomplish the school's mission.
2. Teachers believe all students can learn and expect them to succeed.
3. Teachers use appropriate instructional strategies relevant to the objectives for the curriculum.
4. Teachers allow sufficient time to present fully, demonstrate, and explain new content skills.
5. Teachers allow adequate opportunity to practice and master new skills.
6. Teachers actively monitor student performance, give immediate response, and adjust instruction accordingly.
7. Teachers use a variety of instructional grouping patterns, ranging from whole class to one-to-one instruction.
8. Teachers continually diagnose academic needs and prescribe appropriate educational activities for individual students, considering learning styles and rates of learning.
9. Teachers identify students with special needs and provide appropriate support in class if possible.
10. Teachers use a variety of classroom management skills to create an orderly and comfortable classroom environment conducive to learning.

Students' Roles

1. Students are taught how to learn and value learning.
2. Students believe they can learn.
3. Students understand that they share the responsibility for successful learning.
4. Students are held accountable for doing quality work.
5. Students give evidence of being able to apply what they have learned.

Staff Development

1. Each school has an effective staff development program for all members of the staff.

2. The design of the program is based on academic achievement and social development goals. Needs assessments include recommendations from both the staff and parents.
3. The staff is routinely provided information regarding valid research and current practice.
4. Staff development programs are evaluated for effectiveness.
5. The effectiveness of staff development programs is validated through improved teaching practices.

General Interests

There is concerted effort on the part of the parents, teachers, administrators, and support staff to aid the social and academic development of students.

Social Development

1. School personnel serve as models and reward appropriate behavior.
2. There is a written code of conduct that is cooperatively developed by students, staff, and parents and is followed consistently.
3. Students, staff, and parents accept and share responsibility for discipline.
4. Discipline is used as a tool for learning rather than punishment.
5. Administrators, classroom teachers, support staff, and parents work cooperatively to address the psychological, emotional, and social development needs of students.

Academic Development

1. The accomplishments of students and school personnel are appropriately recognized.
2. Student work is attractively displayed.
3. Attendance by students and staff are high.
4. Students and staff are aware that outstanding performance is expected of them.
5. Students and staff expect to be successful. School personnel believe that all children can learn.

Implementation Process

Implementation begins with orientation and overview sessions with the principal initially, and later with the general faculty. After these sessions the Comer School Improvement facilitator works with the principal to:

- Facilitate a process by which representatives are identified for membership on the SMT
- Collaborate with the SMT members to set standard operating procedures for the team, i.e., agenda setting and distribution of minutes, problem solving procedures, length of meetings
- Facilitate the development of the comprehensive school plan by the SMT and a procedure for monitoring it
- Establish the HSST and a time in which the team can meet to review student cases, discuss programs and procedures that affect teacher and student performance, and generally develop programs and activities that contribute to positive school climate and student success

The work of the SMT and HSST should serve as a model for all committees or work groups established within the school. These groups should be conscious of "no fault" and collaborative problem solving techniques. The guiding principles become second nature to staff and are seen as the "natural" and "right way" to conduct school affairs. They manifest themselves in the classroom, the guidance office, the playground, the cafeteria, and, under the best of circumstances, in the home and community.

66. SOME PRACTICAL BENCHMARKING EXPERIENCE

by Bill King, Best Practices Director
Systems & Computer Technology Corporation (SCT)
Malvern, Pennsylvania

The term *benchmarking* originated in the mid-19th century when land surveys were critical to the westward expansion of our country. Without precise surveys, property ownership rights could not be accurately established. The benchmark was "a mark on a permanent object [such as a metal plate affixed to a granite marker] indicating elevation and serving as a reference in topographic surveys." The definition has been expanded today to designate any "point of reference from which measurements may be made."

The benchmarking process for organizations is laid out earlier in three very simple and basic steps; these are repeated here, with my loose interpretations:

Step 1: Determine: *How good are we?* [This is called "establishing the baseline." You can't know how well you've done at the end if you don't know where you were at the beginning.]

Step 2: Partner with others to find out: *How good can we be?* [This is how you establish your targets.]

Step 3: Plan: *How do we get better?* [Or, how do we get from here to there?]

Determining how good we are is perhaps the hardest part of benchmarking: determining *what* to measure. The *Solutions Fieldbook* addresses this phase thoroughly and accurately, so I will not presume to supplement their work, simply to encourage it. Without doing this critical groundwork, you cannot progress to the next step.

Regarding partnering with others to find out how good we can be, the authors say, "Taking stock of how others do things successfully can be very therapeutic." Indeed, it can be very therapeutic for all parties to do a benchmarking study—each will find things they do very well, which can be shared. The contributor gets a gratifying sense of having helped the recipient(s). But contributors will almost certainly find things they could do better, too, and a better practice flows back to them, in return. It is truly a mutually beneficial (win-win) experience. Hence, it is the concept of *reciprocity*.

It's not data collection for analytical comparative studies. It is evaluating different operative scenarios, identifying the ones among them yielding the best results, and putting them into practice. But this is also not the end of it. The hard part in this step is institutionalizing the change. There will be tremendous resistance to change, and it will take courage and determination on the parts of all concerned to insure the resistance is met with firm resolve. And finally, the importance of the feedback loop for continuous quality improvement cannot be underestimated. What really must happen here is to change the "organizational state of mind," but without ongoing feedback, you cannot know if that's actually taking place. I like to think of it in the simple terms of the (somewhat dated) Total Quality Management (TQM) initiative: "Plan–Do–Check–Act." I first learned that when I joined SCT in 1994, and to this day I think to myself "P-D-C-A" whenever I'm approaching a new benchmarking activity. It is a handy shorthand way to remember the essential ingredients for any successful organizational endeavor. (I wanted to say "human endeavor" there, but that would be beyond the scope of this piece; however, I encourage the reader to consider the concept.)

As for planning the *How do we get better* step, a favorite phrase for a long time has been, "The man with a plan wins." One of my SCT colleagues says it even better, "He who controls the pen controls the situation." This all goes to saying that *something* is better than *nothing*. The person or persons who write down their thoughts and plans and visions and place them out there for others to critique have put a stake in the ground. This forces the recipients to either take issue with the initial document—and make them come up with something better—or to accept it at face value. (Which rarely happens, human nature being what it is.) At least it gives the larger community a starting point for discussion, which will lead to refinements and buy-in. (And buy-in is *very* important, because it leads to implementation success. Without it, the project stands a better than even chance of failure.)

A practical definition of the term "benchmarking" in the context of today's business, government, and educational communities bears repeating: Simply put, "steal shamelessly" describes the concept. This doesn't mean "steal criminally," it means imitate only the best and share your own successes back with them; make best practices out of "pretty good practices."

Chris Bogan and Mike English put it succinctly in their book, *Benchmarking for Best Practices*:[4]

In a world where common sense prevailed, benchmarking would seem prosaic. It is simply the systematic process of searching for best practices, innovative ideas, and highly effective operating procedures that lead to superior performance. What could be more straightforward? No individual, team, or operating unit—no mater how creative or prolific—can possibly parent all innovation. No single department or company [or school] can corner the market on *all* good ideas.

In view of this reality of recognizing human limitations, it makes eminently good sense to consider the experience of others. Those who always go it alone are doomed to perennially reinvent the wheel, for they do not learn and benefit from others' progress. By systematically studying the best business practices, operating tactics, and winning strategies of others, an individual, team or organization can accelerate its own progress and improvement.

To summarize the process of benchmarking for schools, there are four key steps:

1. Determining *whom* to benchmark against.
2. Identifying *what* factors to benchmark and establishing internal baseline data.
3. Determining *how* that standard has been achieved, and comparing your school organization's current practices with the way that the benchmarked organization does similar things.
4. Deciding *which* changes or improvements are to be made to meet or exceed the benchmark. (If any. It may well be that you'll discover your process is better than any other you've identified. That is a valuable finding and should encourage you to share your process with your benchmarking partners.)

By following the solutions outlined in this book, educators, administrators, parents, and most importantly, students will improve their performance. It is a daunting task, but "somebody's gotta do it," and I hope there are many "somebodies" out there who will take it and run with it. Our future as a great nation is at stake.

Some additional thoughts since our national tragedy on September 11, 2001: A good friend who shall remain nameless said to one of us recently, "We must be very careful not to go around as the world's greatest superpower imposing our will on other nations whose values may be different. What happens in fifty years when the Chinese are the world's greatest superpower and *THEY* want to impose *THEIR* value system on *US*?" I thought this was a very astute and sobering comment, and subsequent events to this point are encouraging. The point is, without taking the ideas assembled in this book very seriously, the possibility that the United States could lose its position as the world's greatest superpower is all too real. That itself is enough to start an epidemic in education improvement!

67. BERETTA FIREARMS: BENCHMARKING ORGANIZATIONAL LEARNING

It is helpful to examine the unique history of the Italian gun maker Fabbrice D'Armu Beretta. Seldom are we able to track the 500-year history of one firm. Beretta provides us with a singular perspective. We can look at the impact of technology on its workforce development, management fads, and eventually market changes over an exceptionally long period of time. The important changes in Beretta's long history were triggered by technological episodes that took place outside of the firm.

It is also valuable to look at the effect of these changes on Beretta's production workers. This includes the changing demands for higher-order thinking and work skills. Hopefully the following lessons are not lost on U.S. educators.

Reviewing a company's experience from an unusually long view helps us see five important lessons:

1. The evolution of management thinking
2. How technology affected management behavior
3. How today's technology hastened the return to a modern form of product customization not seen or experienced since the guild craft era
4. The impact of advanced manufacturing processes
5. *Why* the evolution and subsequent demand for a new type of knowledge worker

Given the central role played by war and guns, it is safe to say that Beretta has been a factor in global trade since the earth was last viewed as flat. At about the same time that Christopher Columbus "stumbled" upon the New World, the family firm Beretta was founded. It was in 1492, during what historians called the Guild System era.

At first, all Beretta guns were handmade by master gun makers. The master used calipers, jigs, clamps, and files. An apprentice watched to learn the craft. All activities centered on *fit*. Parts were hand modified to fit tightly with other parts. As a result, every gun was one of a kind. In those days parts were *not* interchangeable. Highly skilled and trained workers, much the same as cabinet and clock case makers of the day, crafted these early instruments of war.

In 1800, the industrial revolution established the English system of then *modern* production. The industrial age brought with it, for the first time, the development of new and uniform tools and universal fabrication (e.g., metal lathes). The new industrial system *separated* the production function from the processes used to make Beretta firearms.

In the 19th century, apprentices were taught proficiency on a particular tool, rather than on a particular gun product. An era of worker specialization was evolving, enabling process improvements to be made independent of which gun products were to be manufactured.

Beretta introduced early mass production. Their workers were expected to have fewer universal skills. But the worker needed to be trained to be more specific and *tool-centered*. This uniformity led to fully interchangeable parts but also to less skilled workers. Such production systems became popular and widespread throughout industrial Europe and then in America.

The American system of production, developed in the 1850s, moved into a new phase. High-volume production of products with interchangeable parts became the order of the day. Driven by mechanization, the workers became interchangeable, but still viewed as only a by-product of production. In the American system, the Beretta product line was pared down to three models. Rigid production processes and worker efficiencies became the rationale for avoiding product customization.

Next, along came Frederick W. Taylor, seeking to refine the early industrial-age production methods. In his book *The Principles of Scientific Management*[5] Taylor discussed his methods. The Taylor Scientific Method, as it became known, sought to make labor as efficient as machine tools; both specialized. Following Taylor's methods, work was redesigned through time-and-motion studies. It used man-machine process interaction to determine the most time- and cost-efficient organization.

With these efficiencies and product shifts, Beretta was able to increase its product catalog from three weapons to ten. Job responsibilities were broken down to specialty-trained workers. Work discretion was replaced with Taylor's "one best way to perform the task." But Beretta management controlled all aspects of work, comparing product and worker performance to preset standards. Taylor's industrial methods have been overtaken by time and modern events. But one piece of Taylor's advice still rings true for teachers and managers.

> This change can be brought about only gradually and through the presentation of many object-lessons to the workman, which together with the teaching which he receives, thoroughly convince him of the superiority of the new over the old way of doing the work. This change in the mental attitude of the workman imperatively demands time.[6]

By the end of World War II (1945), statistical process control had come into wider use. The North Atlantic Treaty Organization (NATO) required M-1 rifle parts with tolerances calling for perfectly interchangeable parts. Beretta responded to this customer's need by building new manufacturing equipment for the task. Beretta used regular sampling for quality control. But only defects were inspected at this time after the product was completed. No best way to operate had yet been found. Quality engineering occurred *at the end* of the production line, while problem-solving teams watched over machine performance. There still remained potential quality gaps in the production process. At the time, the manufacturing process was not yet recognized as needing to be seamless.

By 1976, Beretta began applying W. Edwards Deming's methods of numerical control, then successfully proven as having brought about the postwar "economic miracle" of Japan. Deming's genius was in recognizing that what the Japanese call *kaizen* is deeply ingrained in the culture of a people dedicated to *continuous improvement* in all facets of their lives—product, production, and personal. To this day the brilliance of Deming's methods resides in the fact that it is both a motivator as well as a natural extension of the way the Japanese see life.

Information processing could now be used to automatically and numerically control Beretta machines. It could perform in sequence all of those tasks that had previously taken multiple pieces of equipment. At the time, line workers represented just half of the Beretta total company employment. With new forms of statistical control, it was now possible to increase the management span of control to five times greater while covering several machines at once. The new standardized product demanded a much better trained Beretta worker than at any time since the 18th century.

So another new era began at Beretta. New production equipment and new management methods allowed the company to bid a price *one-half* of that of their U.S. competitors. The transportability of numerical control programs enabled Beretta to meet the stipulation of its customer, the U.S. Army, of delivering guns from fully U.S.-based production.

In the early 1980s, Americans were shocked to learn that the Beretta 9-mm Parabellum won the U.S. Army contract, replacing the historic Colt-45 sidearm. What had been the mainstay of the U.S. military for over 150 years had now fallen to a global competitor—a story often repeated throughout other sectors of the U.S. economy.

With numerical control, Beretta now evolved from a *user* of information to an *information-based* company. Data needed to manufacture products were stored digitally on computers rather than on blueprints, dies, and molds. In 1987, computer-integrated manufacturing (CIM) became the norm at Beretta, linking together the entire company with computer networks to perform computer-aided design (CAD), engineering, and flexible manufacturing systems right on the factory floor. This process used:

- A computer-controlled team of semi-independent workstations connected by automated material handling systems. The looped conveyors carried pallets bearing individual work pieces.
- Supervisory computers, which carried information about these work pieces. They directed the movements of material and components through the manufacturing process and assigned priorities and queue.

- Information-driven machines engineered to react to changing situations by loading the correct numerical programs in the proper machines and continually monitoring results.

At Beretta the effect of computer-integrated manufacturing (CIM) proved startling. First, there was a three-to-one jump in productivity. The Beretta factory floor was now down to 30 machines (which was the lowest in 150 years). Thirty people made up the minimum staffing—fewer people than Beretta employed at the end of the 17th century. Rework had fallen to zero. Staff positions consisting of knowledge-workers now represented two-thirds of the Beretta workforce.

We can now see how Beretta manufacturing had evolved to a service company. Customized products are made available to special market segments—police, military, and gun collectors around the world. In turn, this technology-driven change has raised the demands for highly skilled knowledge-based workers *at every level* of the company.

For the first time since the Guild days, over 300 years ago, Beretta is capable of creating numerous custom products. Customization is almost an unlimited capability today. And Guild Era craftsmanship has returned in a 21st-century model. Beretta has brought us full circle.

68. BENCHMARKING QUALITY IMPROVEMENT

We asked high school principal Rick Utz, "What do you consider the most serious obstacles and the most promising opportunities for moving ISO 9000, Baldrige, or other quality processes ahead into schools on a wider scale?"

His response follows.

The future of the quality movement in schools will be based on the success of those of us who have already taken the first step. The benefits of a quality program are as follows:

- Most schools do their job well, but if you ask them what they do they can't tell you. In this age of accountability, it is very important that we as educators can show in concrete terms what we say we do and to have evidence that we do what we say.

- The quality program also allows us to better monitor our cash flow as to why we spend money on certain programs. Through the quality planning process we have to justify what we do. This is a new concept in education.
- Educators are the best starters of projects known to the world, but we are not great at bringing them to a conclusion. The quality planning gives us more direction than we have ever had before.
- Finally, we [educators] have always added new programs to the schools but have never had a method of doing away with the old programs. ISO 9000 gives us that vehicle.

NOTES

1. Christopher E. Bogan and Michael J. English, *Benchmarking for Best Practices* (New York: McGraw-Hill, 1994).

2. TIMSS Report, April 4, 2001.

3. Debra Viadero, "U.S. Schools Importing Singaporean Texts," *Education Week*, 27 September 2000.

4. Bogan & English, *Benchmarking for Best Practices*.

5. Frederick W. Taylor, *The Principles of Scientific Management* (New York: Harper and Brothers, 1911).

6. Ibid.

Meeting the New Mandates

69. UPDATING THE EDUCATOR'S VIEW

There is now little doubt that the expectations for improved local school performance have changed for good. As with reform movements of earlier years, the local school must meet the needs of its time. In other words, it must respond to a new and more demanding school customer both inside and outside the classroom. At the turn of the 21st century the local school must meet the demands of a global economy, a wider array of cultures in American society, and a far less certain future.

Lest we lightly dismiss such labeling as a harmless exercise in semantics, consider that categorizing certain students and their families as "deprived," "disadvantaged," "uninterested," or "lazy" actually leads, more often than not, to corresponding behavior on the part of both the labeler and the group being labeled. No matter how well-meaning the use of such phrases, they too often are taken to imply a chronic condition, a sort of social fate that may well be passed along to the next generation and the one after that.

Sympathetic terms such as "disadvantaged," no less than doubtful judgments such as "lazy," can work as a self-fulfilling prophecy. Often in subtle ways, we act as if these students will have trouble or will probably fail, and the students become discouraged as they acquire, often without even realizing it, the fear and finally the expectation of defeat.

The tragic consequences of this phenomenon came to our attention by way of experiments on teacher expectations conducted in South San Francisco by Dr. Robert Rosenthal and described in his book,

Pygmalion in the Classroom.[1] In his experiments, teachers were led to believe at the beginning of a school year that certain of their students could be expected to show considerable academic improvement during that year. The teachers thought these predictions were based on tests that had been administered to the student body at the end of the preceding school year. In fact, the students designated as potential "spurters" were chosen at random without reference to test results or to grades. Nonetheless, intelligence tests given after the experiment had been in progress for several months indicated that, on the whole, the randomly chosen students had improved more than the rest.

Rosenthal's study has been well publicized and widely discussed, but have we taken full account of its findings? Keep in mind that the experimental group was chosen randomly and thus, contrary to the teachers' belief, was no different from the control group. When teachers were asked to describe students in each group, however, they found members of the experimental group more attractive, better adjusted, more appealing, and less in need of social approval than members of the control group.

Naturally, some students in the control group also gained in IQ during the year, and Dr. Rosenthal discovered that, on the average, the more a student in the control group gained, the less favorably he was described by his teacher. This inverse ratio between high rate of unexpected pupil gain and an unfavorable teacher attitude provides us with a devastating portrait of the persistence of low expectations on the part of teachers, regardless of student performance. In other words, the teachers knew that members of the control group were not supposed to do well, and they apparently regarded students who forced an exception to that rule as somehow "uppity."

If we consider this finding about teacher expectations together with the charges that IQ tests are culture bound, often failing to detect the full potential of some students, we are faced with the possibility that certain schools, in the words of their sharpest critics, actually make students more stupid.

A sharp-eyed schoolteacher, John Holt, has leveled the much broader charge that students actually decline in enthusiasm, curiosity, and confidence from the very day they start formal school.[2] He sees the present school system as a negative force in learning. This is a striking and terrible indictment.

Our charges are much less broad. We seriously question whether certain schools inadvertently lead many of their students to define themselves as stupid, at least with regard to academic work.

To the extent that this charge is true, though, the situation is intolerable, but is it so surprising? After all, if teachers are put in frustrating or even frightening situations, they are no less inclined than any of us to welcome a scapegoat. Whether the scapegoat is supposedly the stupid or headstrong student or the environment of which he is defined to be a victim, the result comes out the same. The school is excused for the failure. If the student is "disadvantaged," what can the poor helpless school do?

The answer, according to the noted educator and sociologist Kenneth B. Clark, is that with the proper expectations and programs, schools can teach every student what he or she needs to know. In the past few years more and more eyes have been opened to this humiliation, not only by senior educators such as Clark but also by a new breed of writers, teachers, and former teachers who'll tell it like it is. Such books as Nat Hentoff's *Our Children are Dying*, John Holt's *How Children Fail*, Herbert Kohl's *36 Children*, and the award-winning *Death at an Early Age* by Jonathan Kozol,[3] offer devastating indictments of current classroom practices. Grindingly dull, irrelevant, often inexcusable, these outdated classroom practices cry out for remedy. In these and other books the students are shown to be victims of a cruel system that eats away at their confidence and fails to meet their needs. Is it really the children who are failing in this situation? That is what the grading system would seem to suggest.

70. CHANGING EXPECTATIONS

Student Expectations

How can schools stop humiliating the students they are supposed to be teaching? How can they teach these students to expect success in school? First of all, educators need to end their preoccupation with student disabilities. By now we know the litany by heart. Their vocabulary is limited. They cannot think in abstractions. They are not introspective. They prefer physical to mental activity. They lack motivation to succeed in school, and so on.

Instead of always trying to "compensate" for disabilities, why not first identify, develop, and then build on their strengths? In teacher and administrator professional journals there are numbers of testimonials from teachers who work in the inner city and in isolated rural areas, teachers who discover the vast learning potential of their students. The recurring theme that runs through these stories is that the teacher did away with all of the negative things they had been told about the disadvantaged child. The teacher began with an unshakable belief in the youngsters, soon sustained by student achievement. As one teacher put it: "I'm fed up with people who keep saying the disadvantaged child can't learn. My children do have the ability to learn. They have innate talents just like other children do. If those talents have been smothered by economic, social, and cultural deprivation, it's the teacher's job to discover and nurture them."

Public Expectations

This teacher, along with an increasing number of others, now has come to believe that the school has the responsibility not merely to expose each student to a course of instruction, but to give each a real chance to succeed. In the past, schools have not been required to bring about achievement. Schools have too long been thought of as "relatively passive," as an agency expected to provide free public resources. Yet, the United States Supreme Court has recognized that the state does not satisfy its constitutional responsibility if it merely takes people as it finds them, setting equal standards of access. The state must assure each citizen an *effective utilization* of his or her right to a free public education. The effective utilization standard varies with different rights, but the state is obliged to ensure an equal opportunity for an equal educational result.

Like many theories of constitutional law, the effective utilization standard is deliberately vague as well as challenging. It points in a direction and names a goal but leaves the detailed implementation for further negotiation. Ultimately, a citizen has been able to use a right only when he has obtained whatever that right is designed to guarantee.

In the case of learning basic skills such as reading, to which every citizen has a right, we know that the school has made possible an effective utilization of this right only when its students can successfully demonstrate their ability to read. If certain students fail this test, a school might argue that it had done everything humanly possible to teach such students. But the burden of proof must henceforth fall on the school and not, as it now does, on the failing student. Moreover, the school needs to have shown not only that it had provided the failing student with instruction that worked with other students who were in some way similar, but also that no program it could reasonably provide would offer substantial promise of teaching that particular student how to read. In order to effectively argue the latter point, a school official would need to have acquainted him- or herself with new and well-researched programs that are often widely ignored.

The point of this approach is not to elicit a new set of ingenious arguments about the alleged ineducability of many students. The point is, rather, to serve clear notice on the schools that society expects all its children to learn at least the basic skills, and that failures are to be regarded less as the fault of the student or of his social or cultural background than of the school, and that the proper response to failure (as principals are fond of telling troublemakers) is not excuses but reform, and in this case reform by the schools.

71. ACCOUNTABILITY: MEETING STATE AND FEDERAL MANDATES

To understand such mandates calls for an "engineering mind-set." At its best, engineering fosters ingenuity—creativity and resourcefulness.

Let's take a moment to explore some of the major weaknesses of the colleges of education that the engineering mind-set can help overcome. Why is it that technology seemingly finds it so difficult to thrive in education circles?

Throughout the U.S. and around the globe the engineering schools, but not the colleges of education, now include courses in ISO 9000 and Baldrige Performance Criteria in their curriculum. Community colleges have numerous courses in these same quality processes and standards.

Together, we enjoy considerable firsthand experience with engineering design and engineering management principles as well as a broad range of subject matter. Lessinger received his engineering degree before becoming a professional educator. Salowe is a certified planner who has supervised numerous engineering projects.

72. APPLYING ENGINEERING
PRINCIPLES TO CLASSROOM TEACHING

Is it possible to consider "engineering principles" an important phase of classroom teaching? To the majority of educators who train our classroom teachers and administrators in the colleges of education, engineering might signal a cold, technological, and seemingly dehumanizing process. "And," educators might say if pressed (because the topic is rarely discussed), "education is really concerned with the keeping and spread of all that is especially human."

To probe one's personal thoughts and feelings, or, more generally, "looking into or under the surface of things," is called introspection. Let us look, in an introspective way, at engineering and engineers to help answer the questions about education.

Today, wide-ranging, thoughtful discussions are heard at engineering conferences, seminars, and meetings about the changing role of engineers in modern society. Such discussions were rarely heard in the past. How could it be otherwise, considering the social upheaval of the 1960s, the environmental crisis of the 1970s, the political turmoil of the 1980s, and the progression of a totally altered global, information-driven economy in the 1990s, and today, the advent of increased needs for engineering solutions to shore up Americans' safety.

Introspection on the part of engineers parallels an increasing interest in technology on the part of politicians, historians, ethicists, and social scientists. It is hardly news to report that people in all walks of life are waking up to the importance of science and technology in their daily lives. And it is not much of a stretch to argue that engineering is increasingly becoming central to our lives.

The United Nations Human Development Index ranks nations on what they do to meet basic needs: keeping persons healthy, raising education standards, and helping persons earn the income needed to make choices. Most technologically advanced nations achieve the highest ratings.

For all the compassion and goodwill toward others they show, every nation is engaged in a fierce battle to carve out a stake in world commerce. And in each nation the quality of its schools is on the front lines of that battle.

But here we make the case that the application of engineering principles to education, particularly its mind-sets for finding solutions to complex problems, is a major factor in the striving of those front-line "fighters."

We are aware that this observation may meet with stiff resistance among educators. What we are talking about is linking essential courses from the college of engineering with the training of new teachers. That would come as a revolutionary step for most education faculty, and no doubt, for teachers and school administrators. We would dare estimate that a negligible percentage of college education faculty have any engineering background or experience. Florman[4] explains how acceptance of "education as engineering" may depend on the general public's understanding of what engineering is. He writes:

> Yet engineering is not a word one is likely to hear in our communal discussions—for example, on Sunday morning television interview programs. Everybody agrees that we live in an era of "high tech," and that technology has changed our lives. Multimedia, virtual reality, information highway, genetic engineering—these are buzzwords of the day. But real engineers, the people who conceive of computers, and oversee their manufacture, the people who design and build information systems, cars, bridges, airplanes, and so many other things that are central to our lives, are nameless and obscure.

73. MASSACHUSETTS INSTITUTE OF TECHNOLOGY COMMISSION

Commenting on the state of American industry, the MIT Commission reported that the most successful U.S. firms share "an emphasis on competitive benchmarking." And the trend is moving into higher education, with more institutions surveying its administrative and business costs. Unfortunately, as with most new management techniques, many organizations aren't too clear about benchmarking or even how to do it properly. "To attempt benchmarking without a clear understanding may actually lead to negative results."

74. OUTLINE OF STEPS

The following sets out the specific steps required for a successful school improvement effort. School leadership launches such an initiative. The mission is to avoid common mistakes in schools.

Strategic Planning Is Now Mandated for Schools

Strategic planning is now legislated in more states and widely practiced in even more school districts. Dealing straight up with key questions allows a school district to develop more innovative strategies. But even the most brilliant strategy can fail unless carried through. Moreover, many schools are failing to produce genuine performance improvement while costs grow as a percentage of budget. Faculty, in particular, have trouble answering when somebody asks, "What is the value-added benefit of your school's teaching and administrative functions?"

At the core of these issues rest a host of familiar factors: lack of customer focus, slow program development, rising overhead costs, and mediocre quality. Benchmarking, when properly implemented, is a major tool for uncovering solutions to these problems.

In plain language, school benchmarking is a structured approach to creating and driving change into a school organization. Such change comes about by doing process-to-process (or function-to-function) comparisons with other entities (either inside or outside of education) and developing detailed data about performance levels and best practices. In other words, benchmarking is the search for those practices that lead to *superior* performance. Mandated change asks school leaders to ask themselves three key questions:

1. How good are we?
2. How good can we be?
3. How do we get better?[5]

Benchmarking is a change management tool that can broaden the horizons of school leadership and staffs by helping all realize that there are proven better ways. The successful "bench marker" seeks to shed the "not invented here" mind-set and rid school staff of such outmoded notions as, "We're not going to learn anything from other school districts," or, "This district is as good as you can get," or, "There is no such district as outstanding," or, "We're different and can't be compared to anyone else, especially business."

In its place, the benchmarking mind-set is symbolized by attitudes, such as, "We'll borrow good practices shamelessly," or, "We can learn something from anyone," or, "We certainly don't have a corner on all the answers." The benchmarking effort forces colleagues to talk openly with their counterparts in other schools, districts, and communities. Taking stock of how others do things successfully can be very therapeutic.

The introspective process separates fact from fiction. So, finding the better way somewhere else paves the way for new actions. It's much easier to convince the school organization that a better way is doable and not "pie in the sky" if school leadership can point to another school or district already doing it. It saves reinventing the wheel!

TQM, ISO 9000, and Baldrige start their process improvement with self-assessment. This greatly spurs continuous improvement. Never-ending step-by-step improvement is a sound education strategy—if the starting point lies within a reasonable distance of the goal the school is trying to reach.

A mandate leading to benchmarking other schools helps propel the school or district to recognize and achieve situations where a *quantum leap* in performance is needed. Quantum leaps usually call for a "clean sheet of paper" and rethinking basic assumptions about how to operate. Continuous improvement is valuable but it cannot get us there in the absence of fundamental change. The key is answering the question, "How far do we have to go?" Analogous to golf, it's "Which club do I need to pull out of my bag to reach the objective?" The answer depends on how far from the cup you are, your lie on the ground, and how skilled you are in using the club.

75. SCHOOL BENCHMARKING IS NOT . . .

The best way to better understand benchmarking is to look at what it is not. For starters, benchmarking is not comparative analysis, where an analyst looks at how his or her school stacks up to others in terms of measures like the student-faculty ratio, productivity, cost per student, drop-out rates, graduation rates, or student satisfaction. Why? Because this kind of data does not drive change, nor does it help us focus on the practices that lead to superior performance.

Neither is benchmarking process reengineering, which is a method for looking at internal processes and making needed improvements. It applies a variety of techniques, such as quality initiatives spelled out in

Healing Public Schools, the Balanced Scorecard, CRM, and Data Warehousing. For example, when the school wants to improve its registration process, it looks at itself and inwardly works on process steps to fix the problems it finds.

Benchmarking is not a survey. Schools have traditionally gathered data about their own practices and processes compared to those of others. Surveys are commonly used tools for such data gathering and can be extremely useful. They create the opportunity to compare data points on specific items within and between school organizations and may also provide a useful source for longitudinal trending. But the nature of the data gathering is fundamentally different in these respects:

- Surveys have participants. Benchmarking studies have *partners*. A survey participant is selected for a variety of reasons, such as a common geographic area or type of school (e.g., magnet schools) and may frequently request anonymity. A benchmarking partner expects *reciprocity*; to learn something in return for sharing information.
- A major purpose of benchmarking is making friends with other people who are doing specific, analogous-to-your-own-school operations in a better way, sharing information, and perhaps helping each other along the way. After all, the other school may not be as proficient as you are in some other areas.
- The output is different. Surveys generally report aggregated, often average, data from numerous participants. Benchmarked output may also include this type of data but will often detail successful *scenarios* of practices for the process or function.

Many, in fact, completely miss the point of benchmarking. Benchmarking isn't intended as an easily accomplished one-shot effort. Especially, it is not a three-hour show-and-tell session with another school where they tell you what they're doing and you say, "Gee, that's a good idea. We'll copy it!" Then you come back with one or two ideas and try to make a change—but neither an improvement mechanism has been developed nor has a clear path been laid out for future action and results. Nor have any measurements of success typically been put in place. The name of the game with benchmarking is to *institutionalize the improvement ethic*.

76. PERFORMANCE MEASUREMENT

Performance measures for classroom teaching practices and school administrative support still remain the exception rather than the rule in most schools. The field of education talks a lot about "exemplary" or "best" practice, without having determined and measured what is in fact "best."

With big changes demanded in schooling to meet accountability for results, schools must develop competently based standards of best organizational, curricular, and classroom teaching practice to match state-mandated learning standards. Only the systematic review of school processes and practices can give educators the ability to self-diagnose the underlying reasons for unacceptable student learning outcomes. The benchmarking question is, "What process changes could we adopt that have led elsewhere to better teaching outcomes?"

What are needed are mechanisms to make breakthroughs possible to reliable classroom teaching. Benchmarking is a sound tactic. It allows for the free exchange of "best education practices" that have been evaluated in similar situations.

As a standard of comparative excellence, benchmarking is used to measure similar things. The benchmarking process allows the school leadership to compare its practices, processes, and outcomes to others' standards of excellence in a methodical way. Benchmarking also offers a key to gaining support for needed changes. For one thing, a comparison through benchmarking helps identify problems and potential solutions before they negatively impact proposed new programs.

The objective is to aim high, not to lower the floor—to gain results that other approaches have been unable to reach. Benchmarking yields results far greater than those achieved by less formal approaches. Benchmarking also provides focused and useful data, not just anecdotal information, intuition, or opinion; it creates a culture of continuous improvement; it enhances creativity; it opens minds to new ideas; it overpowers the "not invented here" mind-set; and it raises awareness to changes in the outside world.

Benchmarking provides the opportunity for a school organization to see if it really meets its own expectations and to learn why or why not. Possibly the district's expectations are set too low or too vague. Benchmarks enable a school organization to think about current operations and where it is going in solid terms; to set measurable goals that benchmarks can help reach; and to consider the costs and benefits of pursuing a given course of action. Benchmarking has a powerful dispersal potential. Others can immediately see *what* has been done, *why* it was done, the results, and the specific actions that produced the result.

To drive the point home one more time. Benchmarking has four key steps: (1) Determining *whom* to benchmark against, (2) identifying *what* to benchmark and establishing baseline data; (3) determining *how* that standard has been achieved by comparing your school organization's current practices with the way the benchmarked organization does similar things; and (4) deciding *if* to make changes or improvements in order to meet or exceed the benchmark.

77. USING THE BENCHMARKING PROCESS

Following are the key benchmarking steps outlined in *Healing Public Schools*.

1. Determine what to benchmark and establish internal baseline data. The first step is to assess current needs of your school. Ask what results do you want to achieve and by when. Start with a vision of what "doing it well" really means; in other words, what do you consider superior performance? Second, define your own practices and processes down to the smallest detail. For example, when a student fills out a particular form, what becomes of the form? What use is made of the form? Why is a particular piece of information asked for? What is done with each piece of information on that form?

2. What is your benchmark? What standard of excellence are you looking for in this particular practice or process? What other school districts have achieved this excellence? What is the difference between your school's results and the results of the best school organization? For example, you might decide to benchmark a school or a company in your area because they handle telephone inquiries faster, cheaper, and with fewer complaints.

3. Determine how that standard has been achieved, and compare your school's current practices with the way that "best" organization does similar things. In what ways does the other organization do a similar process or a part of a process better than your school?

Why does the way they do the job yield better results, in less time, at less cost? Use analysis to help focus improvement efforts and set expectations for such efforts.

4. Decide to make changes or improvements in order to meet or exceed the benchmark. Benchmarking is most useful when the data are used for more than an academic exercise or comparing one department to another. Data gathering and the entire benchmarking effort are designed to take action, to allow your school to make improvements by thinking about each decision in concrete terms.

These four steps require a background of work to put them into practice. The action plan must eventually include monitoring, specifying: (1) *how* will we know whether the changes are succeeding, (2) *what* measurements are being used, (3) *why* certain data is to be collected, and (4) *what* time intervals will be used for collecting the data.

The benchmark needs to be reevaluated periodically to determine if it remains the "best standard" now used. If not, determine what becomes the new benchmark and begin the effort to reach the new one. The monitoring phase sheds light on a critical aspect of benchmarking that sets it apart from the usual way organizations try to improve. Benchmarking is not a one-time, quick-fix undertaking. It is a continuous learning process.

78. LOOKING FOR BENCHMARK MODELS

Educators normally look only at other schools for "best" practices. This is shortsighted and illustrates another reason for a lack of progress. Successful benchmarking involves looking *outside* of as well as within your own field. In the business world, companies who have successfully benchmarked have liberally borrowed from companies far outside their own industry. For example, Compaq Computer benchmarked Disney World to improve facilities management. Xerox benchmarked L.L. Bean in warehousing and materials handling, Federal Express for billing efficiency, and Cummins Engine for production scheduling—all outside of Xerox's industry. For its manufacturing unit, designed to meet customer emergency needs, Corning Glass benchmarked best-in-class hospital emergency wards to understand how such teams are organized for crises.

Confining benchmarking efforts to school organizations like your own limits your goals and creativity. One's own field is too familiar. This makes it all the more difficult to *see* change with a fresh perspective. Conversely, a benchmarking search of organizations outside of your field *stimulates* creativity because it forces the viewer out of habitual patterns of thought and routine ways of doing things.

Most schools have incomplete information about what is the best practice, if in fact they ever even raise the issue. They might note which elementary grade teacher raised reading scores of students the most, but they would probably not move very aggressively to spread that practice. This type of comparison avoids the question of whether *any* of the departments are as effective as they could be. Best-in-class benchmarking lets schools break free of old habits and from self-imposed limits on performance.

79. REENGINEERING THE CAPABILITIES OF PUBLIC SCHOOLS

The mind-set of educational engineering starts with the assumption that all students can succeed and that with an adequate technology of instruction teachers can lead them toward mastery and a certified sense of accomplishment. What this offers is not another grand manifesto but process improvements through which the school can find programs that work, implement them, and measure the results. The end product of this process is not a new program or a new machine or a new report, but a *capability!*

Benefits of an Educational Engineering Mind-set

First, consider in turn its potential for students, for teachers, and for administrators. Since educational engineering is an approach—a mind-set, broader than any particular program, it soon affects the way students view their own process of learning.

For example, most classes now begin with a vague preview of the material to covered and consist of a series of review sessions, assignments, and tests. There is really nothing much to look forward to. In contrast, most successful commercial enterprises promote their products and services in such a way as to arouse interest before the consumer uses them. We read attractive brochures of a foreign country and begin thinking about a trip; we study the investment pages and contemplate the purchase of some stocks; we pour over a brochure for a new model car before deciding to test-drive one. The actual experience of using the product or service is positively enhanced by an advanced knowledge and anticipation of it.

Student Benefits

In school, where does the student go to find out what is being offered? Most of them enter courses with little notion of what they will study. Little attempt is made to build prior interest in, or to prepare students for, the experience. Why not give them a prospectus setting out the intellectual adventure they are about to undertake? The pre-course materials could highlight things they will learn, the books they will read, ideas they will encounter, and a sample of the assignments they will be asked to complete. Properly done, such a prospectus could arouse intellectual ambition in the students and help their parents better understand and prepare to support what is going on.

Any school could do this, but the link to educational engineering is plain. If the process of innovation requires school officials to define their goals in operational terms as a first step, the school would then be able to share with students not merely vague and admirable objectives, such as the ability to communicate effectively, but specific sets of useful skills. In fact, the spirit of educational engineering has reached the students when, the student begins to say, "I can do that task," instead of saying, "I've had that course." In this process, education is less a program of material to be plod through than a set of useful skills and understandings to be mastered, and that is the way it needs to be treated in planning.

Teacher Benefits

As a frame of reference, educational engineering offers teachers a much wider role. When farmers had nothing more than a horse and a plow, their productivity was limited by their lack of resources and equipment. With a tractor, hybrid seed, modern fertilizers, and a reaper, the farmer sharply increased his yield. In education we are now reaching this same kind of transition, and just as the old-fashioned farmers viewed all the new machinery with deep suspicion, many of us wonder what effect new media of instruction and use of performance data will have on teachers.

Insofar as the new media produce results, the effect is bound to be good. In certain schools, teachers now are failing not because they are untrained or lazy but because they are severely overburdened. Like the old-fashioned farmer who hardly had a moment to eat, teachers need help. In his book *Every Kid a Winner*, Lessinger wrote: "If, as seems clear, some of the functions performed by persons can be performed as well or better through other agencies, teachers could assume versatile, differentiated, human roles in the schools." Instead of leading students through the lock-step of a single program, teachers could assist them in the progress of individualized instruction; teachers could help students discover things for themselves instead of trying to tell them everything; teachers could draw on local development capital through local industry-education partnerships to support process improvements tailored to specific needs.

Teachers can become managers of instruction in tandem with their role as the central presenters of information. Through following the *Healing Public Schools* winning prescription of ISO/Baldrige guidelines and the metrics of the Balanced Scorecard, teachers can operate within a flexibility of form that they have never before enjoyed. Schools will then be able to test process improvements locally before adopting them, teachers will be called on not to initiate untried proposals but rather to take over the operation of processes that are already familiar and successful.

Administrator Benefits

The educational engineering frame of reference can finally ease the persistent problems of desegregation and lower the dropout rate. The solution in each case is the same. If students can begin to master a skill, no matter what their pace of learning, they gain a source of satisfaction and self-respect, and the opportunity, in time, to join their peers in the normal course of instruction. It's when students feel hopeless and discouraged that they may decide to quit school; when they lag far behind their peers, they know they are more of a drag on the class than a contributor to it. In each case, what such students need is rapid, esteem-building progress in learning basic skills.

Until and unless school officials can come around to assure this kind of progress, their level of authority will continue to erode. Student misbehavior will become even more common, as will the use of various forms of power to try and contain it.

There is a sharp distinction between authority and power. Whereas power is derived from simple force, such as the use of police or disciplinary action, authority is derived from respect for the moral purposes of an institution. A tyrant, of whatever magnitude, relies on power in this sense; a leader relies on his authority.

It now seems more clear that, apart from a certain fringe, rebellious youth are demanding that reliance on power be replaced by responsive authority and that our institutions, including our schools, live up to their promises. To win respect as competent educators, schools need to teach students the necessary skills. The educational engineering mind-set is designed to help do just that.

Frame-of-Reference Benefits

In particular, what will educational engineering help schools to do? What are its advantages?

First, process improvements allow decision makers at every level, from the federal government to the local school board, to govern the school as a system instead of dealing with one crisis after another. They can set firm goals and hold others accountable for results. This is performance management.

Second, it will halt the unnecessary waste of dollars on educational failures. When a government experiments and fails, the bureaucracy continues to grow; but when a business fails, it goes out of business and another takes its place. Under educational engineering, if a program does not meet performance criteria, dollars flow back to the state and federal till, and administrators will know which schools should not receive grants until they make changes. The Balanced Scorecard helps provide educators with measurements to match their strategic objectives.

Third, it will stimulate the creation of a much more advanced technology of instruction. Inflexible and invalidated instructional materials and techniques such as present and traditional textbooks and lectures simply aggravate the problems of a group system of teaching and are clearly inadequate for individual instruction. How could such methods possibly provide the feedback that a student needs to improve? Instead, they force students in lockstep and expose them to failure. The Data Warehouse offers the means to implement the strategies we outlined in *Healing Public Schools* and to ride the Balanced Scorecard platform.

Fourth, it will allow educators to match the talents and resources of private industry to local needs, on local terms, under local control, through the intermediary of management support. Customer Relationship Management provides the process improvements to facilitate such wider partnerships.

Fifth, it will foster economy by reducing the cost of effective implementation of successful programs and by highlighting the relatively low cost-effectiveness of some programs now widely used. Performance management based on measurable process data saves employees unnecessary angst and taxpayers unnecessary waste.

Sixth, it will give educational personnel greater incentives for performance. For example, it relieves instructional personnel from having to deal with peripheral issues such as dress codes that interfere with the main job of teaching and learning.

Seventh, it will change the teaching role from mere information transmission to the management of learning. In many classrooms today, the only person actively and consistently engaged is the teacher. What if every student in that classroom were as fully absorbed as the teacher? The teachers' jobs might not be any easier, but they would undoubtedly be more satisfied.

Above all, a process through which good educational practice is forthcoming can become standard practice in a growing number of schools. Some critics say we lack the necessary educational research; others, that the schools are inept even at running the programs they have. Wherever the truth may lie in such charges, the fact remains that the thorniest education problem resides between the research on learning and the routine administration of schools. It is apparent that schools lack a mechanism for applying much of what is already known. There are isolated examples of good practice all over the country, but states, districts, and local schools have no adequate way of standardizing these practices.

80. POLICY VOIDS THAT BLOCK SCHOOL IMPROVEMENT

When the policy initiatives that power school improvement are missing, current efforts cannot pierce the underlying armor of the school culture.

Any reform which leaves the basic structure intact will tend to be assimilated and neutralized. In general the various components of the existing system are so strongly interconnected that any attempt to change one component in isolation will set off a series of compensating adjustments among all the others, mitigating the impact of the reform.[6]

Louisiana provides a striking example. It was way ahead of the rest of the nation in enacting education reform laws and new policies. The titles to the laws and policies promulgated over a 10-year period read like a table of contents to a book summarizing the policy reform efforts of all the other states combined. What has been the result of reform in Louisiana? The following markers tell the sad story:

- Louisiana has the highest illiteracy rate among the 50 states.
- The average ACT (American College Test) scores of Louisiana students rank 27th out of 28 states. (Other states use the Iowa or Stanford Achievement Series.) Louisiana was trailed only by Mississippi. The gap between Louisiana's scores and the national average is larger than it was 10 years ago.
- Louisiana students scored significantly lower than the national average among southern states (Arkansas, Florida, Louisiana, South Carolina, and West Virginia), which participated in the Southern Regional Education Board/National Assessment of Education Progress 11th-grade reading-testing program in 1985–86. Although more than 80 percent of the Louisiana 11th-graders tested said that their grades were mostly As, Bs, and Cs in school, test results indicate that only 37 percent read well enough for college-level work. The program results show that the reading scores of black Louisiana 11th-graders and the nation are equivalent to the average reading score of white 7th-graders nationally.
- Louisiana has the lowest graduation rate among the states—only 54.7 percent of the state's ninth-graders went on the graduate from high school four years later in 1985, according to the U.S. Department of Education. Graduation rate data are not compiled in the same manner by every state, and state officials say many of their students who drop out do later get a GED diploma.
- Louisiana's college freshmen are so unprepared that over half (51.4 percent) of them had to take remedial courses in Louisiana's public colleges and universities despite the fact that they were all high school graduates.

Louisiana's failure to institute genuine reform despite more than a decade of efforts to improve public education confirms how resistant to change—how likely to "assimilate and neutralize" change—school systems can be.

Those who have tried to change the system have time and again seen reform measures watered down, ignored, improperly implemented, taken to court by the teacher unions, repealed, mired down in turf battles and power struggles between public bodies, or not funded (often not because the money was not there but because failing to fund a program is a certain way to kill it).

81. OLD HABITS DIE HARD, BUT . . .

Regrettably, the Louisiana example is not unique. It is an example of the current state of most education reform efforts. In our view, the absence of three highly interdependent education policies account in large part for the poor results of educational reform. Their continued absence or failure to be implemented virtually guarantees continued failure. The three education policies center on: (1) the performance management of breakthrough and control; (2) teacher accountability for knowing and using good practice as regular practice; and (3) administrative logistical support of the teaching and learning process. These policy voids— plus the absence of concern (actually, absence of an acknowledgment of an ongoing, chronic outrage) among staff and leaders—must be addressed.

Policy Void No. 1: The Performance Management of Breakthrough and Control

To restructure education, mastery of both breakthrough and its opposite, control, are essential.

Breakthrough means change. Its performance management is targeted toward a dynamic, decisive movement to a new and higher attainment. The range of breakthrough events is as broad as the human imagination.

Control means staying the course. Its performance management is targeted to sticking to current standards and preventing change.

Breakthrough and control are part of the plan-do-act-revise cycle. The cycle consists of alternating plateaus and gains in performance. Plateaus are the result of control. Gains are the result of breakthrough.

In a dynamic school enterprise, this cycle goes on and on. The differences between breakthrough and control are so great that the decision of whether, at any one time, to embark on breakthrough, or to continue on control, is of cardinal importance. "The choice of breakthrough or control is a decision not only as to the results desired; it is decisive also as to the means." [7]

Policy Void No. 2: Teacher Accountability for Knowing and Using Best Practice

The "soul" of any profession consists of the tools, processes, and materials its members customarily use to fulfill their duties and satisfy their task requirements. In short, a profession relies upon its technologies. Such professional technologies come to life in the *practice* of its members. Taken together, they represent professional practices. In medicine, law, and engineering, it is possible, and often legally mandated, for the professional to distinguish clearly between good practice, poor practice, and malpractice. (See, in Moving Ahead, below, "Are Education Malpractice Suits on the Horizon?" for more detailed discussion.)

Such has never been the case in education. The word *practice* itself is often reserved for learning, as in *practice teaching*. It is seldom invoked for the furtherance of professional mastery, as in a *teaching practice*. Until recently, education lacked an agreed-upon, authoritative body of classroom teaching practice. Now teaching has such an inventory but is not using it.

Whereas the doctor, the lawyer, and the engineer are held personally accountable for knowing and using best practice as their regular practice, the teacher is not. The teacher is left free to ignore or to remain ignorant of what works, or to use tools, processes, and materials that do not (or cannot) contribute to intended standards for student outcomes. A teacher can repeatedly use inadequate technologies with poor results and still enjoy the same professional status as one who is getting results.

Policy Void No. 3: Administrative Logistical Support of the Teaching and Learning Process

Though widely taught in the college business curricula, education lacks an adequate field of logistics. Worse yet, education is unaware of the dimensions of such a field and its value in supporting a teacher's classroom duties. Can we really expect that technology will blossom into student-centered learning in the classroom without giving teachers logistical support?

The contrast between logistical support of teaching duties and tasks and that of other occupations in carrying out their duties and tasks, explains in part why there are such poor results in education. Since the 1880s the standing school practice is to furnish teachers with a chalkboard, and a single textbook for each student in a particular subject. There may be a teacher's guide for the course and a curriculum guide, but often it is either unavailable or out-of-date. Occasionally there is a course syllabus. The teacher may have access to supplemental materials and tools like workbooks, audiovisual equipment, a computer, and a copier.

But most often such tools are rarely available at the moment of need. Yet no teacher, no matter how skilled and credentialed, can know in advance the moment of need in learning. Teachers are expected to order tools, such as visual aide equipment well in advance of need, and then the equipment may not be available in a timely manner or in the amounts required to serve all students adequately; the teacher cannot be sure that the tools are always in working order, and repaired or replaced if previously on the blink.

Teachers often need to buy the tools and materials out of their own pockets, even those prescribed in the official curriculum guide, because they are not supplied. Many of the tools and materials have not been tailored for the particular program and the unique needs of the learners, including the ubiquitous textbook.

The personal computer is the quintessential example of logistical support. With the computer as his or her "assistant" teacher logistical support is available at the point of need: to score tests, to list learning objectives mastered, to make individualized assignments including those needed for quality control, to assign and locate resources required to accomplish an assignment, to provide target completion times and rates of progress, to select and assign alternative lesson approaches, to flag students with entry deficiencies and proficiencies, to provide reports on individual student performance and attendance, to furnish student data profiles for use in student counseling, and to provide feedback for corrective action to the teacher on his or her instructional effectiveness.

By applying educational logistics, teaching can become a partnership between teacher and student in very practical ways. The most important reform of education can come closer to reality: the focus of the classroom can shift dramatically from teaching to learning! Also, with adequate logistical support, it is possible for teachers to move nearer to providing a student-centered learning environment. Given a competent, confident, and caring teacher with logistical support, he or she can meet the needs of individual students.

82. USEFUL DATA HELP SCHOOLS MEET NEW MANDATES

Data warehouse (DW) users get useful information through a user interface. It is such user interfaces that have the most impact on how effective and useful DW is perceived by users. Two criteria for selecting an effective user interface are ease of use and performance. For ease of use, most enterprises turn to the graphical user interfaces (GUIs) that Windows or Mac users are familiar with. For performance, developers need to ensure that the hardware-and-software platform fully supports and is optimized for every chosen user interface.

The key selection criteria for user interface are the *information needs* and the level of *computer literacy* of potential users who will retrieve the needed information from the DW. Users will tend to fall into one of the following four categories:

- *The information-system-challenged*—Users who are hopelessly lost when it comes to information systems. Such users in management roles may rely on their secretaries or assistants to retrieve information for them. Other such users need an extremely easy-to-use and highly graphical interface.
- *The variance-oriented*—Users who are focused on variances in numbers over time. These users mainly want a set of standard reports that they can generate or receive periodically so that they can perform analyses.
- *The number-crunchers*—Users who are spreadsheet fans. They take whatever data is available and refine it, recategorize it, and derive their own numbers for analyzing and managing. Their needs are best met by providing reports or responses to specific queries in a spreadsheet extract format.

- *The technically oriented*—Users who are already familiar with computers and have sufficient motivation to learn and use everything they can get their hands on. These people want to have complete control over the way they retrieve and format information. They are often systems analysts who have moved into an education function. They want to have all of the tools that the Data Warehouse development staff uses.

Most school organizations have all of these categories of individuals, making it advisable to provide each type of DW user interface.

The final decisive factor is that the user interface be able to support access to the data warehouse. If a user interface is easy to use, allows all potential users to get the information they need in the format they need, and does it in an acceptable amount of time, it is the right interface.

83. HOW TO REMEMBER THE DEFINITION OF QUALITY

The following from Philip Crosby[8] gives us a memorable definition of quality:

Quality has much in common with sex. Everyone is for it. (Under certain conditions, of course.) Everyone feels they understand it. (Even though they wouldn't want to explain it.) Everyone thinks execution is only a matter of following natural inclinations. (After all, we do get along somehow.) And of course, most people feel that other people cause all the problems in these areas. (If only they would take the time to do things right.) In a world where more than half the marriages end in divorce or separation, such assumptions are open to question.

84. EDUCATION AND THE FUTURE OF THE NATION

In his best-selling *John Adams*, his biography of our second president, David McCullough shares with readers Adams's profound insight into the role of education.

The more Adams thought about the future of his country, the more convinced he became that it rested on education. Before any great things are accomplished, he [Adams] wrote to a correspondent,

A memorable change must be made in the system of education and knowledge must become so general as to raise the lower ranks of society

nearer to the higher. The education of a nation instead of being confined to
a few schools and universities for the instruction of the few must become
the national care and expense for the formation of the many.[9]

85. THE VALUE OF EDUCATION TO THE AMERICAN WORKER

Former U.S. Secretary of Labor Ray Marshall and Marc Tucker put the
issue of the value of education to the nation in more stark terms in their
book *Thinking for a Living*.

> But the threat is clear. If we do not come to a consensus on the need to es-
> tablish our economy on new principles—the principles of human-resource
> capitalism—then our prosperity will vanish and our democracy will be un-
> der siege. If we can reach beyond our own parochialism to borrow from
> the most creative and successful policies in the world [benchmark], if we
> have the will to reexamine the relevance of deeply entrenched institutions,
> and if we have the courage to take on a multitude of vested interests, then
> we can leapfrog over the best the world has to offer and build a system for
> the development and productive use of our human resources that will be
> without peer. (p. 239)[10]
>
> The only resource we have is ourselves—our energy, our intellect, our
> confidence, and our ability to work with one another to common purpose
> to make American industry and American society the world leaders that
> they once were, and can be again. (p. 256)

86. EDUCATION AND COMMUNITY SUPPORT

In *Head to Head*,[11] Massachusetts Institute of Technology (MIT) professor of management Lester Thurow minces few words when he writes,

> Local governments don't want to pay for first-class schools. They know
> that less than half the population has children in school at any one time,
> that students will leave home and use their skills in different geographic
> regions of the country, and that high taxes necessary to pay for good
> schools would drive industry away. Firms would locate next door and
> free ride on their well-educated workforce. Someone else should make
> the necessary investments. (p. 274)
>
> Communities would agree to quit using schools as a dumping ground
> where they assign social problems that cannot be solved elsewhere. The
> school's prime responsibility is to insure that their students are educated.
> The front lines of the war on crime, drugs, teenage pregnancy, or housing

desegregation should be established elsewhere. Better nutrition, driver's training, and sports are secondary. The energy of our school systems should be focused on education—not dissipated on other goals, no matter how laudable." (p. 279)[12]

87. EDUCATION AND LEADERSHIP

Keynoting the 2001 National Education Summit (October 9, 2001) Louis V. Gerstner, Jr., IBM chairman, said:

I want to remind us all why we're here . . . It's not about books, it's not about buildings, it's not about tests, and it's not about transcripts. . . . [We are] here for one reason, and one reason only.

We're here for the children of America. We're here because we understand, just as the Founding Fathers understood, that absent a healthy, vital system of free public education you can't have an enlightened electorate, which means you can't sustain a working democracy; you can't build a competitive workforce, which means you can't envision a more prosperous future. It's exactly that clear-cut. We have an abiding responsibility to the kids and their future.

. . . If we've learned one thing in this struggle, it is that the schools alone cannot solve this one. This is a national problem. It demands that the entire nation participate in its solution.

88. STARTING AN EPIDEMIC IN SCHOOL IMPROVEMENT

How do we start an "epidemic"—to use Malcolm Gladwell's term—in thinking and action toward improving the quality of schools?

"The paradox of the epidemic: that in order to get one contagious movement, you often have to create many small movements first," writes Gladwell in *The Tipping Point*.[13] It isn't one epidemic focused on one thing. We need thousands of different epidemics, all focused on the groups who have a stake in education.

So where does this leave us? Do we wait for another breast-beating speech by a politician, business leader, book author, or college professor?

Diffusion helps explain how an epidemic moves through a population. The authors have been asked numerous times, "How are we going to get everyone to do what you are proposing?" Simply stated, we're not. But we do acknowledge certain characteristics about educators (or, for that matter, other professional groups) that help us predict how things change.

The Pacesetters

We know that about a one-third of education stakeholders will immediately welcome these proposals and tools. These educators are pacesetters; they lead and want to be at the forefront of creating change in schools. These are the opinion leaders, respected and thoughtful persons who have analyzed the tools of change.

The Fence-sitters

One-third are fence-sitters. This is not all together negative, since these are mostly the skeptics and the deliberate thinkers. They've seen change proposals come and seen them go. They prefer to wait and see. They'll tip toward adoption of these new ideas as the pacesetters begin using these new tools to facilitate change. New tools are highly contagious, and others want to get on board. Pacesetters and those fence-sitters who are first to climb down and adopt these tools are, in fact, visionaries. Most often, they want revolutionary change.

If the goal of the visionary is to make a quantum leap (breakthrough) forward, the goal of the pragmatist is to make a measured movement toward change. Innovations do not slide effortlessly from one group to the next. One might picture a wide chasm between the two groups.

The Head in the Sand

The other one-third would just as soon see change go away (that's part of control). These are the most traditional of all. These are the foot-draggers. They'll eventually get on board or move on to another school district or career.

The Translators

What is eventually needed to complete an epidemic are translators, those who can take the new ideas and information from the highly specialized world of education and translate them into a language the rest of the community stakeholders can understand.

The message about the value of the proposed tools and strategies for finding solutions to seemingly intractable school problems eventually needs to make emotional sense to a wider audience. This is the job for the "mavens, connectors and salesmen," as Gladwell puts it.

So at the end of the day, or the end of a book, the reader is left with the perplexing question: *Where do I fit on the continuum of stakeholders just described?*

- Pacesetter?
- Fence-sitter?
- Foot-dragger?
- Maven, connector, or salesman?
- None of the above?

It's up to the reader to decide and act.

NOTES

1. Robert Rosenthal, *Pygmalion in the Classroom* (New York: Henry Holt, 1968).

2. John Holt, *How Children Fail* (New York: Perseus, 1995).

3. Nat Hentoff, *Our Children Are Dying* (New York: Viking, 1967); John Holt, *How Children Fail*; Herbert Kohl, *Thirty-six Children* (New York: Penguin USA, 1990); Jonathan Kozol, *Death at an Early Age* (New York: New American Library, 1990).

4. Samuel C. Florman, *The Introspective Engineer* (New York: St. Martin's Press, 1996).

5. See section 66, Some Practical Benchmarking Experience.

6. John E. Chubb and Terry E. Moe, *Politics, Markets and America's Schools* (Washington, D.C.: Brookings Institution, 1990).

7. Joseph Juran, *Juran's Quality Handbook,* 5th ed. (New York: McGraw-Hill, 1998).

8. Philip Crosby, *Quality Is Free* (New York: Mentor Books, 1992), pp. 17–18.

9. David McCullough, *John Adams* (New York: Simon & Schuster, 2000), p. 364.

10. Ray Marshall and Marc Tucker, *Thinking for a Living* (New York: Basic, 1992), p. 239.

11. Lester Thurow, *Head to Head* (New York: Warner, 1993), p. 274.

12. Thurow, *Head to Head,* p. 279

13. Malcom Gladwell, *The Tipping Point* (New York: Little, Brown, 2000), p. 192; Leon Lessinger, *Every Kid a Winner: Accountability in Education* (New York: Simon & Schuster, 1970).

Moving Ahead

89. USING THE BENCHMARKING SELF-ASSESSMENT TOOL

The task of every school is to improve the individual learning experiences of each student on a continual basis to master the learning essentials, to take greater responsibility for their learning, to assess their performance against high achievement standards, and to become capable of performing quality work in the 21st century.

Where does your school fit in this picture of continual improvement?

The benchmark scales help schools evaluate their readiness to measure their progress. They also help to provide your school with a self-assessment tool prior to undertaking a benchmarking effort with another school or district.

The benchmark scales focus on goals. They help faculty and staff measure overall effectiveness. The issues are adapted from 2001 Malcolm Baldrige National Quality Criteria for Education.

The scales help faculty and staff identify expectations for growth, establish a vehicle for ongoing self-assessment by the schools, and keep participating school districts and corporate sponsors apprised of the progress of each effective school.

A hallmark of the ideal reliable quality school is accurate evaluation and accountability. The benchmark scales start the process of bringing relevant principles of performance management and quality thinking into education.

Organization of the Benchmark Scales

The benchmark scales raise awareness of *systemic* school improvement. They address seven interrelated and overlapping factors of systemic change: (1) Information and Analysis, (2) Leadership, (3) Student Achievement, (4) Quality Planning, (5) Professional Development, (6) Partnership Development, and (7) Continuous Improvement and Evaluation.

These metrics, extending from one to five horizontally, represent a continuum of your current evaluation related to your school's potential for improvement. A *one* rating located at the left of the scale describes a tradition-minded school that has not yet begun to improve. A *five,* located at the right of the scale, represents your school if it is approaching "world-class quality." The elements between one and five describe how that benchmark scale is conjectured to evolve in a continually improving school. The five in outcomes in each scale is the target.

The benchmark scales are not static. The scales themselves can continuously improve as school leaders and stakeholders learn more about school change and the most effective ways to sustain it.

Where Do You Believe Your School Fits?

Benchmark Scale No. 1: Student Achievement
A Reliable Quality School

1. Does our school identify required student outcomes on which to base curriculum design and assessment methods?

Untrue		Partially True		True
1	2	3	4	5

2. We implement "what works" in classroom teaching; provide relevant learning experiences and performance requirements for students.

Untrue		Partially True		True
1	2	3	4	5

3. Our school integrates technology to align with real-life experiences of students and takes advantage of new instruction methods and tools, such as CD-ROMs and computer networks.

Untrue		Partially True		True
1	2	3	4	5

4. We analyze the needs of our student population, research innovative instructional and curricular strategies, and implement one or more of them.

Untrue		Partially True		True
1	2	3	4	5

5. Our school implements authentic assessment methods such as student portfolios, exhibitions, and performances, which give teachers a better idea of student accomplishments. We provide narrative reports in addition to traditional report cards to note specific evidence of student results.

Untrue		Partially True		True
1	2	3	4	5

6. We disaggregate and analyze student-learning data over time to provide diagnostic information on *every* student; compare this information to measures of student learning to prevent student failures.

Untrue		Partially True		True
1	2	3	4	5

7. Our staff observes the benefits of changes in the classroom, including improved attendance, improved behavior, an increase in student writing, and students actively participating in their own learning.

Untrue		Partially True		True
1	2	3	4	5

8. Our teachers believe that when learning is more relevant and students have more access to technology, students feel their teachers are more caring and the work is challenging and fun.

Untrue		Partially True		True
1	2	3	4	5

Benchmark Scale No. 2: Leadership
A Reliable Quality School:

1. Our school implements shared decision making as school governance and uses this system to make collective decisions on budgets,

curriculum, professional development, and selection of new principals and staff.

	Untrue		Partially True		True
	1	2	3	4	5

2. By participating in decision making, our school staff gains a sense of ownership of the process, takes more responsibility for its actions, and feels a greater sense of collegiality with peers.

	Untrue		Partially True		True
	1	2	3	4	5

3. Our school leadership develops methods to support continuous team building and communication, elements necessary to the shared decision-making process.

	Untrue		Partially True		True
	1	2	3	4	5

4. We customize the structure of shared decision making to fit the school, the staff, the faculty, and the strategic plan.

	Untrue		Partially True		True
	1	2	3	4	5

5. Our school reschedules the workweek to allow teachers time to collaborate, plan, and make decisions; without time to collaborate the school would not have the opportunity to reach a shared vision that is crucial to continuous improvement.

	Untrue		Partially True		True
	1	2	3	4	5

6. We learn how to conduct effective meetings and reach consensus in order to make change possible.

	Untrue		Partially True		True
	1	2	3	4	5

7. Our school serves as a resource for information and expertise, shares its results with other schools, school districts, hosts visitors to campus, and provides in-service training for other schools on various topics.

	Untrue		Partially True		True
	1	2	3	4	5

Benchmark Scale No. 3: Quality Planning
A Reliable Quality School:

1. Our school develops a mission, vision, school goals, and values and beliefs about student learning.

Untrue		Partially True		True
1	2	3	4	5

2. We develop at least a three-year (five-year is better) action plan to guide our continuous improvement efforts.

Untrue		Partially True		True
1	2	3	4	5

3. We learn that a comprehensive quality plan makes the difference between implementing change and adopting change.

Untrue		Partially True		True
1	2	3	4	5

4. Our school finds that when our plans outline the school vision, the entire school community gains a clearer understanding of what they can do to support the change efforts.

Untrue		Partially True		True
1	2	3	4	5

Benchmark Scale No. 4: Information and Analysis
A Reliable Quality School:

1. Our school knows its students and faculty and community demographics, perceptions, and needs; the information from these analyses helps our school set goals, meet client needs, and ensure problem solving of the root causes as opposed to the symptoms.

Untrue		Partially True		True
1	2	3	4	5

2. We track student achievement results by ethnicity and other categories appropriate to each school situation to ensure that *every type—and thus all* students—receive what is needed to increase individual achievement.

Untrue		Partially True		True
1	2	3	4	5

3. Our school analyzes individual student achievement subcategories over time for diagnostic purposes; uses this data for decision making and to evaluate the impact of its efforts.

Untrue		Partially True		True
1	2	3	4	5

Benchmark Scale No. 5: Professional Development and Management
A Reliable Quality School:

1. Our school engages staff in professional development and training to support acquiring and using new classroom skills. Such activities increase teacher effectiveness in applying new approaches to increasing student achievement.

Untrue		Partially True		True
1	2	3	4	5

2. Our teaching staffs conduct action research on their implementation of new instructional and assessment skills and strategies. This research covers a broad range of subject areas and helps teachers predict the impact of their actions on student achievement.

Untrue		Partially True		True
1	2	3	4	5

3. Our school commits itself to long-term, sustainable professional development activities and training related to the school mission statements and goals, rather than one-day-type in-service activities that take a "cafeteria" approach to professional development.

Untrue		Partially True		True
1	2	3	4	5

4. Our school discovers that professional development activities and training have their greatest impact when they are planned in advance and become a priority on the school calendar.

Untrue		Partially True		True
1	2	3	4	5

5. We learn that peer coaching, combined with the acquisition of new skills, is the most efficient, positive, and supportive way to implement new classroom strategies.

Untrue		Partially True		True
1	2	3	4	5

Benchmark Scale No. 6: Partnership Development
A Reliable Quality School:

1. Our school plans for and establishes partnerships with community groups and local businesses to bring real-world examples into class-rooms, to help the schools acquire goods and services, to provide training, and to support staff with "success stories" that reflect well on the entire community.

Untrue		Partially True		True
1	2	3	4	5

2. Our school develops partnerships with parents to support student learning. Our school uses parents as classroom aides and as liaison with the community and offers special classes to parents; we add parents to our shared decision-making council; we have set up par-ent rooms at the schools where parents know they are welcome and safe.

Untrue		Partially True		True
1	2	3	4	5

3. We have learned the best way to increase parent involvement is to get parents and business people who are already school volunteers to help recruit others like them.

Untrue		Partially True		True
1	2	3	4	5

4. Our school has learned that structuring a partnership that is win-win is the most effective way to establish strong partnerships.

Untrue		Partially True		True
1	2	3	4	5

Benchmark Scale No. 7: Continual Improvement and Evaluation
A Reliable Quality School:

1. Our school collects school data on an ongoing basis to document the results of current activities and to use the knowledge gained in our continuous improvement process.

Untrue		Partially True		True
1	2	3	4	5

2. We use responses from parents, students, and teacher questionnaires to modify our processes.

Untrue		Partially True		True
1	2	3	4	5

3. We report positive results from using school portfolios as a framework to analyze continuous improvement. Our school finds that the information gathered validates chosen approaches and clarifies the next steps to be taken.

Untrue		Partially True		True
1	2	3	4	5

4. We receive help to develop and analyze a number of information collection and evaluation systems to better understand the impact of our continuous improvement efforts. These systems include:

- Teacher evaluation systems

Untrue		Partially True		True
1	2	3	4	5

- Control charts of a variety of data on students and teacher

Untrue		Partially True		True
1	2	3	4	5

- Follow-up survey of graduates

Untrue		Partially True		True
1	2	3	4	5

- Satisfaction surveys from parents

Untrue		Partially True		True
1	2	3	4	5

- Program evaluations

Untrue		Partially True		True
1	2	3	4	5

5. Our database systems identify areas where our school processes need to be improved or redirected to achieve school goals.

Untrue		Partially True		True
1	2	3	4	5

90. THINGS TO REMEMBER

There are five critically important things to remember about the shift in context from an industrial-based national economy to an electronically driven, knowledge- and information-saturated, world economy:

1. We now live in a world of *interdependent* communities.
2. Interdependent communities are—*at the same time*—competitors and collaborators. An apt term for this interdependence is *coopetition*.
3. Human capital is central in the global transformation.
4. Continuous improvement of human capital is key to competitive superiority (American Kaizen).
5. Persons and enterprises most likely to meet these demands practice lifetime learning.

Lester Thurow, MIT professor of management, gives us two frameworks for capturing the meaning of this contextual shift: *plate tectonics* from geology and *punctuated equilibrium* from biology.[1]

> In geology the visible earthquakes and volcanoes are caused by the invisible movement of the continental plates floating on the earth's molten inner core. . . . Corporate downsizing rocks human foundations (expectations about their economic futures) as profoundly as any earthquake. (p. 6)
>
> Normally evolution proceeds at a pace so slow that it is not noticeable on a human time scale. . . . But occasionally something occurs that biologists know as "punctuated equilibrium." The environment suddenly changes and what has been the dominant species rapidly dies out to be replaced by some other species. (p. 7)

Putting the Focus on Schools

Schools are the focus of greater attention because there is now more evidence that we can do something constructive about them. Schools are creatures of government. As citizens in a democracy, we also have a political "tool kit"—a potentially powerful set of methods and mindsets that can result in improvement. We also refer the concepts and modalities described in our *Solutions Fieldbook* to the elected officials—governors, mayors, congressmen, state legislators, school board members. It is they who determine the statutes, rules, regulations, and dollars spent and withheld. In the final analysis, the major tool in a democracy is the capacity to shape attitudes and mobilize public opinion.

Schools bear the brunt of concern because they are the most important institution and potential influence—after the family—in the lives of children and their future in society and the workplace. It is abundantly clear that heavier burdens are now placed on the schools.

Rationing Resources

There is a direct relationship between learning and earning. Learning is the *ration card* to entry and sharing in a higher living standard.

Rationing, unknown to younger Americans, is familiar enough to students and witnesses of World War II. During that war, many essential goods were scarce in America. The war effort took priority for raw materials, foodstuffs, oil products, and other essentials. Because such scarcities bring inflation, America needed a means of holding price levels in check and for a fair way of distributing essential goods to people. Each American family and business was issued ration cards to allocate access *to* scarce necessities, such as sugar, gasoline, and tires.

In 1973, the Middle East oil crisis forced Americans to once again experience the basic lessons of scarcity, elevated prices, and distribution. A rationing system was quickly put in place, using odd and even license-plate numbers to equitably allocate limited supplies of gasoline. It was not uncommon to sit in your car for an hour or more in line just to receive ten gallons of gasoline.

In a knowledge economy, driven by cognitive processing of information, learning is the rationing system that helps open the gates to individuals and the chance for gaining a higher share of the nation's wealth. The new relationship between the factors of production—physical capital, financial capital, and human capital—shows that:

- *Human capital*—knowledge and skills—becomes the basic energy to drive the other factors of production. It takes human ingenuity to get the most out of raw materials, money, and other workers, and
- *Knowledge and skill*s are the new form of capital accumulation. For example, a physician's education has greater economic potential than a high school diploma.

Learning, schools, and continuous learning determine an individual's *access to* the chances for gaining wealth and the *potentially* proportionate share of a higher standard of living.

This is the point that the principal of Denver's North High School, an inner-city school, made with an effective device. The school, with the city's highest dropout rate, introduced a new weapon to get kids to "think" before quitting. It was called a "certificate of dropping out."

Each student was required to sign a disclaimer acknowledging, "I realize that I will not have the necessary skills to survive in the 21st century." Principal Joe Sandoval presented the disclaimer to the first two students and both changed their minds. Said the principal, "It's like a brick went down their throat" when they realized the consequences of their decisions. Students who want to drop out must also bring their parents to a conference.

This is powerful stuff. But the question is more fundamental than that. Can our public schools assure those students who remain in school that they will have the necessary skills to survive in the 21st century? We think they can improve themselves enough to deliver these results. Some already have.

> To be fully effective in achieving potential productivity improvements, technological innovations also require a considerable amount of human investment on the part of workers who have to deal with these devices on a day-to-day basis. On this score, we still may have not progressed very far. Many workers still possess only rudimentary skills in manipulating advanced information technology. In these circumstances, firms and employees alike need to recognize that obtaining the potential rewards of the new technologies in the years ahead will require a renewed commitment to effective education and training, especially on-the-job training. This is especially the case *if we are to prevent the disruptions to lives* and the nation's capacity to produce that arise *from mismatches between jobs and workers*. We need to improve the preparation for the job market our schools do, but even better schools are unlikely to be able to provide adequate skills to support a lifetime of work. Indeed, *the need to ensure that our labor force has the ongoing education and training necessary to compete in an increasingly sophisticated world economy is a critical task for the years ahead*. [Emphasis added]
>
> —Alan Greenspan, Chairman, Federal Reserve Board
> Senate Finance Committee testimony, 20 February 1996

Clearly, higher levels of knowledge and skills are the needed engines for creating new wealth as well as getting a piece of any new prosperity. Schools and business together with families and community need to become the engines to power learning in this fast-changing information- and knowledge-driven global economy.

91. ARE EDUCATIONAL MALPRACTICE SUITS ON THE HORIZON?

In the "Leave No Child Behind" Act of 2002, the president and Congress have recognized that education is central to our quality of life. Yet, concerns about the effectiveness of the public educational system continue to surface. An educational system that leaves students functionally illiterate after they have completed the available programs evidently has serious flaws.

The success of American society depends on the quality of education. More and more leaders, from Washington, Adams, and Jefferson to Bush, Clinton, and Bush, have come to recognize that education is central to our economic strength and security, our creativity in the arts and letters, our invention in the sciences, and the perpetuation of our cultural values. Education is the key to America's international competitiveness.

Similarly, in 1954, the United States Supreme Court in *Brown v. Board of Education* stated that "today, education is perhaps the most important function of state and local governments." Education not only prepares students for professional training but also sets the foundation of good citizenship.

Despite this recognition of education's importance—to both students and society—some public schools fail to instill the needed skills for productivity and survival in a contemporary society. That is why we have set forth the needed system reforms and the tools available to set measurable goals and step-by-step process improvements in this book. We know we need sweeping, fundamental changes in our education system and that these changes must come not just from teachers and students but also from all Americans, their communities, their business and civic groups, and state, local, and federal government.

The courts may play an important role in effecting the needed changes to attain the goals of this new legislation. The current legislation attempts to restructure education. It includes powerful incentives for teacher performance and improvement and some real consequences for persistent failure. The exact role the courts may need to play in creating further incentives or greater consequences has not yet been established. Earlier, we reviewed tort reform actions thus far aimed at educational malpractice, as well as discussing the elements that make up good practice, poor practices, and malpractice.

For decades, the public schools skirted the issue of racial integration through adherence to "separate but equal" clauses and principles. The United States Supreme Court finally was prodded to step in and tear segregation down. Now, the public schools need to reform their processes and systems so as to raise the level of all student performance. Otherwise, the public schools may expect that a maze of education malpractice actions cannot be very far behind. It comes down to getting results. It's either "pay me now or pay me later!" as the expression goes.

Educational Malpractice

"Educational malpractice" is the failure to adequately educate a student; it includes the improper or inadequate instruction, testing, placement, or counseling of a child.[2] Educational malpractice claims can be divided into two distinct categories: (1) failure to provide an adequate education, and (2) misclassification and improper placement within the school system. To date no court has recognized a cause of action for a failure to provide an adequate education. While there exist a variety of theories upon which recovery may be based, the most popular theory lies in the tort principles of negligence.

Traditionally, a person alleging a cause of action for negligence must prove four basic and necessary elements: duty, breach of duty, causal connection, and injury. First, the law must recognize a duty requiring the defendant's conduct to conform to certain standards (standard of care) to protect others against unreasonable risks. Second, the defendant must breach that duty. Third, there must be a reasonably close causal connection between the defendant's conduct and the injury to the plaintiff. Fourth, actual loss or damage to the plaintiff must be demonstrated.

Duty Owed

Courts have refused to recognize a cause of action for educational malpractice because of the absence of a workable standard of care. The court in *Peter W. v. San Francisco Unified School District* (discussed earlier) held that no workable standard of care exists to measure an educator's teaching methods. It explained that the science of pedagogy promotes a multitude of conflicting views and approaches to educating students, and determining the "correct" method would be an impossible task.

Standard of Care for the "Professional Educator"

Although critics have urged the courts to adopt a "workable" standard of care, the courts have been unable to find such a standard. Because "Leave No Child Behind" legislation emphasizes placing more responsibility on educators, at some point the courts may be compelled to accept the standard of care set forth for professionals. This standard of care requires that professionals possess and use the knowledge, skill, and care ordinarily employed by members of that particular profession in good standing.

Courts have applied this professional standard of care to cases involving doctors, dentists, pharmacists, psychiatrists, veterinarians, lawyers, architects and engineers, accountants, abstractors of title, chiropractors, karate teachers, pilots, and nurses. The court in *Donohue v. Copiague Union Free School District* (discussed earlier) suggested that "[i]f doctors, lawyers, architects, engineers and other professionals are charged with a duty owing to the public whom they serve, it could be said that nothing in the law precludes similar treatment of professional educators." In fact, the new legislation and educators themselves refer to educators as "professionals." Thus far, however, the majority of the courts have held educators only to a lesser, *quasi-professional* standard.

Some critics argue that educators should be held to the same standard applied to other professionals in light of educators' numerous responsibilities. These responsibilities include selecting materials to carry out mandatory curriculum objectives, establishing standards of performance, organizing instruction along with selecting appropriate instructional techniques, and measuring and evaluating the accomplishments of students.

One of the objectives of the 2002 legislation is to give educators—principals and teachers—the discretion to make more decisions. This would provide educators with greater flexibility to innovate new methods of teaching, to use resources in more productive ways, and to provide alternate entrance paths for gifted professionals who wish to teach. But with this increased flexibility comes the educator's responsibility toward his or her pupils. Flexibility would be improved but would also require a more finely tuned status of "professional."

There are several practical considerations that differentiate educators from other recognized professionals such as doctors and lawyers. First, an educator is a public servant who receives his salary from the community budget. The salary schedule of teachers reflects *only* their level of education and experience, rather than their reputation or status. Parental recognition of an educator's experience or teaching excellence will generally not affect the educator's salary. Better teachers do not get paid more than average or even unreliable teachers. Second, the client exercises significant control over the hiring and firing of professionals such as lawyers and doctors. To date, students and parents exercise only a limited amount of control over educators; parents normally do not perceive teachers as their employees. Since the new legislation calls for parents to exercise their level of "customer satisfaction" in their child's progress in learning, the parent is allowed, and in fact encouraged, to transfer their child to a different school.

But until a "workable" standard of care is determined to be applicable to educators, the courts will continue to deny educational malpractice claims. The new legislation invites the determination of standards of care.

Policy Consideration against the Recognition of a Duty

Applying a standard of care to educators is not without its problems. For example, in *Peter W. v. San Francisco Unified School District*, the court relied on public policy considerations for not recognizing a duty. It said that the recognition of a duty is "the sum total of those considerations of policy which lead the law to say that the particular plaintiff is entitled to protection."

The recognition of *a duty to adequately educate* would expose educators to countless claims—real or imagined. This burden would not only cost society time and money, but would also discourage prospective new instructors. The 2002 legislation recognizes that key to restructuring the nation's public education system is attracting and keeping quality teachers who have the educational skills and knowledge of up-to-date technology. Recognizing the potential of educational malpractice claims down the road would require administrators to tighten the policies on hiring and certification of potential educators. Yet, the legislation encourages adoption of policies to attract more qualified teachers from diverse backgrounds.

The court in *Donohue* argued that "an educational malpractice claim would constitute unwarranted judicial intrusion not only into broad educational policies but also more importantly, into the day-to-day implementation of these policies." Such an intrusion runs counter to the need to allow educators greater flexibility to innovate new ways to improve learning. The desire for increased flexibility, coupled with the inherently imprecise nature of education, directly conflicts with the rigidity and absolute nature of court-made rules. Therefore, the courts have thus far resisted applying a single standard of care to educators.

Remaining Elements of Negligence

Even if a plaintiff is able to establish a workable standard of care, he must still satisfy the remaining three elements of negligence: breach of duty, causal connection between the defendant's conduct and the resulting injury to plaintiff, and actual loss or damage to plaintiff.

Breach of Duty   Assuming a professional standard of care, the plaintiff must establish that the defendant failed to use known and available educational alternatives.[3] An "expert witness," someone who is an expert in the profession, such as a teacher or administrator, must establish this proof. However, problems are sure to arise since educators disagree widely on what philosophies and methods of education are most appropriate. The choice between various methods of education depends on myriad specific factors. Therefore, expert witnesses could readily be located to support each side of the case.

Also, because of the different approaches taken by the various districts and states, the locality rule, which requires the expert witness be an expert in the same geographic location as the defendant, would seem to be necessary. (Some jurisdictions have discarded the "locality rule" altogether, having noticed that in medical malpractice suits physicians from the same area are reluctant to testify against a colleague.) There is little reason to believe that educators would be less reluctant to testify against another educator in the same geographic area.

To further complicate the finding of a breach of duty, the new legislation has stressed the desire to give educators greater flexibility to serve the needs of a diverse body of students. The potential of subjecting educators' unproven methods to education laypersons (judges and juries) and experts who have different theories of education may stifle innovation and creativity. Therefore, the question remains: Are the courts in any position to determine "the correct way" to educate and when an educator has breached his duty to educate?

Causal Connection between Conduct and Injury   The plaintiff seeking a negligence claim must also prove that the educator's breach of duty was a factual and proximate cause of plaintiff's injuries. The defendant's conduct is considered the factual cause of the injury if (1) the event would not have occurred but for the defendant's conduct (the "but for" test), and (2) defendant's conduct is more than an insignificant contribution to the result (the "substantial factor" test). Factual causation in education is very difficult, if not impossible, to prove because of the multitude of factors involved, such as the student's motivation, attitude, temperament, and past experience, along with other mental, social, and economic factors.

Proximate cause deals with how far the courts will extend liability. A defendant's conduct is the *proximate cause* if it is so closely connected with the result, and of such significance, that the law is justified in imposing liability. If a car broadsides your car and its driver disregards a stop sign, the proximate cause is pretty clear. In education, the whole host of factors outside the educator's control, which influence a student's ability to learn, complicate proving proximate cause. Clearly the act of one particular teacher in a school system cannot cause a student to graduate from high school functionally illiterate. As an Alaskan court explained, "The level of learning that a child might have reached if an educator had not breached his duty is impossible to assess; therefore, the determination of proximate cause is beyond the court's ability."

Injury   The final element necessary for the tort of negligence is actual loss or damage suffered by the plaintiff. As stated in *Donohue,* "Who can in good faith deny that a student who upon graduation from high school cannot comprehend simple English—a deficiency allegedly attributable to the negligence of his educators—has not in some fashion been 'injured'?" However, some courts have thus far refused to recognize injury resulting from a failure to educate as an "injury" within the meaning of tort law.

Court recognition of educational deficiency as tort injury creates two basic problems. First, the plaintiff has lost what amounts to an "expectancy interest," or a failure to receive a benefit. The issue of not receiving an adequate education is analogous to the 1928 issue resolved in New York in *H. R. Moch Co., Inc. v. Rensselaer Water Co.*, where the court held that a municipal contractor's failure to furnish sufficient water to adequately fight fires was a denial of a benefit, not a commission of a legal wrong. What was lost was an *expectancy interest*, for which the court does not recognize a right of redress. Likewise, in an educational malpractice suit the injury to the plaintiff is the lost expectancy interest.

Second, a calculation of damages for nonlearning would be virtually impossible. Damages would be based on future earnings, which are mere expectations and are highly speculative. In one case, Sioux Indian children were denied recovery for lost educational benefits because the amount of the loss could not be determined with sufficient accuracy. Education to a particular level does not guarantee a particular income, and damages resulting from a lack of education are difficult to assess. Therefore, the task of proving actual injury continues to be an obstacle for those who advocate recognition of educational malpractice as a legal cause of action.

Conclusion

Clearly, many policy considerations are at the center of a court's decision of whether to recognize a claim for educational malpractice. The "Leave No Child Behind" legislation encourages restructuring of the public education system to make teachers and administrators more accountable. However, in light of the many other aspirations set forth in the legislation, this plea for increased accountability must be balanced with the need for greater flexibility. To date, the courts have been unable to adequately balance these seemingly contradictory needs.

Judicial recognition of the cause of action for "educational malpractice" would certainly burden an education system that is already inadequate. While holding educators accountable for their actions is considered necessary, deciding the extent and enforcement of standards to increase accountability should not be left to the courts. Such issues are largely political and are properly left to the legislative process.

The hoped-for improvements sought by "No Child Left Behind" legislation requires all Americans to take part in the restructuring of the public education system. All parties—students, parents, educators, and legislators—need to take concrete steps to police themselves in order to improve public education. If key education stakeholders do not decide to take the necessary steps to restructure and reform the faltering public school system, they run the risk that the courts, with all the unintended consequences accompanying such an action, may be asked to decide it for us.

92. MISTAKES MADE AND LESSONS LEARNED

Industry has learned that when a company fails to innovate its end is near. We think business will most likely be around in 50 years. Kids will also be around, and so too will the challenges of helping them develop.

We are less convinced that schools, as we have come to know them, will be around. Schools that fail to adapt to the needs of our society will perish and will be replaced by new learning institutions. The initial move will likely come from corporate sponsorship driven into the education field because their employees lack the requisite skills to thrive in their world of work. Some will be private and some public; some cyberschools will be created to meet the needs of 21st-century business.

Business and community leaders now see more clearly the patterns and forces calling for changes in their schools. They are able to make persuasive arguments and presentations for school personnel and community audiences. They can generate common understanding and common commitments to a significantly improved future. What improvements are we looking for in the next decade?

We want schools to offer more avenues of learning and provide greater opportunities for students to reach their educational potential at their own pace. Meaningful learning will prepare them for the information and knowledge age. Thinking and reasoning skills will sustain learning for their lifetime. Only if our efforts, and the results of those efforts, are seen by education stakeholders to be of high quality can American public education survive into the future.

We Need Process Improvement

We need systems thinking and process planning teams. We have used these successfully for years. Such teams focus on improving the essential processes that are used in the system. We use teams to document work instructions and standard operating procedures. While such documentation is important, the real value comes from the *quality discussions* and *systems thinking*. This helps bring clarification and understanding of the processes and helps identify those processes needing to be updated. Documenting the processes enables us to thoughtfully step back and view the system from a distance. Too often, we find that educators become trapped inside the system, making it difficult to see things needing fixing. This results in duplicate effort with little value added to the objectives and goals of the school system.

We Need to Benchmark Best Practices

Strategic planning is legislated in more states. It is also widely practiced in more school districts. Dealing straight away with key issues helps a school district develop innovative strategies. In spite of forward thinking, even a brilliant strategy fails unless successfully executed. Too many schools fail to practice real performance improvement. School faculty has trouble answering, "What is the value-added benefit of our functions?"

The core of the issue rests on a host of familiar factors: lack of customer focus, slow program development, rising overhead costs, and mediocre quality. Benchmarking "best practices" is a major step toward solving these problems.

Benchmarking business practices or other processes used in other schools means we borrow as many good practices as we can uncover. It flows from the fact that our organization can learn something from someone else and that we are far from having all the answers in such changing and dynamic times. The benchmarking process helps us talk more freely with our colleagues as well as talk more openly with our counterparts in other schools, districts, and communities. Learning how others do things successfully is very therapeutic for us.

Benchmarking separates fact from fiction, so finding better ways somewhere else helps pave the way for new actions. It's much easier to convince the school organization that a better way is doable and not "pie in the sky" if school leadership can point to another school or district already doing it. It saves reinventing the wheel!

Benchmarking propels the school or district to recognize and achieve situations where a *quantum leap* in performance is needed. This opens minds to new ideas and to rethink how to operate.

We Need to Institutionalize Improvement

We are out to *institutionalize the improvement ethic*. Benchmarking quality system improvements is not intended as an easily accomplished one-shot deal. It is especially not a three-hour show-and-tell session with another school or a business, where they tell you what they're doing and you say, "Gee, that's a good idea. We'll copy it!" An improvement mechanism needs to be developed and a clear path laid out for future action and results.

Accountability Means Big Changes

Let's not kid ourselves; for schools to meet increased accountability standards there will need to be big changes. It means that schools must drive to develop competently based standards of organizational, curricular, and classroom teaching practice to match state-mandated learning standards. And a thorough review of school processes and practices must give educators the ability to self-diagnose the underlying reasons for unacceptable student learning. The benchmarking question is, "What process changes could we adopt that have led to better teaching outcomes elsewhere?"

Why We Can No Longer Leave Children Behind

The "Leave No Child Behind" Act of 2002 is about the future lives of American children and America as a nation. The objective is to aim high: to gain results that other approaches have been unable to reach.

We know that the strategies described in these pages yield results far greater than those achieved by less formal approaches. They provide focused and useful data, not just anecdotal information, intuition, or opinion. They create a culture of continuous improvement and enhance creativity. They open minds to new ideas. They overpower the "not invented here" mentality and raise the awareness to changes in the outside world.

Improving the Future of Education

In adapting to new demands, schools need the benefits of more research on learning. But we must not delay action, or the means to support it, until we fully understand the mysteries of learning. School leaders already know much more than they're willing to put into practice. Studies, reports, and education research give us ample evidence of how to improve school performance.

Quality processes are still unique to schooling, but we predict that this will not remain so for much longer. Using such process helps induce improvement. But it takes activists—promoters, believers, and sponsors of change.

Mental blocks are the greatest barrier to change, whether it be benchmarking "best practices" or tracking quality process improvement criteria. It is a psychological obstacle as much as a technical barrier. No solution, no matter how strong the evidence, can be adopted and nurtured until teachers, administrators, and school board members learn to overcome their desensitized state to chronic school problems.

What Is the Future for Schools?

We have too much scrap in education! Scrap is poor quality, waste, and rework. Human capital, as Lester Thurow, Robert Reich, Ray Marshall, Alan Greenspan, and a host of others persuasively argue, is destined to be the source of a nation's comparative economic advantage in the 21st century. For too many persons, the American Dream is a fading mirage. These persons are the "scrap" of an information- and knowledge-age economy.

Exaggeration? Once upon a time the U.S. economy provided plenty of jobs for those with limited knowledge skills. But that economy is fast disappearing and it is not likely to come back!

Money and Schools

Many criticize school operations as if it were a "business," and yet the real error is in not using a "businesslike" approach to schools. The main difference between the public and the private sector is that the latter must identify the cost per unit of meeting standards—including direct costs, indirect costs, and the cost of scrap.

If one airliner in four crashed between takeoff and landing, how many people would continue to fly? If one car in four went out of control, causing a fatal accident or permanent injury, how long would it be before we would demand something be done about it?

Schools produce a far more important "product" than airliners or cars and trucks. How long can we look the other way and permit this level of disgraceful failure? If concern for student performance is not the school's main concern, maybe citizens need to become more aware of the money it really takes to make students into successful learners and achievers.

In the End . . .

For every child who fails to be effectively prepared to earn a living or share in the benefits and obligations of American citizenship, *all of us* pay the price in taxes, social unrest, increased crime, and greater vulnerability in a competitive global economy.

In the end, the student is deprived of any realistic chance to reach his or her full potential, and so too is the nation deprived.

NOTES

1. Lester C. Thurow, *The Future of Capitalism* (New York: William Morrow,1996).

2. W. Page Keeton et al., *Prosser and Keeton on the Law of Torts*, 5th ed. (St. Paul, Minn.: West Publishing, 1984), p. 131.

3. Keeton et al., supra, n. 131, 132.

What Works in Education?

We know a great deal about "what works" in education. They are the equivalent of successful plays in a football coach's playbook or a baseball manager's game plan. Thirty-three such "plays" appear in the first-ever book of good practice published under the title *What Works* (1986) by the U.S. Department of Education. They serve as a model for good practice—authoritative practice—verified by actual tryout in schools over long periods of time. The topics are:

1. Curriculum of the Home	18. Student Ability and Effort
2. Reading to Children	19. Managing Classroom Time
3. Independent Reading	20. Direct Instruction
4. Counting	21. Tutoring
5. Early Writing	22. Memorization
6. Speaking and Listening	23. Questioning
7. Developing Talent	24. Study Skills
8. Ideals	25. Homework: Quantity
9. Getting Parents Involved	26. Homework: Quality
10. Phonics	27. Assessment
11. Reading Comprehension	28. Effective Schools
12. Science Experiments	29. Discipline
13. Storytelling	30. Unexcused Absences
14. Teaching Writing	31. Effective Principals
15. Learning Mathematics	32. Teacher Supervision
16. Estimating	33. Rigorous Courses
17. Teacher Expectations	

1—CURRICULUM OF THE HOME: WHAT WORKS

Research Finding:

Parents are their children's first and most influential teachers. What parents do to help their children learn is more important to academic success than their family economic situation.

Highlights:

- Parents can do many things at home to help their children succeed in school. Unfortunately, recent evidence indicates that many parents are doing much less than they might. American mothers on average spend less than half an hour a day talking, explaining, or reading with their children. Fathers spend less than 15 minutes.
- They can create a "curriculum of the home" that teaches their children what matters. They do this through daily conversations, household routines, attention to school matters, and affectionate concern for their children's progress.
- Conversation is important. Children learn to read, reason, and understand things better when their parents:

  - Read, talk, and listen to them,
  - Tell them stories, play games, share hobbies, and
  - Discuss news, TV programs, and special events

- In order to enrich the "curriculum of the home," some parents:

  - Provide books, supplies, and a special place for studying,
  - Observe routine for meals, bedtime, and homework, and
  - Monitor the amount of TV time and doing after-school jobs.

- Parents stay aware of their children's lives at school when they:

  - Discuss school events,
  - Help children meet deadlines, and
  - Talk with their children about school problems and successes.

Research on both gifted and disadvantaged children shows that efforts at home greatly improve student achievement. When parents of disadvantaged children take the above steps, their children can do as well at school as children of more affluent families.

2—READING TO CHILDREN: WHAT WORKS

Research Finding:

The best way for parents to help their children become readers is to read to them—even when they are a very young. Children benefit most from reading aloud when they discuss stories, learn to identify letters and words, and talk about the meaning of words.

Highlights:

- The specific skills required for reading come from direct experience with written language. At home, as in school, the more reading the better.
- Parents can encourage their children's reading in many ways. Some tutor informally by pointing out letters and words on signs and containers. Others use more formal tools, such as workbooks.
- Children whose parents simply read to them perform as well as those whose parents use workbooks or have had training in teaching.
- The conversation that goes with reading aloud to children is as important as the reading itself.
- When parents ask children only superficial questions about stories, or do not discuss the stories at all, their children do not achieve as well in reading as the children of parents who ask questions that require thinking and who relate the stories to everyday events.
- Kindergarten children who know a lot about written language usually have parents who believe that reading is important and who seize every opportunity to act on that conviction by reading to their children.

3—INDEPENDENT READING: WHAT WORKS

Research Finding:

Children improve their reading ability by reading a lot. Reading achievement is directly related to the amount of reading children do in school and outside.

Highlights:

- Independent reading increases both vocabulary and reading fluency.
- Unlike using workbooks and performing computer drills, reading books gives children practice in the "whole act" of reading, that is, both in discovering the meanings of individual words and in grasping the meaning of an entire story.
- American children do not spend much time reading independently at school or at home.
- In the average elementary school children spend just seven to eight minutes a day reading silently.
- At home, half of all fifth-graders spend only four minutes a day reading. These same children spend an average of 130 minutes a day watching television.
- The amount of leisure time spent reading is directly related to children's reading comprehension, the size of their vocabularies, and the gains in their reading ability.
- Reading at home can be a powerful supplement to class work.
- Parents can encourage leisure reading by making books an important part of the home, by giving books or magazines as presents, and by encouraging visits to the local library.

Another key to promoting independent reading is making books easily available to children through classroom libraries. Children in classrooms that have libraries read more, have better attitudes about reading, and make greater gains in reading comprehension than children in classrooms without libraries.

4—COUNTING: WHAT WORKS

Research Finding:

A good way to teach children simple arithmetic is to build on their informal knowledge. This is why learning to count everyday objects is an effective basis for early arithmetic lessons.

Highlights:

- Young children are comfortable with numbers; "math anxiety" comes in later years. Just watching the enjoyment children get from songs and nursery rhymes that involve counting is ample evidence of their natural ease.

- Early counting activities set the stage for later and formal exposure to arithmetic.
- Counting is not limited to merely reciting strings of numbers. It also includes matching numbers to objects and reaching totals (for example, counting the number of apples sitting on the table).
- Children learn to do arithmetic by first mastering different counting strategies, beginning with rote counting (1, 2, 3, 4), and progressing to memorized computations (2 x 2 = 4). As children learn the facts of arithmetic, they also learn to combine those facts by using more sophisticated strategies. As their skills grow, they rely less and less on counting.

When teachers begin by using children's informal knowledge, then proceed to more complex operations, children learn more readily and enjoy it.

5—EARLY WRITING: WHAT WORKS

Research Finding:

Children who are encouraged to draw and scribble "stories" at an early age will later learn to compose more easily, more effectively, and with greater confidence than children who do not have this encouragement.

Highlights:

- Even toddlers, who can hardly hold a crayon or pencil, are eager to "write" long before they acquire the skills in kindergarten that formally prepare them to read and write.
- Studies of very young children show that their carefully formed scrawls have meaning to them and that this writing actually helps them develop language skills.
- Research suggests that the best way to help children at this stage of their development as writers is to respond to the ideas they are trying to express.
- Very young children take the first steps toward writing by drawing and scribbling or, if they cannot use a pencil, they may use plastic

or metal letters on a felt or magnetic board. Some preschoolers may write on toy typewriters; others may dictate stories into a tape recorder or to an adult, who writes them down and reads them back.

- For this reason, it is best to focus on the intended meaning of what very young children write, rather than on the appearance of the writing.

Children become more effective writers when parents and teachers encourage them to choose the topics they write about, then leave them alone to exercise their own creativity. The industriousness of such children has prompted one researcher to comment that they "violate the child labor laws."

6—SPEAKING AND LISTENING: WHAT WORKS

Research Finding:

A good foundation in speaking and listening helps children become better readers.

Highlights:

- When children learn to read, they are making a transition from spoken to written language.
- Reading instruction builds on conversational skills: the better children are at using spoken language, the more successfully they will learn to read written language.
- To succeed at reading, children need a basic vocabulary, some knowledge of the world around them, and the ability to talk about what they know. These skills enable children to understand written material more readily.
- Research shows a strong connection between reading and listening. A child who is listening well shows it by being able to retell stories and repeat instructions.
- Children who are good listeners in kindergarten and first grade are likely to become successful readers by the third grade.
- Good fifth-grade listeners are likely to do well on aptitude and achievement tests in high school.

- Parents and teachers need to engage children in thoughtful comment on all subjects—current events, nature, sports, hobbies, machines, family life, and emotions—in short, on anything that interests children. Such comments should not be limited to reading selections that are part of class work.
- Conversing with children about the world around them will help them reflect on past experiences and on what they will see, do, and read about in the future.

Speaking English at school is especially important for children who have not grown up speaking English.

7—DEVELOPING TALENT: WHAT WORKS

Research Finding:

Many highly successful individuals have above average but not extraordinary intelligence. Accomplishment in a particular activity is often more dependent upon hard work and self-discipline than on innate ability.

Highlights:

- High academic achievers are not necessarily born "smarter" than others, nor do people born with extraordinary abilities necessarily become highly accomplished individuals.
- Parents, teachers, coaches, and the individuals themselves can influence how much a mind or talent develops by fostering self-discipline and encouraging hard work.
- Most highly successful individuals have above average but not exceptional intelligence. A high IQ seems less important than specializing in one area of endeavor, persevering, and developing the social skills required to lead and get along well with others.
- Studies of accomplished musicians, athletes, and historical figures show that when they were children, they were competent, had good social and communication skills, and showed versatility as well as perseverance in practicing their skill over long periods.

- Most got along well with their peers and parents. They constantly nurtured their skills. And their efforts paid off.
- Developing talent takes effort and concentration. These, as much as nature, are the foundation for success. Consider the story of golfer Tiger Woods and his nurturing father.

8—IDEALS: WHAT WORKS

Research Finding:

Belief in the value of hard work, the importance of personal responsibility, and the importance of education itself contribute to greater success in school.

Highlights:

- The ideals that children hold have important implications for their school experiences.
- Children who believe in the value of hard work and responsibility and who attach importance to education are likely to have higher academic achievement and fewer disciplinary problems than those who do not have these ideals. They are also less likely to drop out of school.
- Such children are more likely to use their out-of-school time in ways that reinforce learning.
- High school students who believe in hard work, responsibility, and the value of education spend about three more hours a week on homework than do other students. This is a significant difference since the average student spends only about five hours a week doing homework.
- Parents can improve their children's chances for success by emphasizing the importance of education, hard work, and responsibility and by encouraging their children's friendships with peers who have similar values.
- The ideals that students, their parents, and their peers hold are more important than a student's socioeconomic and ethnic background in predicting academic success.

9—GETTING PARENTS INVOLVED: WHAT WORKS

Research Finding:

Parental involvement helps children learn more effectively. Teachers who are successful at involving parents in their children's schoolwork are successful because they work at it.

Highlights:

- Most parents want to be involved with their children's schoolwork but are unsure of what to do and how to do it. Many say they would welcome more guidance and ideas from teachers.
- It takes more than occasional parent-teacher conferences and school open houses to involve parents. Teachers who are successful at promoting parent participation in the early grades use specific strategies.
- Some teachers ask parents to read aloud to the child, to listen to the child read, and to sign homework papers.
- Others encourage parents to drill students on math and spelling and to help with homework lessons.
- Still other teachers encourage parents to discuss school activities with their children and suggest ways parents can help teach their children at home.
- A simple home activity might be alphabetizing books; a more complex one would be using kitchen supplies in an elementary science experiment.
- Teachers meet parents' wishes for face-to-face contact by inviting them to the classroom to see how their children are being taught.
- Firsthand observation shows parents how the teacher teaches and gives parents ideas on what they can do at home.

10—PHONICS: WHAT WORKS

Research Finding:

Children get a better start in reading if they are taught phonics. Learning phonics helps them to understand the relationship between letters and sounds and to "break the code" that links the words they hear with the words they see in print.

Highlights:

- Until the 1930s and 1940s, most American children learned to read by the phonics method, which stresses relationships between spoken sounds and printed letters.
- Children learned the letters of the alphabet and the sounds those letters represent. For several decades thereafter, however, the "look-say" approach to reading was dominant: children were taught to identify whole words in the belief that they would make more progress if they identified whole words, as adults seem to.
- Recent research indicates that, on the average, children who are taught phonics get off to a better start in learning to read than children who are not taught phonics.
- Identifying words quickly and accurately is one of the cornerstones of skilled reading.
- Phonics improves the ability of children both to identify words and to sound out new ones.
- Sounding out the letters is the first tentative steps of a toddler: it helps children gain a secure verbal footing and expand their vocabularies beyond limits of basic readers.
- Because phonics is a reading tool, it is best taught in the context of reading instruction, not as a separate subject to be mastered.
- Good phonics strategies include teaching children the sounds of letters in isolation and in words (s/i/t), and how to blend the sounds together (s-s-i-i-t).
- Phonics should be taught early but not overused.
- If phonics instruction extends for too many years, it can defeat the spirit and excitement of learning to read.

Phonics helps children pronounce words approximately, and it is a skill they can learn by the end of second grade. In the meantime, children can learn to put their new phonics skills to work by reading good stories and poems.

11—READING COMPREHENSION: WHAT WORKS

Research Finding:

Children get more out of a reading assignment when the teacher precedes the lesson with background information and follows it with a review of its major points.

Highlights:

- Young readers, and poor readers of every age, do not consistently see connections between what they read and what they already know. When they are given background information about the principal ideas or characters in a story before they read it, they are less apt to become sidetracked or confused and are more likely to understand the story fully. Afterwards, a question-and-answer session clarifies, reinforces, and extends their understanding.
- Good teachers begin the day's reading lesson by preparing children for the story to be read—introducing the new words and concepts they will encounter.
- Many teachers develop their own introductions or adapt those offered in teachers' manuals. Such preparation is like a road map: children need it because they may meet new ideas in the story and because they need to be alerted to look for certain special details. Children who are well prepared remember a story's ideas better than those who are not.
- In the comments after the reading lesson, good teachers ask questions that probe the major elements of the story's plot, characters, theme, or moral. ("Why did Pinocchio's nose grow? Why did he lie? What did his father think about his lying? Did their feelings for each other change?")
- Such questions achieve two purposes: (1) to check students' understanding of what they have just read, and (2) to highlight the meanings and ideas students should look for in future reading selections. These questions lay the path for later appreciation of literature theme and style.
- When children take part in a thought-provoking story and comments, they understand more clearly that the purpose of reading

is to get information and insight, not just to decode the words on a page.

12—SCIENCE EXPERIMENTS: WHAT WORKS

Research Finding:

Children learn science best when they are able to do experiments, so they can witness "science in action."

Highlights:

- Reading about scientific principles or having a teacher explain them is frequently not enough. Cause and effect are not always obvious, and it may take an experiment to make that clear. Experiments help children actually see how the natural world works.
- Scientific explanations sometimes conflict with the way students may suppose that things happen or work.
- Most students would probably think that a basketball will fall faster than a ping-pong ball because the basketball is larger and heavier. Unless a teacher corrects this intuitive assumption by having the students perform an experiment and see the results, the students will continue to trust their intuition, even though the textbook or the teacher tells them the effect of gravity on both objects is exactly the same and that both will reach the floor at the same instant.
- Many students have misconceptions even after taking a science course because they have not had opportunities to test and witness the evidence that would change their minds.
- To clear up misconceptions, students need to be given the chance to predict the results they anticipate in an experiment. For example, the mistaken idea that the basketball will fall faster than the ping-pong ball can be tested experimentally.
- The teacher can then explain why the original hypothesis was faulty. In this way experiments help students use the scientific method to distinguish facts from opinions and misconceptions.

13—STORYTELLING: WHAT WORKS

Research Findings:

Telling young children stories can motivate them to read. Story-telling also introduces them to cultural values and literary traditions before they can read, write, and talk about stories by themselves.

Highlights:

- Elementary school teachers can introduce young students to the study of literature by telling them fairy tales such as the "Three Billy Goats Gruff" or "Beauty and the Beast" and myths such as "The Iliad."
- Even students with low motivation and weak academic skills are more likely to listen, read, and write, and work hard in the context of storytelling.
- Stories from the real tradition celebrate heroes who struggle to overcome great obstacles that threaten to defeat them. Children are neither bored nor alienated by learning literature through story-telling; they enjoy, understand, and sympathize naturally with the goats on the bridge, Beauty in a lonely castle, and Hector and Achilles outside the walls of Troy.
- With the help of skillful questioning, they can also learn to reflect on the deeper meanings of these stories.
- Children also benefit from reading stories aloud and from acting out dramatic narration, whether at home or at school. Parents can begin reading to their children as infants and continue for years to come.
- Storytelling can ignite the imaginations of children, giving them a taste of where books can take them.
- The excitement of storytelling can make reading and learning fun and can instill in children a sense of wonder about life and learning.

14—TEACHING WRITING: WHAT WORKS

Research Finding:

The most effective way to teach writing is to teach it as a process of brainstorming, composing, revising, and editing.

Highlights:

- Students learn to write well through frequent practice. A well-structured assignment has a meaningful topic, a clear sense of purpose, and a real audience.
- Good writing assignments are often an extension of class reading, highlights, and activities; not isolated exercises.
- An effective writing lesson contains these elements:

  - Brainstorming: Students think and talk about their topics. They collect information and ideas, frequently much more than they will finally use. They sort through their ideas to organize and clarify what they want to say.
  - Composing: Students compose a first draft. This part is typically time-consuming and hard, even for very good writers.
  - Revising: Students reread what they have written, sometimes collecting responses from teachers, classmates, parents, and others. The most useful teacher response to an early draft focuses on what students are trying to say, not the mechanics of writing. Teachers can help most by asking for clarification, comment on vivid expressions or fresh ideas, and suggesting ways to support the main thrust of the writing. Students can then consider the feedback and decide how to use it to improve the next draft.
  - Editing: Students then need to check their final version for spelling, grammar, punctuation, other writing mechanics, and legibility.

Prompt feedback from teachers on written assignments is important. Students are most likely to write competently when schools routinely require writing in all subject areas, not just in English class.

15—LEARNING MATHEMATICS: WHAT WORKS

Research Finding:

Children in early grades learn mathematics more effectively when they use physical objects in their lessons.

Highlights:

- Numerous studies of mathematics achievement at different grade and ability levels show that children benefit when real objects are used as aids in learning mathematics. Teachers call these objects "manipulatives."

- Objects that students can look at and hold are particularly important in the early stages of learning a math concept because they help the student understand by visualizing. Students can tie later work to these concrete activities.
- The type or design of the objects used is not particularly important; they can be blocks, marbles, poker chips, and cardboard cutouts—almost anything. Students do as well with inexpensive or home-made materials as with costly, commercial versions.
- The cognitive development of children and their ability to understand ordinarily move from the concrete to the abstract. Learning from real objects takes advantage of this fact and provides a firm foundation for the later development of skills and concepts.

16—ESTIMATING: WHAT WORKS

Research Finding:

Although students need to learn how to find exact answers to arithmetic problems, good math students also learn the helpful skill of estimating answers. This skill can be taught.

Highlights:

- Many people can tell almost immediately when a total seems right or wrong. They may not realize it, but they are using a math skill called estimating. Estimating can also be valuable to children learning math.
- When students can make good estimates of the answer to an arithmetic problem, it shows they understand the problem. This skill leads them to reject unreasonable answers and to know whether they are "in the ballpark."
- Research has identified three key steps used by good estimators; these can be taught to all students:

  ▪ Good estimators begin by altering numbers to more manageable forms—by rounding, for example.

  ▪ They change parts of a problem into forms they can handle more easily. In a problem with several steps, they may rearrange the steps to make estimation easier.

- They also adjust two numbers at a time when making their estimates. Rounding one number higher and one number lower is an example of this technique.

- Before students can become good at estimating, they need to have quick, accurate recall of basic facts. They also need a good grasp of the place value system (ones, tens, hundreds, etc.)
- Estimating is a practical skill; for example, it comes in very handy when shopping. It can also help students in many areas of mathematics and science that they will study in the future.

17—TEACHER EXPECTATIONS: WHAT WORKS

Research Finding:

Teachers who set and communicate high expectations to all their students obtain greater academic performance from those students than teachers who set low expectations.

Highlights:

- The expectations teachers have about what students can and cannot learn may become self-fulfilling prophecies. Students tend to learn as little—or as much—as their teachers expect.
- Students from whom teachers expect less are treated differently. Such students typically

  - Are seated farther away from the teacher,
  - Receive less direct instruction,
  - Have fewer opportunities to learn new material, and
  - Are asked to do less work.

- Teachers also call on these students less often and the questions they ask are more likely to be simple and basic than thought-provoking. Typically, such students are given less time to respond and less help when their answers are wrong.
- When teachers give these same students the chance to answer more challenging questions, the students contribute more ideas and opinions to class discussions.

18—STUDENT ABILITY AND EFFORT: WHAT WORKS

Research Finding:

Children's understanding of the relationship between being smart and hard work changes as they grow older.

Highlights:

- When children start school, they think that ability and effort are the same thing; in other words, they believe that if they work hard they will become smart. Thus, younger children who fail believe it is because they didn't try hard enough, not because they have less ability.
- Because teachers tend to reward effort in earlier grades, children frequently concentrate on working hard rather than on the quality of their work. As a result, they may not learn how to judge how well they are performing.
- In later elementary grades, students slowly learn that ability and effort are not the same.
- They come to believe that lower ability requires harder work to keep up and that students with higher ability need not work so hard. At this stage, speed at completing tasks replaces effort as the sign of ability; high levels of effort may even carry the stigma of low ability.
- Consequently, many secondary-school students, despite their ability, will not expend the effort needed to achieve their potential. Underachievement can become a way of life.
- Once students begin believing they have failed because they lack ability, they tend to lose hope for future success. They develop a pattern of academic hopelessness and stop trying. They see academic obstacles as insurmountable and devote less effort to learning.
- Teachers who are alert to these beliefs in youngsters will keep their students motivated and on task. They will also slowly nudge their students toward the realism of judging themselves by performance.

Teachers will set high expectations and insist that students put forth the effort required to meet the school's academic standards. They will make sure slower learners are rewarded for their progress and abler students are challenged according to their abilities.

19—MANAGING CLASSROOM TIME: WHAT WORKS

Research Finding:

How much time students are actively engaged in learning contributes strongly to their achievement. The amount of time available for learning is determined by the instructional and management skills of the teacher and the priorities set by the school administration.

Highlights:

- Teachers must not only know the subjects they teach, they must also be effective classroom managers. Studies of elementary school teachers have found that the amount of time the teachers actually used for instruction varied between 50 and 90 percent of the total school time available to them.
- Effective time managers in the classroom do not waste valuable minutes on unimportant activities; they keep their students continuously and actively engaged.
- Good classroom managers perform the following time-conserving functions.

  - Planning class work: choosing the content to be studied, scheduling time for presentation and study, and choosing those instructional activities (such as grouping, seatwork, or recitation) best suited to learning the material at hand.
  - Communicating goals: setting and conveying expectations so students know what they are to do, what it will take to get a passing grade, and what the consequences of failure will be;
  - Regulating learning activities: sequencing course content so knowledge builds on itself, pacing instruction so students are prepared for the next step, monitoring success rates so all students stay productively engaged regardless of how quickly they learn, and running an orderly, academically focused classroom that keeps wasted time and misbehavior to a minimum.

When teachers carry out these functions successfully and supplement them with a well-designed and well-managed program of homework, they achieve three key goals:

1. They capture students' attention.
2. They make the best use of available learning time.
3. They encourage academic achievement.

20—DIRECT INSTRUCTION: WHAT WORKS

Research Finding:

When teachers explain exactly what students are expected to learn and demonstrate the steps needed to accomplish a particular academic task, students learn more.

Highlights:

- The procedure stated above is called "direct instruction." It is based on the assumption that knowing how to learn may not come naturally to all students, especially to beginning and low-ability learners.
- Direct instruction takes children through learning steps systematically, helping them see both the purpose and the result of each step. In this way, children learn not only a lesson's content but also a method for learning that content.
- The basic components of direct instruction are

  1. Setting clear goals for students and making sure they understand those goals,
  2. Presenting a sequence of well-organized assignments,
  3. Giving students clear, concise explanations and illustrations of the subject matter,
  4. Asking frequent questions to see if children understand the work, and
  5. Giving students frequent opportunities to practice what they have learned.

- Direct instruction does not mean repetition. It does mean leading students through a process and teaching them to use that process as a skill to master other academic tasks.

Direct instruction has been particularly effective in teaching basic skills to young and disadvantaged children, as well as in helping older and higher-ability students to master more complex materials and to develop independent study skills.

21—TUTORING: WHAT WORKS

Research Finding:

Students tutoring other students can lead to improved academic achievement for both student and tutor and to positive attitudes toward coursework.

Highlights:

- Tutoring programs consistently raise the achievement of both the students receiving instruction and those providing it.
- Peer tutoring, when used as a supplement to regular classroom teaching, helps slow and underachieving students master their lessons and succeed in school.
- Preparing and giving the lessons also benefits the tutors themselves because they learn more about the material they are teaching.
- Of the tutoring programs that have been studied, the most effective include the following elements:

  1. Highly structured and well-planned curricula and instructional methods
  2. Instruction in basic content and skills (grades 1-3), especially in arithmetic
  3. A relatively short duration of instruction (a few weeks or months)

When these features were combined in the same program, the students being tutored not only learned more than they did without tutoring, they also developed a more positive attitude about what they were studying. Their tutors also learned more than students who did not tutor.

22—MEMORIZATION: WHAT WORKS

Research Finding:

Memorizing can help students absorb and retain the factual information on which understanding and critical thought is based.

Highlights:

- Most children at some time memorize multiplication tables, the correct spelling words, historical dates, and passages of literature such as the poetry of Robert Frost or the sonnets of Shakespeare.
- Memorizing simplifies the process of recalling information and allows its use to become automatic. Understanding and critical thought can then build on this base of knowledge and fact. Indeed, the more sophisticated mental operations of analysis, synthesis, and evaluation are impossible without rapid and accurate recall of bodies of specific knowledge.
- Teachers can encourage students to develop memory skills by teaching highly structured and carefully sequenced lessons, with frequent reinforcement for correct answers. Young students, slow students, and students who lack background knowledge can benefit from such instruction.
- Teachers can teach "mnemonics," that is, devices and techniques for improving memory. For example, the mnemonic "Every Good Boy Does Fine" has remained generations of music students that E, G, B, D, and F are the notes to which the lines on a treble staff correspond.

Mnemonics help students remember more information faster and retain it longer. Comprehension and retention are even greater when teachers and students connect the new information being memorized with previous knowledge.

23—QUESTIONING: WHAT WORKS

Research Finding:

Student achievement rises when teachers ask questions that require students to apply, analyze, synthesize, and evaluate information in addition to simply recalling facts.

Highlights:

- Even before Socrates, questioning was one of teaching's most common and most effective techniques. Some teachers ask hundreds of questions, especially when teaching science, geography, history, or literature.
- Questions take different forms and place different demands on students. Some questions require only factual recall and do not provoke analysis. For example, of more than 61,000 questions found in the teacher guides, student workbooks, and tests for nine history textbooks, more than 95 percent were devoted to factual recall. This is not to say that questions meant to elicit facts are unimportant.
- Students need basic information to engage in higher-level thinking processes and comments. Such questions also promote class participation and provide a high success rate in answering questions correctly.
- The difference between factual and thought-provoking questions is the difference between asking: "When did Lincoln deliver the Gettysburg Address?" and asking: "Why was Lincoln's Gettysburg Address an important speech?"
- Each kind of question has its place, but the second one intends that the student analyze the speech in terms of the issues of the Civil War.
- Although both kinds of questions are important, students achieve more when teachers ask thought-provoking questions and insist on thoughtful answers.

Students' answers may also improve if teachers wait longer for a response, giving students more time to think.

24—STUDY SKILLS: WHAT WORKS

Research Finding:

The ways in which children study influence strongly how much they learn. Teachers can often help children develop better study skills.

Highlights:

- Research has identified several study skills used by good students that can be taught to other students. Average students can learn how to use these skills. Low-ability students may need to be taught when, as well as how, to use them.

- Some examples of sound study practices include:
  - Good students adjust the way they study according to several factors:
    - ▲ The demand of the material,
    - ▲ The time available for studying,
    - ▲ What they already know about the topic,
    - ▲ The purpose and importance of the assignment, and
    - ▲ The standards they must meet
  - Good students space learning sessions on a topic over time and do not cram or study the same topic continuously.
  - Good students identify the main idea in new information; connect new material to what they already know, and draw inferences about its significance.
  - Good students make sure their study methods are working properly by frequently appraising their own progress.
  - When low-ability and inexperienced students use these skills, they can learn more information and study more efficiently.

25—HOMEWORK—QUANTITY: WHAT WORKS

Research Finding:

Student achievement rises significantly when teachers regularly assign homework and students conscientiously do it.

Highlights:

Extra studying helps children at all levels of ability. One research study reveals:

- When low-ability students do just one to three hours of homework a week, their grades are usually as high as those of average-ability students who do not do homework.
- When average-ability students do three to five hours of homework a week, their grades usually equal those of high-ability students who do homework.

Homework boosts achievement because the total time spent studying influences how much is learned. Low-achieving high school students study less than high achievers and do less homework. Time is not the only ingredient of learning, but without it little can be achieved.

Teachers, parents, and students determine how much, how useful, and how good the homework is.

- American teachers say they assign about 10 hours of homework each week—about 2 hours per school day.
- High school seniors report they spend only 4 to 5 hours a week doing homework, and 10 percent say they do none at all or have none assigned.
- In contrast, students in Japan spend about twice as much time studying outside school as American students.

26—HOMEWORK—QUALITY: WHAT WORKS

Research Finding:

Well-designed homework assignments relate directly to class work and extend students' learning beyond the classroom. Homework is most useful when teachers carefully prepare the assignment, thoroughly explain it, and give prompt discussion and criticism when the work is completed.

Highlights:

To make the most of what students learn from doing homework, teachers need to give the same care to preparing homework assignments as they give to classroom instruction.

- When teachers prepare written instructions and discuss homework assignments with students, they find their students take the homework more seriously than if the assignments are simply announced.
- Students are more willing to do homework when they believe it is useful, when teachers treat it as an integral part of instruction, when it is evaluated by the teacher, and when it counts as a part of the grade.

- Assignments that require students to think, and are therefore more interesting, foster their desire to learn both in and out of school.
- Such activities include explaining what is seen or read in class; comparing, relating, and experimenting with ideas; and analyzing principles.

Effective homework assignments do not just supplement the class-room lesson; they also teach students to be independent learners. Homework gives students experience in following directions, making judgments and comparisons, raising additional questions for study, and developing responsibility and self-discipline.

27—ASSESSMENT: WHAT WORKS

Research Finding:

Frequent and systematic monitoring of students' progress helps students, parents, teachers, administrators, and policymakers identify strengths and weaknesses in learning and instruction.

Highlights:

Teachers find out what students already know and what they still need to learn by assessing student work.

- They use various means, including essays, quizzes and tests, homework, classroom questions, standardized tests, and parents' discussions.
- Teachers can use student errors on tests and in class as early warning signals to point out and correct learning problems before they worsen.
- Student motivation and achievement improve when teachers provide prompt feedback on assignments.

Students generally take two kinds of tests: classroom tests and standardized tests.

- Classroom tests help teachers find out if what they are teaching is being learned; thus, these tests serve to evaluate both student and teacher.

- Standardized tests apply similar gauges to everyone in a specific grade level. By giving standardized tests, school districts can see how achievement progresses over time.
- Such tests also help schools find out how much of the curriculum is actually being learned.
- Standardized tests also reveal problems in the curriculum itself. A recent international mathematics test showed that U.S. students had encountered only 70 percent of what the test covered.

28—EFFECTIVE SCHOOLS: WHAT WORKS

Research Finding:

The most important characteristics of effective schools are strong instructional leadership, a safe and orderly climate, school-wide emphasis on basic skills, high teacher expectations for student achievement, and continuous assessment of pupil progress.

Highlights:

One of the most important achievements of education research in the last 20 years has been identifying the factors that characterize effective schools, in particular the schools that have been especially successful in teaching basic skills to children from low-income families. Analysts first uncovered these characteristics when comparing the achievement levels of students from different urban schools. They labeled the schools with the highest achievement as "effective schools." Schools with high student achievement and morale show certain characteristics:

- Vigorous instructional leadership
- A principal who makes clear, consistent, and fair decisions
- An emphasis on discipline and a safe and orderly environment
- Instructional practices that focus on basic skills and achievement
- Collegiality among teachers in support of student achievement
- Teachers with high expectations that all students can and will learn
- Frequent review of student progress

Effective schools are places where principals, teachers, students, and parents agree on the goals, methods, and content of schooling. They are united in recognizing the importance of a coherent curriculum, public recognition for students who succeed, promoting a sense of school pride, and protecting school time for learning.

29—DISCIPLINE: WHAT WORKS

Research Finding:

Schools contribute to their students' academic achievement by establishing, communicating, and enforcing fair and consistent discipline policies.

Highlights:

For 16 of the last 17 years, the public has identified discipline as the most serious problem facing its schools. Effective discipline policies contribute to the academic atmosphere by emphasizing the importance of regular attendance, promptness, respect for teachers and academic work, and good conduct.

Behavior and academic success go together. In one recent survey, for example, high school sophomores who got "mostly A's" had one-third as many absences or incidents of tardiness per semester as those who got "mostly D's." The same students were 25 times more likely to have their homework done and 7 times less likely to have been in trouble with the law. Good behavior as a sophomore led to better grades and higher achievement as a senior.

The discipline policies of most successful schools share these traits:

- Discipline policies are aimed at actual problems, not rumors.
- All members of the school community are involved in creating a policy that reflects community values and is adapted to the needs of the school.
- Misbehavior is defined. Because not everyone agrees on what behavior is undesirable, defining problems is the first step in solving them. Students must know what kinds of behavior are acceptable and what kinds are not.

- Discipline policies are consistently enforced. Students must know the consequences of misbehavior, and they must believe they will be treated fairly.
- A readable and well-designed handbook is often used to inform parents and students about the school's discipline policy.

30—UNEXCUSED ABSENCES: WHAT WORKS

Research Finding:

Unexcused absences decrease when parents are promptly informed that their children are not attending school.

Highlights:

Absences are a major problem at all levels of school. Students who miss a lesson lose an opportunity to learn. Too many missed opportunities can result in failure, dropping out of school, or both. Research indicates:

- Parents want to hear promptly if their children have poor grades, are creating discipline problems, or have unexcused absences.
- Schools have different ways of letting parents know when their children aren't in school. Some use staff members to check attendance records and phone the parents of absent students. Others have begun using automatic calling devices that leave a recorded message with parents.
- The usual message is a request to contact the school about the absence. These devices can be programmed to call back if no answer is received. Schools using such devices report substantial increases in attendance.

Good attendance in school is another example of the connection of time and learning. Just as homework amplifies learning, regular attendance exposes students to a greater amount of academic content and instruction. Students, of course, must concentrate on their lessons in order to benefit from attendance.

31—EFFECTIVE PRINCIPALS: WHAT WORKS

Research Finding:

Successful principals establish policies that create an orderly environment and support effective instruction.

Highlights:

Effective principals have a vision of what a good school is and systematically strive to bring that vision to life in their schools.

- School improvement is their constant theme.
- They scrutinize existing practices to assure that all activities and procedures contribute to the quality of the time available for learning.
- They make sure teachers participate actively in this process.
- Effective principals make opportunities available for faculty to improve their own teaching and classroom management skills.

Good school leaders protect the school day for teaching and learning. They do this by keeping teachers' administrative chores and classroom interruptions to a minimum.

Effective principals visibly and actively support learning.

- Their practices create an orderly environment.
- Good principals make sure teachers have the necessary materials and the kind of assistance they need to teach well.
- Effective principals also build morale in their teachers. They help teachers create a climate of achievement by encouraging new ideas; they also encourage teachers to help formulate school teaching policies and select textbooks.
- They try to develop community support for the school, its faculty, and its goals.

In summary, effective principals are experts at making sure time is available to learn and at ensuring that teachers and students make the best use of that time.

32—TEACHER SUPERVISION: WHAT WORKS

Research Finding:

Teachers welcome professional suggestions about improving their work, but they rarely receive them.

Highlights:

When supervisors comment constructively on teachers' specific skills, they help teachers become more effective and improve teachers' morale.

- Yet, typically, a supervisor visits a teacher's classroom only once a year and makes only general comments about the teacher's performance.
- This relative lack of specific supervision contributes to low morale, teacher absenteeism, and high faculty turnover.

Supervision that strengthens instruction and improves teachers' morale has these elements:

- Agreement between supervisor and teacher on the specific skills and practices that characterize effective teaching
- Frequent observation by the supervisor to see if the teacher is using these skills and practices
- A meeting between supervisor and teacher to discuss the supervisor's impressions
- Agreement by the supervisor and teacher on areas for improvement
- A specific plan for improvement, jointly constructed by teacher and supervisor

Principals who are good supervisors make themselves available to help teachers. They make teachers feel they can come for help without being branded failures.

33—RIGOROUS COURSES: WHAT WORKS

Research Findings:

The stronger the emphasis on academic courses, the more advanced the subject matter, and the more rigorous the textbooks, the more high school students learn. Subjects that are learned mainly in school rather than at home, such as science and math, are most influenced by the number and kind of courses taken.

Highlights:

Students often handicap their intellectual growth by avoiding difficult courses. In order to help young people make wise course choices, schools are: increasingly requiring students to take courses that match their grade level and abilities; seeing to it that the materials used in those courses are intellectually challenging.

The more rigorous the course of study, the more a student achieves, within the limits of his capacity. Student achievement also depends on how much the school emphasizes a subject and the amount of time spent on it.

The more time expended, the higher the achievement. Successful teachers encourage their students' best efforts.

Where does your school fall on the following scales?

A Survey On Continuous Improvement

1. Our school leadership and staff recognize and desire to promote continuous improvement as a means to achieve high performance.

1	2	3	4	5
Untrue		Partially True		True

2. The school's operations ensure that each student achieves the skills necessary to pursue a life path of his or her choosing.

1	2	3	4	5
Untrue		Partially True		True

3. School operations ensure that each student will be capable of pursuing a high-skilled career.

1	2	3	4	5
Untrue		Partially True		True

4. Our school programs ensure that each student possesses learning skills to ensure her/his abilities to negotiate changes in career or other life interests.

1	2	3	4	5
Untrue		Partially True		True

On Classroom Performance

1. The school's classroom experiences ensure a result that each student can pursue, as desired, higher levels of education for a lifetime.

1	2	3	4	5
Untrue		Partially True		True

2. School leadership and teachers are dedicated to the premise that each student will play a responsible role as a citizen in her/his community.

1	2	3	4	5
Untrue		Partially True		True

3. Each party (school, parents, businesses) realizes significant benefits by the achievement of high performance and each pledges support to the quality schools initiative in the local school district.

1	2	3	4	5
Untrue		Partially True		True

4. Each realizes that, without the total support of all parties, the quality schools initiative will likely not achieve its intended outcomes.

1	2	3	4	5
Untrue		Partially True		True

On Administration

1. The school board, the superintendent, and any participating institution of higher education all pledge their dedicated efforts to the school quality initiative.

1	2	3	4	5
Untrue		Partially True		True

2. The superintendent, senior staff, and board members demonstrate a strong commitment to quality through active leadership and participation in quality planning and training efforts.

1	2	3	4	5
Untrue		Partially True		True

3. Procedures are identified and established to maintain effective leadership that represents key stakeholders of the system.

1	2	3	4	5
Untrue		Partially True		True

4. The leadership actively participates in the networking activities of the local school network.

1	2	3	4	5
Untrue		Partially True		True

5. Based on our locally developed strategic plan, our system has committed the necessary human and financial resources from all available sources to support the plan.

1	2	3	4	5
Untrue		Partially True		True

6. The district has completed a system-based self-assessment utilizing the aligned management system approach based on quality criteria.

1	2	3	4	5
Untrue		Partially True		True

7. Periodic updates are submitted to the district on key activities and results as required by a data tracking system developed for annual reporting, including but not limited to work plans and financial reports.

1	2	3	4	5
Untrue		Partially True		True

On State Support

1. The state department of education provides leadership for the overall development and coordination of the quality schools effort with your local school systems, local businesses, and the higher education community.

1	2	3	4	5
Untrue		Partially True		True

2. The department of education assists local school systems, businesses, and communities in developing effective business/education partnership(s) for their quality initiative.

1	2	3	4	5
Untrue		Partially True		True

3. The district continues to work with statewide leadership in the business, education, and policy-making communities to advance the quality initiative.

1	2	3	4	5
Untrue		Partially True		True

4. District staff continues to assist in identifying and securing human and financial resources to assist with the implementation of the statewide and local plans for quality schools.

1	2	3	4	5
Untrue		Partially True		True

On School Business Partner(s)

The following requirements relate to your school district business partner(s):

1. Your business partner has committed a senior-level officer to participate on the district's quality leadership effort.

1	2	3	4	5
Untrue		Partially True		True

2. Your business partner has identified and provided available resources, expertise, and training opportunities to advance the strategic plan for the district.

1	2	3	4	5
Untrue		Partially True		True

3. The business partner provides opportunities for its employees and other community members to become knowledgeable of the quality schools effort and how they can support this effort.

1	2	3	4	5
Untrue		Partially True		True

4. The business partner maintains and reinforces its corporate commitment to pursuing quality with its own employees, customers, and suppliers.

1	2	3	4	5
Untrue		Partially True		True

5. All parties in the quality schools initiative agree to accept and enthusiastically exercise their roles by complying with the foregoing requirements.

1	2	3	4	5
Untrue		Partially True		True

About the Authors and Contributors

Allen E. Salowe is a consultant, educator, and author. He is principal of A. E. Salowe & Associates and has consulted widely to public and private clients. He is formerly an adjunct professor of economics at Webster University. In 1997, he was named a senior fellow of the Florida Institute of Education (a Type I Regents Education Improvement Center), and in 1991 he was named a senior fellow of the Florida Center for Electronic Communication (a Type II University Research Center). Salowe served a three-year term, the last as president, of the Plainfield, New Jersey, School Board, immediately following the urban riots of the sixties.

Salowe has been senior vice-president, planning, for ITT Community Development Corporation; senior operations executive for ITT Consumer Services Group; and group planning director for Champion International. Over a 40-year business career he held numerous positions in strategic, tactical, financial, and operations planning. He has served as economic advisor to more than 30 Florida Community Development Districts in their infrastructure planning and financing. He holds an M.B.A. from Nova Southeastern University and a B.A. in economics from the University of Miami. He also holds the certified planner designation from the American Institute of Certified Planners (AICP).

Leon M. Lessinger received a B.S. in mechanical engineering from North Carolina State University and a B.A. in psychology, M.Ed. in educational psychology, and Ed.D. in educational administration from the University of California, Los Angeles. He is a licensed clinical psychologist in California. Lessinger has also served as a public school teacher, a counselor, a principal, and an assistant superintendent and superintendent of three California school systems.

He served as associate U.S. commissioner for elementary and secondary education in Washington, D.C., under Presidents Johnson and Nixon. In his more than 50-year career in education, he has held endowed chairs as a professor at Georgia State University and the University of North Florida. He was a professor and dean of the College of Education at the University of South Carolina. Lessinger has conducted research for the State of California and has been a consultant to state departments of education, school systems, and leading companies.

Roger Kaufman, professor and director, Office for Needs Assessment and Planning, at Florida State University, is also research professor of engineering management at Old Dominion University and director of Roger Kaufman & Associates. He holds a Ph.D. in communications from New York University, an M.A. from Johns Hopkins University, and a B.A. from George Washington University. Prior to entering higher education Kaufman held senior advisory positions with Douglas Aircraft, US Industries, Bolt, Beranek & Newman, Martin Baltimore, and Boeing and served two terms on the secretary of the navy's advisory board on education and training. Kaufman consults to public and private clients around the globe. He is a fellow of the American Psychological Association, a fellow of the American Academy of School Psychology, and a diplomate of the American Board of Professional Psychology. He holds the "Member for Life" honor of the International Society for Performance Improvement and that organization's Thomas F. Gilbert Professional Achievement Award.

His 35 books include *Mega Planning*, *Strategic Planning Plus*, and *Strategic Thinking* (rev. ed.), and he coauthored *Useful Educational Results: Defining, Prioritizing, and Accomplishing* and the *Strategic Planning and Thinking Field Book*. He has published more than two hundred articles on strategic planning and improving quality performance.

William N. Kiefer is an educator with over 25 years experience. He has been a teacher, school psychologist, and program coordinator for early childhood education, elementary principal, secondary principal, and central office administrator. Currently, he is the coordinator of planning and quality systems in the office of the superintendent of the school district of Lancaster, Pennsylvania.

Under Kiefer's leadership, Lancaster was the first U.S. school district to be registered to the ISO 9001 Quality Standard. Kiefer's books include *I Like It When You Help Me Learn to Read,* coauthored with Morris E. Krape Jr., and *Putting Kids First with Quality: Implementing ISO 9001 in Public Education*, in manuscript.

In addition to his work in school reform, Kiefer is a major general in the U.S. Army Reserve. His career with the U.S. Army has spanned 34 years of command and staff positions. He is a recognized speaker on leadership. Kiefer holds B.A. and M.S. degrees in psychology from Millersville University and an Ed.D. in educational administration from Walden University.

William R. King is director of best practices for Systems & Computer Technology Corporation (SCT), a Pennsylvania-based software and technology services solutions provider. He has more than 35 years of information technology industry experience, including 26 years managing information technology services organizations in postsecondary education.

King has served as staff director of information technology for the Florida House of Representatives and as CIO at Florida Atlantic University. In his current role, he is responsible for business process benchmarking and improvement of SCT practices. King earned his B.S. degree in business administration at State University of New York–Empire State College and completed graduate courses in business at State University of New York–Albany and in advanced computer graphics at Florida Atlantic University.

Leslie L. Kossoff is a leading organizational thinker and consultant. Her firm, Kossoff Management Consulting, has been providing guidance in the areas of executive and management development and organizational strategy and excellence since the mid-1980s. She has assisted a range of Fortune 100 clients as well as nonprofit organizations in the public and private sectors.

Kossoff enjoys an outstanding reputation as an invited speaker at professional and educational conferences throughout the United States. During her long-term alliance with W. Edwards Deming, she assisted in his client consultations and presented at his seminars on implementation obstacles and strategies. Deming declared Kossoff "quite simply, one of the best at implementation."

Kossoff is the author of two books, *Executive Thinking: The Dream, the Vision, the Mission Achieved* (Palo Alto, Calif.: Davies-Black Publishing, 1999) cited as one of the top ten books of 1999 by *Management General* and a main selection of the Doubleday Executive Program Book Club, and *Managing for Quality: How to Implement and Manage a Business Strategy of Continuous Improvement*, 3rd ed. (Kossoff Management Consulting, 1998).

Jane Lockett is national principal in the IBM Global Services Business Intelligence Practice. She ensures that client expectations are met and is viewed as an industry expert in the public sector. Lockett fosters teamwork between IBM and clients by encouraging solutions that are supported by skills that best represent her client's interests. Her strengths are leadership, mentoring and guiding a vision, and supporting a can-do approach for any team.

Prior to IBM, Lockett consulted for five years with other computer corporations, as well as national and state professional organizations, supporting the public sector. Lockett has extensive public speaking experience and has averaged more than two dozen public speaking engagements a year over the past 15 years.

Lockett taught business and English in high school and college for 11 years in Illinois. Her peers chose her as a leader for her innovative use of technology in the classroom. She has held state and national offices in professional education organizations. Lockett also worked for 11 years in business, supporting banking, finance, manufacturing, and the printing industries. She has published numerous articles relating to education and technology in the public sector. Lockett was recognized with an International Consulting Engagement award in 1997 and received leadership recognition for her entire nine years with IBM. In 1980 Lockett published two textbooks to teach elementary children the fundamentals of computer programming.

Lockett holds an M.S. in education and business and a B.S. in education, business, and English from Eastern Illinois University. She has attended professional development sessions at MIT and graduate sessions at the College of Education at Harvard.